FACTBOOK
—OF—
BRITISH
HISTORY

FACTBOOK
— OF —
BRITISH
HISTORY

THE RED HOUSE

Authors
Jean Cooke
Theodore Rowland-Entwistle

Editor
Frances M. Clapham

This edition published in 1994
by The Red House, Witney
Oxford OX8 5YF
Originally published in 1984

© Grisewood & Dempsey Ltd 1984,
1990, 1992

ISBN 1 871745 09 8

Printed in Italy by New Interlitho
S.p.A. – Milan

Contents

Early Britain

The early story of Britain falls in the period known as *prehistory*, before there was any written history. Archaeologists, people who delve into that remote past, have discovered traces of some very early form of people, who lived near what is now Clacton-on-Sea in Essex, and used flint tools. They existed about 500,000 years ago. They have also found remains of other early people who lived near Swanscombe, in Kent, about 200,000 years ago.

But the story of Britain does not really begin until after the end of the last Ice Age. The ice began to retreat about 10,000 years ago, and by then there were people living in Britain, making stone axes. At that time they could still cross from France by land, but as the ice melted it released more water into the sea until, about 8000 years ago, the last land bridge disappeared and the English Channel was formed. But people still came to Britain. They built primitive villages, and dug huge banks to make hill forts. About 4750 years ago they started to build the vast stone structure we know as Stonehenge, one of the most remarkable prehistoric stone structures in the world. At about the same time, the Pharaoh Khufu was building the Great Pyramid in Egypt. Britain was still a pretty backward place compared with Egypt and other major civilizations.

Left: This gigantic outline of a horse carved into the Berkshire downs probably dates from the Iron Age but nobody knows its significance.
Below: Skara Brae, a neolithic settlement on Mainland, Orkney.

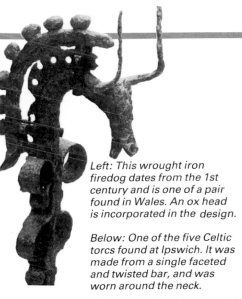

Left: This wrought iron firedog dates from the 1st century and is one of a pair found in Wales. An ox head is incorporated in the design.

Below: One of the five Celtic torcs found at Ipswich. It was made from a single faceted and twisted bar, and was worn around the neck.

Silbury Hill

One of the greatest prehistoric mysteries in Britain is Silbury Hill in Wiltshire. Stone Age men built it between 3000 and 2500 BC. It is the biggest artificial hill in Europe, and is 40 metres high. Archaeologists reckon that if 700 men had worked on it they could not have built it in less than ten years. But nobody knows what its purpose was. The most likely theory is that it was a tomb, but though traces of a *barrow*, or burial mound, have been found under it, no grave has been discovered. Silbury Hill may also have had some religious significance.

ELSEWHERE IN THE WORLD

Early dates in this period are all approximate

BC

20,000 Cave paintings at Lascaux, France
8000 Domestication of cattle and pigs
7000 First settlement at Jericho
3100 First Dynasty rules Egypt
2700 Great Pyramid built
2500 Civilizations flourish in Indus Valley, Pakistan, and in Crete
2350 Yao Dynasty in China
1400 Knossos in Crete destroyed
1250 Exodus: Jews leave Egypt
1000 David becomes king of Israel
776 First Olympic Games in Greece
746 Tiglath-Pilesar III rules Assyria
753 Foundation of Rome
605 Nebuchadrezzar rules Babylon
563 Birth of the Buddha
559 Cyrus II founds Persian Empire
500 Bantu tribes spread in East Africa
480 Battles of Thermopylae and Salamis
336 Alexander the Great becomes king of Macedonia
321 Maurya dynasty in India
221 Ch'in dynasty in China
51 Julius Caesar conquers Gaul
23 Augustus, first Roman emperor
5 Birth of Jesus Christ

AD

30 Crucifixion of Jesus
45 Paul begins to preach to Gentiles
58 Buddhism introduced into China
70 Destruction of Jerusalem
135 Diaspora: final dispersal of the Jews into exile
285 Emperor Diocletian divides Roman Empire into East and West
300 Maya civilization flourishes in Central America
476 Barbarians conquer Rome: end of the Western Roman Empire

Megaliths

Megaliths – huge standing stones – are found scattered throughout northern Europe. Sometimes the stones are found in rows, as at Carnac in Brittany. Nobody knows the purpose of these alignments but stone circles are better understood. They were probably used for religious worship.

Stonehenge, on Salisbury Plain, was built in three stages, beginning about 2750 BC and ending about 1300 BC. In the second stage of the building a ring of 80 bluestones was erected. These blue rocks were brought from the Prescelly Mountains in southern Wales, a journey of about 390 km. They were probably floated on rafts to a landing place on the river Avon, which lies 3 km from Stonehenge. The huge sandstone

Maiden Castle in Dorset, south-west England. This ridge overlooked the countryside around, and was a good place to live. In the 2000s BC Stone Age people built huts and a ditched enclosure for their animals there. At this time the country round was wooded marsh, and the ridge provided farmland. About 2000 BC a vast long barrow (burial mound) was built on the highest point. A little later Bronze Age people settled there. By about 1500 BC the bogs and swamps below had dried out and the land could be farmed. The ridge was deserted until the 5th century BC when a fort was built there, surrounded by walls of earth and chalk with a wide, deep ditch outside them. Maiden Castle became a permanent settlement with stone and wooden huts.

blocks in the centre were dragged from Avebury, 30 km away. Avebury has a much older and larger stone circle but it is less well preserved.

Islands of Tin

Britain first became known to the classical world of Greece and Rome as the Cassiterides, the Islands of Tin. The Ancient Britons mined tin in Cornwall from about 1900 BC. That was the beginning of the Bronze Age in Britain, bronze being an alloy of copper and tin. The tin was apparently taken from the mines to the island of Ictis, probably St Michael's Mount. From there Phoenician traders took it by sea to sell in Greece and Rome. Some tin is still mined in Cornwall.

Left: A Bronze Age beaker found in Kent. Immigrants from the Rhineland, known as the Beaker Folk, are thought to have introduced these objects to Britain.

Below: The megaliths or standing stones at Callanish on the isle of Lewis in the Outer Hebrides date from about 2000 BC.

Note: Dates in this period are all approximate

BC

510,000 to 310,000 Early people using flint tools near Clacton-on-Sea
200,000 Swanscombe Man in Kent
125,000 Last period of glaciation (ice cover) begins
100,000 Paviland Man in South Wales
40,000 Early people live in caves at Cresswell Crags, Derbyshire
24,000 Last interstadial (pause in Ice Age) begins
13,000 Warm period ends; ice cap moves over most of Britain again
10,000 Stone-axe factory set up at Grimes Graves, Norfolk
8000 Ice cap again begins to retreat
6000 Rising sea-level forms English Channel, cutting Britain off from continental Europe
3100 Stone Age village established at Skara Brae, Orkney
3000-2500 Silbury Hill, Wiltshire, built
2750 Stonehenge, Wiltshire, begun
2500 Skara Brae abandoned
Settlers at Windmill Hill, Wiltshire, make first British pottery
2000 Weaving first known in Britain
1900 Beaker Folk arrive in Britain; they make and use bronze
1300 Stonehenge completed
800 First Celts invade
500 Iron Age begins in England
350 Celts from Germany settle in Ireland
310 Greek navigator Pytheas of Massilia sails around Britain
250 Parisi from France invade Yorkshire
200 Celts settle in Taymouth and Moray Firth areas
100 Lake villages flourish at Glastonbury and Meare, Somerset
75 Belgic tribe Catuvellauni settle at Colchester

The Roman Invasions

The first Roman invasion of Britain was led by Gaius Julius Caesar, the governor of the Roman province of Gaul (France). He landed near Dover in 55 BC, but storms damaged his ships and after some fierce fighting with the Britons he had to retreat. A second invasion with a larger force the next year was more successful, and Caesar forced the Britons to submit to him.

Revolt in Gaul and civil war in Rome took Caesar away, never to return. Almost a hundred years later, in AD 43, the Emperor Claudius sent four legions to conquer the island. Claudius himself came over, and the next year entered the British town of Camulodunum (Colchester) in triumph. Resistance was led by the British chief Caratacus for the next seven years.

Boudicca's Revolt

In AD 60 Prasutagus, king of the Iceni, a Norfolk tribe, died and left his fortune jointly to his two daughters and the Roman emperor. The Romans proceeded to take over the kingdom, and ill-treated the girls and their mother Boudicca (Boadicea). Boudicca, outraged, led a fierce revolt. The Iceni burned Camulodunum (Colchester), Verulamium (St Albans) and London and slaughtered many Romans. The Romans rallied under their governor and won a bloody battle, probably at Fenny Stratford, Buckinghamshire.

A reconstruction of a Roman villa at Rockbourne, Hampshire. The interior would have been decorated with frescoes and mosaics in the Mediterranean style. The lack of fortifications shows how successfully the Romans had established peace.

A section of Roman road in Yorkshire. Planned by military engineers and built by soldiers, each road followed the most direct route possible. Most Roman buildings in Britain were soon destroyed, but some of their roads can still be seen while many modern roads follow Roman routes.

Hadrian's Wall

The Romans gradually extended their conquest of Britain northwards until they reached what is now Scotland. There they were hampered by the bleak countryside and the fierce Pictish tribes of the north.

In 122 the Emperor Hadrian visited Britain, and decided to establish a firm northern frontier for the Roman province. So he ordered a wall to be built across the country, from the river Tyne to the Solway Firth. Hadrian's Wall took seven years to complete, and a great deal of it still remains. It is 117 km long. It consisted of a stone wall about 4.5 metres high, with a ditch on the north side. Every 1.5 km were small forts, called milecastles, and there were 16 major forts as well. A second ditch, the *vallum*, was later dug to the south.

55 Julius Caesar invades Britain near Dover, but has to retreat
54 Caesar raids again with five legions and reaches Essex

AD

43 Four Roman legions under Aulus Plautius invade Britain
Emperor Claudius arrives in Britain and captures Camulodunum
?45 Vespasian (later emperor) captures Vectis (the Isle of Wight)
47 Ostorius Scapula defeats the Iceni in East Anglia
48 Romans begin conquest of Wales
51 Caradog (Caratacus), king of the Silures, is defeated and taken to Rome
61 Romans conquer Anglesey, stronghold of the Druids
Revolt of the Iceni under Queen Boudicca (Boadicea) is suppressed
78 Julius Agricola arrives to become governor of Britain
81 Agricola reaches the Forth and establishes northern frontier
84 Agricola defeats the Picts at Mons Gropius, in the Highlands
100 In Ireland, Firbolgs (early inhabitants) led by Caibre Cinn Cait ('Cat-head') revolt against Celts. Celtic leader Tuathal forms united kingdom of Meath and Connacht
115 Romans withdraw northern frontier to Tyne-Solway line
119 Caledonian clans revolt, wiping out Roman Ninth Legion
123 Emperor Hadrian builds his great wall on Tyne-Solway line
143 Romans build a new wall (Antonine Wall) from Forth to Clyde
163 Romans withdraw to Hadrian's Wall
200 In Ireland, Conn Céd-cathach (Conn of the Hundred Fights) becomes Ard-Rí (High King) at Tara

15

Britain Under Attack

The Romans had to keep soldiers in Britain all the time to guard it against attack. From about AD 280 on, Saxon pirates began raiding the shores of Britain, while at the least sign of weakness in the Roman defence the Picts were ready to pour over Hadrian's Wall in the north.

To guard against the Saxons, the Romans built a chain of forts around the coast from Norfolk to the Isle of Wight. The forts were under the command of an officer known as the Count of the Saxon Shore.

These defences held off the raiders for many years. But in 367 the Picts, the Saxons and the Scots of northern Ireland joined forces to make a concerted attack. They overran the Wall, and killed the Count of the Saxon Shore. But the Romans restored order, and made treaties with some of the tribes north of the Wall.

Early Christians

Nobody knows when Christianity was first established in Britain, but it was some time before AD 200. It was probably brought to Britain by Roman soldiers or civilian settlers from Gaul. In 287 a Romano-Briton named Alban, living at Verulamium, sheltered a Christian fleeing from persecution and was put to death. From this event comes Verulamium's present name of St Albans. By 325, when the Emperor Constantine made Christianity Rome's official religion, England already had three bishops, at Lincoln, London and York.

Opposite: The Lunt near Coventry, a partial reconstruction of a typical Roman fort made of timber and turf. As they advanced across the country the Romans built a number of such temporary forts, from which to subdue the surrounding area.

Below: A map of Roman Britain showing the main towns, roads and forts. A fully equipped Roman soldier could march 30 miles (58 kilometres) a day on these roads, which were built as straight as possible. The network of roads enabled later invaders to overrun Britain with great speed.

16

The High Kings of Ireland

The early history of Ireland is a mixture of fact and legend that is hard to unravel. Some of the earliest peoples were small, dark people from Spain, known to legend as Firbolgs. Later, Celts invaded and controlled the country.

There were many small Celtic kingdoms in Ireland. The first great leader was Cormac, who ruled over Meath and Connacht. He made himself *Ard-Rí* (High King), and set up a national assembly at Tara Hill, in Meath. An even more powerful ruler was Niall of the Nine Hostages, who was Ard-Rí from 380 to 405. His descendants were Ard-Rí until 1003.

208 Emperor Septimius Severus arrives; invades Caledonia
211 Severus dies at York
275 In Ireland, Cormac MacArt rules as Ard-Rí at Tara (to 300)
280 Saxon pirates begin raiding Britain
284 Emperor Diocletian makes Britain part of the Prefecture of Gaul
287 St Alban martyred for sheltering a fugitive Christian
Marcus Aurelius Carausius, admiral of the English Channel fleet, briefly becomes emperor in Britain
287-296 Chain of forts built from the Wash to the Isle of Wight, as part of the Saxon Shore system
306 Emperor Constantius campaigns in Scotland; he dies, and his son Constantine is proclaimed at York
314 Bishops from Lincoln, London and York attend the Council of Arles (assembly of the Roman Church)
324 Christianity becomes official religion of the Roman Empire
325 British bishops attend Council of Nicaea, first world-wide council of the Christian Church
332 The Three Collas, descendants of Conn of Tara, defeat Fergus of Ulster
366 Picts raid as far as London
367 Saxons, Picts and Scots all raid Britain
Spanish-Roman general Theodosius drives the Picts back beyond Hadrian's Wall
380-405 Niall of the Nine Hostages is Ard-Rí at Tara
383 Magnus Clemens Maximus, British-born governor of Britain, fails to make himself emperor of Rome
396 Picts invade northern Britain
397 St Ninian founds the monastery of Candida Casa (White House) at Whithorn in Galloway

After the Romans

The years following the collapse of the Roman Empire in AD 476 are often known as the Dark Ages. The name is given to them partly because so little is known about what was happening at that time, and partly because the end of the strong Roman rule of law and order meant that life in Western Europe was hard and dangerous. The Dark Ages began in Britain much earlier than in the rest of Europe, when the last of the Roman legions left in 406.

Britain was already being attacked by Saxon pirates. The attacks grew stronger and more frequent. For a time the Romano-British people fought them off. Memories of that grim struggle are contained in the legends of King Arthur. The Arthur of the story books is an invention: he was not a knight in shining armour, with ideals of chivalry. But historians are now pretty certain that there was a person called Arthur. He was probably *dux bellorum* – a war leader, commander-in-chief of a mobile army, who fought a long guerrilla war against the invaders.

However, it was the pirate raiders who eventually won. Saxons, Jutes and Angles swarmed into the country from northern Germany. From the Angles comes the name England – Angle-land. Later invaders were the Northmen, the fierce Vikings who settled in northern and eastern England and left their mark in place names containing old Norse words such as *by*, a village, or *thwaite*, a clearing.

Left: An enamelled bronze plaque from the Sutton Hoo ship burial, which may be that of an East Anglian king. The Anglo-Saxons were fierce warriors but they were also skilled craftsmen.

Below: Three early English kings; Alfred (871-99), Edgar (959-75) and Aethelred (978-1016).

A page from the Book of Kells, a copy of the Latin Gospels made by Celtic monks in Ireland in about AD 800. Like many Celtic books made at the time it was decorated with complicated abstract patterns.

The Learned Monks

One of the worst features of the Dark Ages was that the barbarian rulers of Europe and Britain were not scholars. Few could even read or write. They destroyed many priceless manuscripts, and much of the accumulated knowledge of the Greeks and Romans was lost.

However, scholarship was kept alive in the monasteries of the Christian Church. Monks studied medicine and wrote history. In their *scriptoria* they copied books and sent them to other monasteries. Above all, they studied the Bible and the writings of the Holy Fathers, men who led the Church in its early days.

ELSEWHERE IN THE WORLD

405 St Jerome completes Latin translation of the Bible (the Vulgate)
410 Alaric and Goths sack Rome
433 Attila becomes ruler of the Huns
451 Battle of Châlons: Romans and Visigoths defeat the Huns
476 Goths conquer Rome: end of the Western Roman Empire
527 Justinian emperor of Byzantium (the Eastern Roman Empire; to 565)
552 Buddhism reaches Japan
570 Birth of Muhammad
590 Gregory I, the Great, Pope (to 604)
619 Persians occupy Egypt (to 629)
632 Death of Muhammad
635 Muslims begin conquest of Syria and Persia
639-642 Arabs conquer Egypt
655 Battle of the Masts: Arab naval victory over Byzantine fleet
674 Arab armies reach the Indus River
Arabs capture Crete
700 Arabs capture Tunis
711-718 Moors conquer most of Spain
787 Harun al-Raschid caliph at Baghdad (to 809)
800 Frankish ruler Charlemagne crowned as emperor of the West
841 Northmen (Vikings) invade what is now Normandy
900 Mayas move into Yucatán
907 Civil war in China
911 Viking leader Hrolf the Ganger is granted lands in France: formation of Normandy
960 Sung Dynasty in China
962 Otto I first Holy Roman Emperor
1000 Empire of Ancient Ghana at its height about this time
1002 Viking Leif Ericsson explores coast of North America
1054 Split between Roman and Eastern Orthodox Churches

19

The End of Roman Rule

Two things combined to bring about the end of Roman rule in Britain. One was civil war, as rival generals fought to become emperor. The other was increasing attacks by barbarian tribes from northern Europe. Slowly legions were withdrawn from Britain to protect other parts of the Roman Empire. The last legion left in 406. Four years later, when the Romano-British appealed for help, the Emperor could only reply: 'Take steps to defend yourselves.'

Britain had been Roman for four centuries. The Romans gave it a good system of roads. Life centred around large villas, the equivalent of the 'stately homes' of later years. The country had settled government, many Christian churches, and prosperous farms. All this was soon to change.

Hengest and Horsa

With the Romans gone, the Picts broke through Hadrian's Wall and raided England frequently and savagely. According to tradition the Romano-British chief Vortigern invited a group of Jutish mercenaries to come and drive the Picts away. They arrived, led by two brothers, Hengest and Horsa (meaning respectively 'horse' and 'mare'). Some historians think the names, and the brothers, are fictitious.

The Jutes drove off the Picts, and then drove off Vortigern too, taking his kingdom of Kent. Horsa was killed in battle, but Hengest went on to fight the Welsh. Within the next few years hundreds of Saxons and Angles landed, conquered or killed the Britons, and settled the land. Many of the Britons fled westwards, to Wales and Cornwall.

Arthur and his knights of the Round Table. Hardly anything is known of the real man behind the legend but it is probable that he was a military commander rather than a king. His greatest victory was at Mount Badon but nobody knows where this was; Badbury Rings in Dorset is a likely site. Arthur is first mentioned in the 8th century by the Welsh writer Nennius who describes him as 'dux bellorum', war leader. In the 12th century he became the subject of many tales. The Arthurian legend flourished above all in France where it gradually lost its Celtic flavour and became more courtly in style.

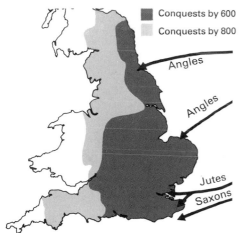

Conquests by 600
Conquests by 800

Following the departure of the Romans, Britain was invaded by Germanic tribes. Angles and Saxons came from the coasts of Denmark and Germany. Jutes came either from their original home in Jutland or from their more recent settlements in Friesland and on the lower Rhine.

St Patrick

In the early 400s a 16-year-old Romano-British lad named Patrick was carried off to Ireland and made a slave. He escaped and trained as a Christian priest, and some thirty years later he went back to Ireland as a bishop and a missionary. There were already a few Christians in Ireland; Patrick's preaching converted almost all the island.

Many legends later grew up around Patrick, who became Ireland's patron saint. One claimed that he banished all the snakes from Ireland, which has none. In fact snakes never reached Ireland after the Ice Age; the sea rose and made it an island at a time when Britain was still attached to the European mainland.

401 St Patrick sold into slavery in Ireland by pirates
406 Roman legions leave Britain
407 Romano-Briton Constantine proclaims himself 'emperor'
410 Emperor Honorius tells the British Rome can no longer defend them
432 St Patrick begins mission to Ireland
440 About this time Saxon invaders begin to settle permanently
449 British ruler Vortigern invites Saxons to help repel the Picts; Jutes Hengest and Horsa respond
450 Treasure buried at Mildenhall, Suffolk (discovered 1942)
455 Jutes rebel against Vortigern; Horsa killed at Aylesford
457 Hengest defeats the Britons at Crayford, and conquers all Kent
475 Wansdyke (defensive earthwork) in western England built about now
477 South Saxons arrive in England
495 West Saxons arrive in England
500 Traditional date of Saxon defeat by Britons under Arthur at Mount Badon
540 Welsh poets Aneurin, Taliesin, and Llywarch Hên flourish
Bubonic plague reaches Britain
547 Anglian chief Ide founds kingdom of Bernicia
563 St Columba founds Iona monastery
575 Convention of Drumceat – Irish council of kings and abbots
577 West Saxons defeat Welsh at Deorham (now Dyrham, Avon)
588 Aethelric creates the kingdom of Northumbria
597 St Augustine arrives on a mission from Rome, and founds a monastery at Canterbury
598 King Aethelbert of Kent baptised
600 Saxons, Angles and Jutes control most of England

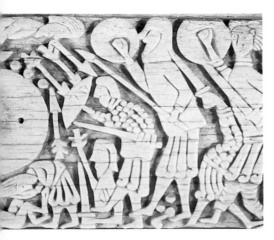

Above: Part of the Franks casket, a whalebone box which was made in Northumbria in the 8th century. The carvings on it depict a curious mixture of barbarian and Christian subjects.

The Chroniclers

Much of what we know about life in Britain during the Dark Ages comes from chronicles and histories written by monks. One of the most important sources is the *History of the English Church and People*, completed in 731 by a monk at Jarrow, the Venerable Bede. Bede spent his whole life at Jarrow, teaching and writing.

The other major work is the *Anglo-Saxon Chronicle*, begun sometime in the 800s by monks at Winchester and continued there and at other monasteries up to the coronation of Henry II in 1154. The chroniclers drew largely on Bede for their early material (from AD 1), but their later work was written year by year as events took place.

The Synod of Whitby

Even in the Dark Ages Christians argued fiercely about the form their Church should take. In England some followed the teachings of the Celtic Church, brought from Ireland by St Columba and others. The rest followed the ideas of Rome and the Pope, brought to England by St Augustine. In 664 a synod (conference) was held at Whitby in Yorkshire, and Church leaders decided to follow the Roman rule, thus uniting the Christians in Britain with the rest of Europe.

The Lindisfarne Gospel. This illuminated Latin manuscript was written by Eadfrith of Lindisfarne shortly before 700, during a period of intense creative activity within the Church. It shows a very skilful fusion of Anglo-Saxon, Irish and Mediterranean styles.

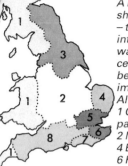

A map of England showing the heptarchy – the seven kingdoms into which the country was divided by the 7th century. Wessex had become the most important kingdom by Alfred's reign.
1 Celtic Territories (not part of the heptarchy)
2 Mercia 3 Northumbria 4 East Anglia 5 Essex 6 Kent 7 Sussex 8 Wessex

The Making of England

The Angles, the Saxons and the Jutes were basically the same people, with the Saxons dominant. In Europe they had been vulnerable to attack from other peoples, but in Britain they had a chance to lead safer, more settled lives.

The Anglo-Saxons occupied the land which is now England, and they were the real creators of England. Although their kings fought each other, the land was basically settled and peaceful. The Saxons were mostly farming folk and few lived in towns. Under each king there were three classes: noblemen; churls, who were freemen or yeomen, many of them owning land; and slaves. A slave was worth eight oxen.

Most people lived in wooden houses. They grew barley, oats and wheat for food, and flax for making linen. Sheep were kept for their wool as much as for their meat, and the Saxons also kept cattle, pigs and goats.

Towns were centres for trade, and also for defence in time of war. Craftsmen made pottery and glass, and metalworkers included skilled jewellers.

601 First York Minster built
604 First church of St Paul, London
613 Northumbrians defeat Britons near Chester
620 Northumbrians annex Isle of Man Northmen (Vikings) invade Ireland
627 Bishop Paulinus converts Edwin of Northumbria to Christianity
633 Edwin, now Bretwalda of Britain, killed at Hatfield Chase, Yorks.
635 Lindisfarne monastery established St Aidan bishop of Northumbria
642 Oswald of Northumbria killed in battle against Penda of Mercia
650 Epic poem *Beowulf* written
655 Penda killed in battle; final decline of paganism in Britain
660 Sutton Hoo ship burial
664 Synod of Whitby: Roman form of worship replaces Celtic form
665 St Wilfrid made bishop at York
669 Theodore of Tarsus appointed as archbishop of Canterbury
673 Theodore reforms monasteries and curbs Saxon divorce customs Abbot Benedict Biscop sets up libraries at Wearmouth and Jarrow
674 First glass windows installed in English churches
681-6 St Wilfrid converts people of Sussex to Christianity
684 Caedwalla, pagan king of Wessex, begins career of conquest St Cuthbert bishop of Hexham
690 King Ine of Wessex's laws are written down by the clergy
700 Lindisfarne Gospels completed
704 Aethelred of Mercia abdicates to become a monk
716 Aethelbald becomes king of Mercia (until 747)
731 Venerable Bede completes *History of the English Church and People*
750 Gregorian Church music in England

Above: Offa's Dyke. During his reign as King of Mercia, Offa masterminded the building of this formidable earthwork, designed to keep the Welsh at bay.

Below: A Mercian penny issued during King Offa's reign. He was the first king to issue a royal coinage bearing his name.

Kenneth MacAlpin

The early inhabitants of Scotland formed a number of tribes, each with its own leader. By the AD 600s these tribes had united to form two kingdoms north of the Clyde-Forth line. Most of the north was Pictavia, the land of the Picts. To the west lay Dalriada, the kingdom of the Scots who had moved there from Ireland. South of the Clyde-Forth line lay Strathclyde, extending from the Clyde south into modern Cumbria, and Bernicia, extending from the Forth to the Tyne.

In 843 Kenneth MacAlpin (son of Alpin), King of Scots, claimed the throne of Pictavia through his grand-mother, a Pictish princess. From his time onwards all the land north of the Clyde-Forth line was united and came to be called Scotland.

The Northmen
In the late 700s the former Anglo-Saxon pirates, now settled in England, the land they had made their own, received the first of a series of shocks – raids by the Northmen, pirates from Scandinavia. These Northmen were known as *Vikings*, from a Norse word meaning pirate. The monks who wrote the *Anglo-Saxon Chronicle* referred to them as 'the heathen' or 'the force'.

The Vikings were bold warriors, fierce and cruel. They sailed in longships, graceful vessels each of which carried a square sail and oars to cope with all weathers. They were well disciplined and loyal to one another. But in their raids they slaughtered, burned and robbed. They carried off all the most beautiful women, and took men to sell as slaves. In their churches the Saxons prayed: 'From the fury of the Norsemen, good Lord deliver us.'

Egbert
The first king who could claim to be ruler over all England was Egbert, king of Wessex from 802 to 839. He enlarged Wessex to include Kent, Sussex, Surrey and Cornwall, and defeated the powerful Mercian kingdom in the battle of Ellandun (Wroughton, in Wiltshire). Thereafter Mercia and Northumbria acknowledged Egbert as *Bretwalda* (Lord of Britain).

757 Offa becomes king of Mercia (until 796); Mercia at most powerful
760 Book of Kells: Latin gospels
768 Churchman Alcuin teaches theology at York, under Offa's patronage
774 Offa becomes effectively supreme ruler in England
782-5 Offa builds defensive wall (Offa's Dyke) to keep out the Welsh
787 Vikings raid Wessex: first recorded raid of Northmen on England
790 Offa founds St Alban's abbey
793 Offa annexes East Anglia; Northmen sack Lindisfarne
794 Vikings raid Scottish isles
795 First Viking raid on Ireland
796 Offa of Mercia dies
798 Cenwulf of Mercia ravages Kent
802 Egbert king of Wessex (to 839)
806 Vikings sack monastery on Iona
810 Welsh monk Nynniaw (Nennius) compiles *Historia Britonum*, with first mention of Arthur
815 Egbert defeats the Cornish Britons
821 Cenwulf of Mercia dies: Mercian domination comes to an end
825 Egbert defeats Beornulf of Mercia at Ellandun (Wroughton, Wilts.)
829 Egbert conquers Mercia and forces Northumbria to submit: he is supreme king in England
831 Thorgest the Viking settles in Ireland as a king
834 Kenneth MacAlpin becomes king of the Scots (to 863)
839 Egbert dies; his son Aethelwulf becomes king of Wessex (to 858)
843 Kenneth MacAlpin defeats the Picts and unites the Picts and Scots
851 Danes raid Canterbury
856 Aethelbald rebels against his father, King Aethelwulf of Wessex
858 Aethelwulf dies; Aethelbald, then his brother Aethelbert (860-865), succeed

Alfred the Great

The Vikings would have conquered the whole of England but for the efforts of one man: Alfred the Great, King of Wessex. Alfred was the youngest of four sons of King Aethelwulf of Wessex, who spent most of their lives fighting the invaders. Alfred carried on the struggle after he came to the throne in 871. At one stage the Danish Vikings overwhelmed Alfred's forces, and he spent some months hiding in the Isle of Athelney, among the marshes of Somerset. But he recovered, and defeated the Danes at the battles of Ashdown and Edington. The Danes agreed to divide the country with him.

Alfred built a fleet to defend his shores and, freed from campaigning, devoted his time to reforming the law and encouraging scholarship. He himself translated several works from Latin into Anglo-Saxon.

Opposite: The Alfred Jewel was found at Athelney in Somerset and is thought to have belonged to Alfred the Great. It bears the Anglo-Saxon inscription 'Alfred had me made'.

Part of a Viking tomb, found in St Paul's churchyard in London. The Vikings were not just raiders; many of them settled in Britain.

The Danelaw

The Vikings who invaded England in the mid-800s came from Denmark. They were led by Ivar the Boneless and Ubbe, sons of the semi-legendary Danish leader Ragnar Lodbrok ('Hairy-breeches'). The Danes came prepared to stay. They conquered Northumbria and East Anglia, and spread across Mercia. Only the southern kingdom of Wessex held out against them.

The northern part of England, north of a line from London to Chester, became Danish, and was later called the *Danelaw* – the region where the law of the Danes prevailed.

The Triumph of Wessex

Alfred's son Edward the Elder was as skilful a general as his father. In his 25-year reign he defeated the Danes several times, and by the time he died he ruled over all England south of the river Humber. The Danish settlers of East Anglia and the Midlands submitted to him, and the Welsh princes also acknowledged him as their overlord.

Edward's son Aethelstan was a worthy descendant of his father and grandfather, defeating a coalition of Vikings, Scots and Irish Celts at the battle of Brunaburgh.

860 Danes sack Winchester
863 Constantine II king of Scots (to 897)
865 Aethelbert dies; succeeded by his brother Aethelred I (to 871)
869 Danes occupy East Anglia and kill its last king, St Edmund
870 English first use calibrated candles to measure time
871 Alfred the Great succeeds his brother Aethelred I (to 899)
878 Alfred defeats Danes near Chippenham; Peace of Wedmore divides England between Danes (Danelaw) and Saxons
889 Donald I king of Scots (to 900)
890 Alfred establishes regular navy
899 Alfred dies; succeeded by his son Edward the Elder (to 924)
900 England divided into shires
913 Edward takes Essex from Danes
919 Danes defeat Irish at Dublin
924 Aethelstan succeeds his father Edward (to 939)
926 Aethelstan annexes Mercia and Northumberland
937 Aethelstan defeats Scots and allies at battle of Brunaburgh
939 Aethelstan dies; is succeeded by his brothers Edmund (to 946) and Edred (to 955) and Edmund's sons Edwig (to 959) and Edgar (to 975)
959 St Dunstan archbishop of Canterbury
965 English invade Celtic kingdom of Gwynedd
967 Cuilean king of Scots (till 971)
971 Kenneth II king of Scotland (to 995)
973 Edgar acclaimed king of England (to 975)
975 St Edward the Martyr king of England (to 978)
978 Edward murdered; half-brother Aethelred II king (to 1016)
980 Danes begin almost yearly raids

Aethelred the Evil-Counselled

Three strong kings – Alfred, Edward the Elder and Aethelstan – made the Anglo-Saxon kingdom of England strong. A succession of weak rulers lost it. The weakest was Aethelred II, who came to the throne in 978 when his half-brother Edward the Martyr was murdered. Aethelred was known as the *Unraed* – redeless, or evil-counselled. Later generations translated the word as 'unready', and he was that too.

Serious Danish raids began again almost at once. The battle of Maldon, in Essex, was a grim defeat for the Saxons. Acting on bad advice, Aethelred bought off the Danes with an ever-increasing series of bribes, raised by a tax known as *Danegeld*: £10,000 in silver in 991, £16,000 in 994, £24,000 in 1002, and £36,000 in 1006.

Still the Danes were not satisfied. In 1013 their invading King, Sweyn, was proclaimed king of England. Aethelred fled to Normandy, the home of his wife, Emma. This marriage had been the first of England's links with Normandy.

The Danish Kings

Sweyn died in 1014. Aethelred came back, but died in 1016. For a few months his warrior son, Edmund Ironside, fought the Danes, but he died suddenly, and Sweyn's son Cnut (Canute) became king.

Cnut was a strong, if harsh, ruler, who brought peace to England. He was

The battle of Stamford Bridge: When the King of Norway and Tostig Godwinsson invaded in the north, Harold hastily raised an army and defeated them in a surprise attack on their camp at Stamford Bridge.
Meanwhile William of Normandy landed at Pevensey and within a few days Harold was defeated at Hastings.

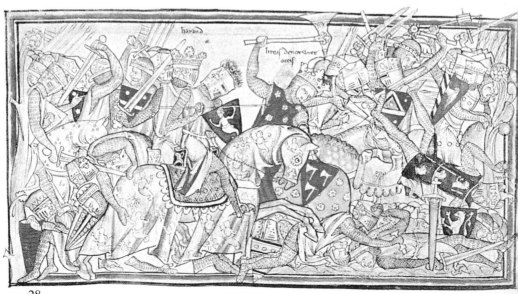

also king of Denmark, and he conquered Norway. He was succeeded in turn by two of his sons, Harold I, known as Harefoot, and Harthacnut. Within seven years these two loutish and ignorant men were dead.

Edward the Confessor

After the Danish kings a Saxon again sat on the English throne. Edward, son of Aethelred II and Emma of Normandy, was a gentle, pious man, Norman by upbringing. He was so devout that his people called him 'the Confessor', and though he was married he lived like a monk and refused to produce an heir.

The government of the land was in the hands of a Wessex earl, Godwin, and when he died in 1053 his son Harold Godwinsson took over.

The Last Saxon King

Harold Godwinsson, Earl of Wessex, was the last Saxon king of England. He had no right to the throne by descent, but he was the most powerful man in England, governing it for a dozen years and marrying the King's sister.

According to the Normans, Harold was shipwrecked on the coast of France in 1064, came into Duke William's hands, and swore a solemn oath to help William to the English Crown – which Edward the Confessor had apparently promised him. But on his deathbed Edward named Harold as his heir, and the Witan, the Saxon council, agreed. Harold probably reckoned that his oath, obtained under duress, was not binding. He took the throne; William invaded; Harold was killed at Hastings.

991 Aethelred raises £10,000 by tax, Danegeld, to buy off Danes
Danes defeat English at Maldon
994 Olaf of Norway and Sweyn of Denmark besiege London
995 Constantine IV king of Scotland
997 Kenneth III king of Scotland (to 1005)
999 Malachy II, High King of Ireland, and Brian Boru defeat the Danes
1003 Brian Boru High King of Ireland
1005 Malcolm II king of Scotland (to 1034)
1013 Danes master England
1014 Brian Boru defeats Vikings at Clontarf, but is killed
Sweyn dies; son Cnut is king
1016 Aethelred dies; succeeded by son Edmund Ironside, who dies; Cnut king of England (to 1035)
1034 Duncan I king of Scotland (to 1040)
1035 Cnut dies; succeeded as king of England by son Harold I Harefoot
1040 Harold I dies; succeeded by half-brother Harthacnut (to 1042)
Macbeth kills Duncan I in battle, becomes king (to 1057)
1042 Edward, son of Aethelred, becomes king (to 1066)
1057 Duncan's son Malcolm kills Macbeth
1058 Malcolm III Canmore king of Scots (to 1093)
1066 Edward the Confessor dies; Witan offers throne to Harold II
Appearance of Halley's Comet
Tostig and Harold Haardraade of Norway invade northern England; defeated at Stamford Bridge by Harold II
William of Normandy invades Sussex; defeats and kills Harold II at Hastings, becomes king (to 1087)

The Normans

In the 600 years since the Saxon pirates began to settle amid the ruins of the old Roman province of Britain, their descendants had made their land of England one of the wealthiest and best-governed in western Europe. The country had even absorbed the latest raiders, the Danes. The King, Edward the Confessor, was a man of peace. All was about to change. Because Edward had no son to take his place, the storm clouds were gathering. Once again the Northmen threatened. Harold Haardraade of Norway, aided by Earl Godwin's renegade son Tostig, Earl of Northumbria, was waiting to pounce. So too was William, Duke of Normandy.

William won the contest, and for the next hundred years England was under Norman kings. The Normans imposed many of their customs and their language on the English. They were, indeed, conquerors. But they gave England what she badly needed: a succession of strong, capable kings. And in the end it was England and the English people who conquered. They absorbed the Normans completely. English law prevailed, and so did the English language, enriched with a smattering of Norman-French words.

The Normans brought about one major change. They ended England's insularity. Henceforth England was very much a part of Europe as a whole, and indeed until 1558 the English kings owned a part of France – at times the major part.

Scotland and Ireland retained their independence under the Norman kings. Wales already had links with the Saxon kings, and within a few years the Normans overran the southern part of Wales. But for some centuries northern Wales held out.

THE NORMANS

WILLIAM I
1066–1087

Robert II Duke of Normandy	WILLIAM II 1087–1100	HENRY I 1100–1135	Adela

Emperor m. Matilda m. Geoffrey
Henry V   of Anjou

STEPHEN
1135–1154

HENRY II Plantagenet m. Eleanor of
1154–1189   Aquitaine

Part of the Bayeux tapestry, which tells the story of the Norman invasion and conquest of England. On the right is the death of Harold.

SCOTTISH KINGS

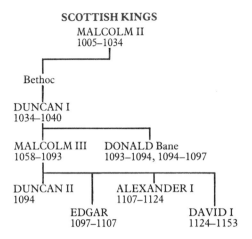

MALCOLM II
1005–1034

Bethoc

DUNCAN I
1034–1040

MALCOLM III   DONALD Bane
1058–1093   1093–1094, 1094–1097

DUNCAN II   ALEXANDER I
1094   1107–1124

         EDGAR   DAVID I
         1097–1107   1124–1153

The Battle of Hastings

An army of perhaps 8000 men conquered England for William. They were a ragamuffin crew, for to make up the numbers of his own Norman knights and barons William recruited adventurers from other parts of Europe.

The Saxon army Harold brought to oppose the invasion was probably little bigger, for the battle of Hastings lasted eight hours, a long time for a medieval battle, and the two armies must have been closely matched. Harold and many of his men were weary from the victory of Stamford Bridge and a six-day forced march back to London.

ELSEWHERE IN THE WORLD

1068 Fujiwara clan loses power in Japan
1071 Seljuk Turks overrun Asia Minor
1072 Normans conquer Sicily
1073 Gregory VII becomes Pope
1075 Gregory demands exclusive right to appoint bishops: clash with Holy Roman Empire begins
1076 Synod of Worms declares Pope Gregory VII deposed
     Gregory excommunicates Henry IV, Holy Roman Emperor
1077 Henry does penance at Canossa
1080 Gregory again excommunicates Emperor Henry IV
1082 Henry IV besieges Rome
1088 Urban II becomes Pope
1090 Assassin sect formed in Persia
     Ancient Ghanaian Empire collapses
1094 Spanish hero Rodrigo Diaz, 'El Cid', conquers Moorish kingdom of Valencia
1096 First Crusade begins
1099 Crusaders capture Jerusalem
1106 Henry V, Holy Roman Emperor
1115 St Bernard founds abbey of Clairvaux, France
1119 Knights Templars established
1122 Concordat of Worms ends dispute over appointing bishops
1125 Lothair II, Holy Roman Emperor
1127 Sung dynasty in China
1130 Innocent II becomes Pope
1135 Chimu culture in Peru flourishes at this time
1138 Conrad III, Holy Roman Emperor
1143 Portugal wins independence from Spain
1147-49 Second Crusade; it fails
1150 Great temples at Angkor Wat built about this time
1142 Frederick Barbarossa, Holy Roman Emperor

William the Conqueror

The man who overthrew the Saxons and has been known ever since as 'the Conqueror' was tough. He had to be, to survive. William was the illegitimate son of Duke Robert of Normandy and a tanner's daughter, Arlette. When Robert died William was only seven. Life was hard for any minor succeeding to an inheritance. It was much worse for a bastard. By the time he was 20 William had put down one major rebellion by his barons, and he had to overcome several more.

William's claim to England was based on the fact that he was related to Edward the Confessor through Emma of Normandy, Aethelred II's wife, and on a promise by Edward that he should inherit.

Though he was a harsh and sometimes cruel man, even the monks writing the *Anglo-Saxon Chronicle* could say: 'Good peace he made in this land, so that a man of any account might fare over the kingdom with his bosom full of gold unmolested.'

The keep or White Tower is the original part of the castle built in London by William the Conqueror and his son William Rufus. Skilful siting of castles helped the Normans to control England. Their earliest castles were simple, quickly built fortifications of earth mounds and wooden palisades.

Domesday Book

Domesday Book was a survey of England, drawn up by order of William the Conqueror. The survey was carried out in 1085, so that the King could find out exactly what his new realm consisted of. He could also check that none of his followers had seized land they should not have done, and exactly what rents and fees the land should bear. 'Domesday' comes from the word *dom*, meaning assessment.

It was so thorough that, as the horrified monks of the *Anglo-Saxon Chronicle* commented, 'there was not a single hide nor rod of land, nor, further, it is shameful to tell, though it seemed to him no shame to do it, not an ox, a cow, a pig was left out'.

A page from Domesday Book giving details of part of Bedfordshire.

1066	Edward the Confessor dies; Witan offers throne to Harold II
	Appearance of Halley's Comet
	Tostig and Harold Haardraade of Norway invade northern England; defeated at Stamford Bridge by Harold II
	William of Normandy invades Sussex; defeats and kills Harold II at Hastings, becomes king (to 1087)
1068	William quells revolts in north and west, lays the north waste
1070	Malcolm III invades Northumbria
	Lanfranc archbishop of Canterbury
	Hereward the Wake heads a rising in the fen country
1071	William subdues fen rebellion
1072	William raids Scotland
1073	Lincoln cathedral begun
1077	First English Cluniac monastery founded at Lewes, Sussex
	Rochester cathedral and St Albans abbey-church begun
1078	Tower of London begun
	Pope Gregory VII sends legates to reorganize Church in England
1079	William I's son Robert Curthose begins castle that gives Newcastle-upon-Tyne its name
1081	William I leads expedition to St David's, in Wales
1085	Cnut IV of Denmark prepares to invade England: William brings large army of mercenaries from Normandy to repel him; attack abandoned
1086	Domesday Survey completed
1087	William dies at Rouen: Robert succeeds to dukedom of Normandy, William II Rufus to English throne (to 1100)
	Abbey-churches begun at Tewkesbury and Gloucester

33

king   bishop   baron   knights   yeoman   serf

The Feudal System

The term 'Feudal System' is a modern name for the way of life of the Middle Ages, and in particular the way people held their land. It was introduced into England by William I.

The name comes from the word *feu*, meaning a free right to land in return for services. The feudal system produced a pyramid-like structure of society. The king held all the land, but granted most of it to his barons in return for service. They in turn granted some of their land to lesser nobles or knights, who sublet to yeomen, and lesser freemen. At the bottom of the pyramid were the serfs, slaves working for their keep.

The basis of tenure (holding) was, at the top of the scale, by knight service. The knight had to follow his lord to war for 40 days a year, armed and on horseback, and bring with him a specified number of soldiers. Bishops, abbots and other leading men of the Church, who also held land under the feudal system, might send substitutes in their place. But they, and other lords, often sent payment in money or goods, known as scutage, instead. With such

money the king could hire professional soldiers.

At the lower level, freemen held their land in return for working on their lord's farms for part of their time. In their spare time they farmed their own lands. They too might be called on to fight if necessary. Other payments were also laid down: for example, when a man died his heir had to pay a form of inheritance tax before he could take over the lands.

The feudal system had its own system of justice. The king held courts, and so, for legal matters on their own estates, did the lower landholders.

In England, the feudal system gradually died out, and it was finally abolished in the reign of Charles II. The king's courts, with judges and justices of the peace appointed by the king, took over the administration of justice throughout the country.

The feudal system was a two-way affair. Although the lower ranks owed service to their overlords, they were given a certain amount of protection by them. This was important in an age where armed strength was misused to gain power.

34

The Real Macbeth

The murderous tyrant whom Shakespeare has made famous as Macbeth was in real life a very different person. He was Maelbeatha, and he was a grandson, through his mother, of Malcolm II of Scotland. He defeated his cousin King Duncan I in battle, and killed him in revenge for the murder of his wife's brother by Duncan's grandfather. 'Lady Macbeth' was the Princess Gruoch, a descendant of Malcolm I, with a strong claim to the throne. Macbeth ruled for 17 years, and seems to have been a strong and good king. He was eventually killed in battle by Duncan's son, Malcolm III.

Malcolm III was called Canmore, meaning 'Big Head'. He married a Saxon princess, Margaret, who was canonized as a saint in 1250.

William Rufus, from a list of kings drawn up in the 13th century. He was a good ruler but squandered large sums of money raised by levying heavy taxes. A chronicler wrote of him: 'He was hateful to almost all his people, and odious to God.'

1088 Norman barons led by Bishop Odo rebel against William II; English militia help to crush revolt
1089 William begins campaign to wrest Normandy from his brother Robert
1090 Most of Wales comes under Norman rule
Ely and Norwich cathedrals begun
1091 Malcolm III of Scotland invades England, but has to do homage
1092 William takes Cumbria from Scots
Walcher of Malvern observes an eclipse of the Moon (in Italy)
1093 Anselm of Bec becomes archbishop of Canterbury
Malcolm III killed while invading England: Donald Bane succeeds him (to 1097)
Durham cathedral begun
1094 Revolt in north-west Wales
Duncan II, son of Malcolm III, drives out Donald Bane, but is killed after eight months
1095 Anselm quarrels with William and goes to Rome
Robert de Mowbray, Earl of Northumberland, rebels, but is defeated
1096 Normans conquer South Wales
William lends Robert funds for a crusade, with Normandy as security for the loan
1097 Edgar, son of Malcolm III, deposes and succeeds Donald Bane (to 1107); he accepts William as his overlord
Revolt by the Welsh
1098 Magnus III of Norway seizes Isle of Man, Orkneys and Hebrides
1099 William holds his first court at Westminster
William invades and conquers Maine in northern France

The Red King

The Conqueror left Normandy to his eldest son, Robert, and England to the next son, William II. The new King was known as 'Rufus' because of his ruddy complexion. Like his father he was harsh, tough and capable. But there the resemblance ended. William II was cruel and immoral.

William extorted from his subjects all the taxes and dues he could. Several times his barons rebelled in support of Robert of Normandy. William suppressed these revolts with the aid of the *fyrd*, the old Saxon part-time army. Eventually Normandy came into William's hands: Robert pawned it to his brother for money to go on crusade.

Henry Beauclerk

William II was shot while hunting in the New Forest. Nobody knows if the arrow that killed him was shot deliberately or not. His younger brother Henry at once seized the throne. He began by riding straight to Winchester, then the capital, and taking possession of the royal treasury. He was a scholarly man, known to later generations as 'Beauclerk'; he became a strong king, called 'the Lion of Justice'.

Six years later, tired of attempts to put Robert on the throne, Henry invaded Normandy and defeated Robert at the battle of Tinchebrai. Robert was imprisoned in England for 28 years until his death.

Durham cathedral's nave, with its massive, geometrically patterned or fluted columns and rounded arches, dates from the late 11th and early 12th centuries.

1100 William Rufus slain while hunting in New Forest; succeeded by younger brother, Henry I (to 1135)
Henry marries Matilda, daughter of Malcolm III of Scotland
Archbishop Anselm recalled from Rome
Gloucester candlestick cast by lost wax process: medieval masterpiece
1101 Robert of Normandy, back from the crusades, invades England, but is bought off (Treaty of Alton)
1102 Henry suppresses a revolt by Robert of Bellême, ally of Robert of Normandy
1103 Anselm quarrels with Henry and goes into exile again
Magnus Barefoot of Norway invades Ulster, but is killed
1104 A monk of Malmesbury, Saewulf, describes pilgrimage to Jerusalem
1106 Henry defeats and captures Robert at battle of Tinchebrai, and gains Normandy; Robert imprisoned for life
1107 King Edgar of Scotland dies; succeeded by his brother, Alexander I (to 1124)
Synod of Westminster: Henry gives up his right to invest bishops and abbots, and is reconciled with Archbishop Anselm
1109 Anselm dies
Henry at war with Louis VI of France
1110 Henry betrothes his eight-year-old daughter Matilda to the Holy Roman Emperor Henry V, and raises heavy taxes for her dowry
Bad weather ruins the crops
Earliest known miracle play performed at Dunstable, Bedfordshire, about this time

Right: Henry I dreams of an uprising; in fact, his rule brought England a time of peace. He revived the Saxon courts of justice and it was said that in his time no man dared to harm another. Offenders were fined – a useful source of revenue.

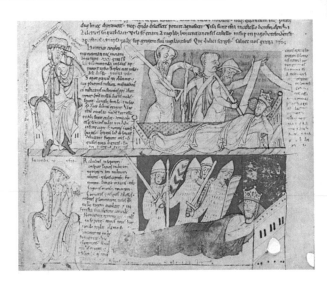

Below: The Great Seal of Henry I. Henry was an outstandingly efficient administrator; it was said: 'In his days no man dared to wrong another. He made peace for man and beast.' He increased the use of royal writs which conveyed his will to all parts of his kingdom.

Birth of Officialdom

The Civil Service, the body of officials who run the country, owes its origin to Henry I. The Curia Regis, or royal court, then consisted of the most important barons, some of them men who would rebel at any excuse. Henry created a class of loyal administrators from the servants of his royal household: the chamberlain, who looked after the royal bedchamber; the marshal, who controlled the royal stables; the treasurer; and the steward, under whose care came the ushers and other attendants. Henry's chancellor, or secretary, now issued writs for the sheriffs, or shire-reeves, who administered the counties. The chief officer of the state was the justiciar, who was the equivalent of today's Lord Chief Justice, but also acted as regent when the king was absent from the country. With these men Henry set up strong rule.

The White Ship

Henry I made himself popular with his Saxon subjects by marrying Edith (also known as Matilda), the daughter of Malcolm Canmore of Scotland. For Edith's mother Margaret was a Saxon princess, daughter of Edgar the Aethling, the last Saxon claimant to the throne.

The eldest of their children, Matilda, was married at the age of 12 to the Holy Roman Emperor Henry V, ruler of Germany. William, the only son, and his sister Adela were drowned when they were returning from Normandy to England in a vessel called *The White Ship*. The crew, many of whom were drunk, ran the vessel on the rocks, and only one person survived. Henry was so grief-stricken at the news that, it is said, he was never again seen to smile.

Below: A silver penny of Henry I's time.

1112 Henry I suppresses revolt by his Norman barons, and imprisons the ringleader, Robert of Bellême
1114 Henry's daughter Matilda marries the Holy Roman Emperor Henry V
Chichester cathedral is begun
Henry leads an army into Wales and makes peace with the Welsh
Ralph of Rochester becomes archbishop of Canterbury
1116 Peterborough minster is burned
1117 William Clito, son of Duke Robert of Normandy, leads revolt against Henry's rule in Normandy, supported by Louis VI of France
1118 *Leges Henrici Primi*, a collection of laws, made about this time
1119 Henry defeats Louis VI at the battle of Brémule
Archbishop Thurstan of York exiled for defying the King
Henry's son William marries the 12-year-old daughter of Count Fulk of Anjou
1120 Prince William is drowned in *The White Ship* off Harfleur
Choir of Gloucester abbey-church collapses
Henry and Louis VI of France make peace
Southwell minster is begun
Archbishop Thurstan is reconciled with Henry
1121 Henry marries again; his bride is Adeliza of Louvain
1122 Henry creates Robert of Caen, one of his bastard sons, earl of Gloucester
1123 Rahere, the King's jester, founds Augustinian priory of St Bartholomew, London
1124 Alexander III of Scotland dies; succeeded by brother, David I (to 1153)
First Scottish coinage

The Growth of Towns

William the Conqueror and his two sons gave England some 70 years of firm rule and overall peace. There were no more invasions or pirate raids by fierce Viking warriors. In these more settled conditions the towns in England began to grow.

William and his knights were followed to England by traders, Churchmen, craftsmen, and a host of attendants and servants. Many of these newcomers settled in the bigger towns, such as London, Norwich and Winchester. It was in the towns that the more prosperous of the ordinary citizens, neither barons nor serfs, began to assert their independence.

The seal of Stephen. Civil war raged between him and Matilda; both were bad rulers who could not control the powerful barons. All law broke down, the countryside was ravaged and people were tortured. Matilda's greatest asset was her son, Henry of Anjou, a formidable soldier who as Henry II brought peace and justice back to England.

Matilda and Geoffrey

The wreck of *The White Ship* cost Henry I his only legitimate son, and therefore his heir. He married again, but had no more children. So he pinned his hopes on his daughter, Matilda, now the widow of Henry V of Germany (who died in 1125). Twice he persuaded his reluctant barons to swear to stand by Matilda. For the future Queen's greater security he married her to Geoffrey, Count of Anjou, the most powerful state in northern France. This marriage angered the barons, who had insisted that she should not marry outside England without their consent.

Geoffrey bore as his badge a sprig of broom – *planta genista* in Latin. From this came his name of Plantagenet. Geoffrey was also one of the first people known to have borne a coat-of-arms: the three lions which still appear on the royal arms of England.

Contemporary chronicles describe Matilda as having 'the nature of a man in the frame of a woman'. She was, by all accounts, fierce and proud. Confusingly, she is sometimes called Maud.

St Bartholomew's

The important teaching hospital of St Bartholomew in London, and the neighbouring church of St Bartholomew the Great in Smithfield, owe their origin to Henry I's jester, Rahere. Rahere was rather more than an ordinary jester: he was a minstrel, and later he became a churchman. He founded an abbey at Smithfield – of which the church is all that remains – and the hospital, to fulfil a vow.

Stephen of Blois

Although there was no law to say that a woman could not inherit the throne of England, or the dukedom of Normandy, the barons generally felt that in an age of armed might a man made the best ruler. So despite promises to Henry they were reluctant to see his daughter Matilda become queen. Some of the barons had other motives too. For the other possible claimant to the throne was Henry I's nephew Stephen of Blois, son of the Conqueror's daughter Adela and the French Count of Blois. And Stephen was a pleasant, good-natured man who was likely to let the barons have their own way.

The race went to the swift. Stephen was the first to arrive in London after Henry died. Aided by his brother Henry, Bishop of Winchester, he quickly won the support of the Church, and only three weeks after Henry died Stephen was crowned.

Geoffrey of Monmouth

Soon after the death of Henry I a book called *Historia Regum Britanniae*, 'History of the Kings of Britain', was published. Its author was a cleric named Geoffrey Arthur, known also to later generations as Geoffrey of Monmouth, who was created bishop of St Asaph in 1151.

Geoffrey's 'History' is a mixture of a little fact with a great deal of fiction, and includes the legend of Lear and much of the Arthurian legend as well. It contains the prophecies of the Arthurian wizard Merlin, in which people believed for many years.

1125 Monk William of Malmesbury writes *Gesta regum Anglorum*, history of England
Emperor Henry V dies

1126 Adelard of Bath translates astronomical tables of al-Khwarizmi from Arabic into Latin

1127 Henry persuades his barons to accept his daughter Matilda as heir to the English throne

1128 Widowed Matilda marries again, to Geoffrey Plantagenet, son of the count of Anjou
England's first Cistercian monastery founded at Waverley, Surrey. David of Scotland founds Holyrood abbey, near Edinburgh

1129 Fulk, Count of Anjou, goes to Palestine: Geoffrey takes over rule of Anjou, Maine and Touraine

1130 Earliest surviving annual returns: pipe roll of the Exchequer
Ancrene Riwle, manual in English for the guidance of anchoresses (female hermits)

1131 Tintern abbey founded

1133 St Bartholomew's Fair first held at Smithfield (the 'smooth field'), London; held annually for 700 years

1135 Henry I dies in Normandy
Stephen of Blois, nephew of Henry, crosses to England and seizes the throne, helped by many barons (to 1154)
Foundation of Fountains abbey in Yorkshire

1136 Welsh prince Gruffydd ap Cynan heads an uprising
King Stephen gives Cumberland to David of Scotland, who recognizes Stephen as rightful king
Matilda claims the throne
Glasgow cathedral begun

A Weak King

The Normans provided England with 60 years of rule by three harsh but strong kings. The last Norman king, Stephen, was weak, and that lack of strength and his disputed claim to the throne at once plunged the country into a devastating war.

After the war was over and Stephen confirmed as king he still proved quite incapable of controlling the barons. He tried to gain their support with extravagant gifts, but they realized that they could act as they liked.

The last pages of the *Anglo-Saxon Chronicle* paint a vivid picture of the 19 unhappy years of Stephen's reign, and the way in which the barons rebelled against him. 'When the traitors perceived that he was a mild man, gentle and good, and did them no justice . . . they oppressed the wretched men of the land hard,' wrote the monk compiling the *Chronicle*. He added: 'The land was all ruined with such deeds, and they said openly that Christ slept, and his angels.'

Fighting at the time of the civil war – an illustration from a 12th-century Bible produced at Bury St Edmunds in eastern England. Although it illustrates an event in Palestine in the 6th century BC, the artist has shown the soldiers wearing the armour and carrying the weapons that were familiar in his own time.

The Civil War

Unchecked by King Stephen, the more turbulent barons built castles where they liked, and went round raiding and robbing. They tortured and killed people for their money, burned houses and towns and laid farms waste.

Matilda was supported in her fight for the throne by her half-brother Robert, Earl of Gloucester. Robert was the bastard son of Henry I, but rather than claim the throne for himself he chose to support his half-sister.

The Scots decided to join in the fray, and invaded northern England. They were repelled by an English army hurriedly got together by the aged but warlike Archbishop of York, Thurstan. His troops carried the banners of St Cuthbert, St John of Beverley and St Wilfred, all much revered in the north country. The men of the north fell on the Scots at Northallerton and slew 12,000 of them. This bloody slaughter is known as the battle of the Standard.

Homage

Homage was a declaration of loyalty made by a tenant to his landlord. He placed his hands between those of his lord and said 'I become your man for the lands which I hold of you'. Kings had to do homage for lands they held in other countries. For example, several Scottish kings did homage to English kings for the earldom of Huntingdon, while English kings paid homage to French monarchs for their French territories.

Peers still pay homage to the sovereign at present-day coronations.

1137 Gruffydd dies; succeeded by son Owain as prince of Gwynedd (to 1170)
Kirkwall cathedral, Orkney, begun
About now Geoffrey of Monmouth writes his largely fictional *History of the Kings of Britain*
Stephen wins campaign in Normandy against Geoffrey of Anjou

1138 Robert, Earl of Gloucester, begins civil war in support of Matilda. David of Scotland supports her, but is defeated at battle of the Standard, near Northallerton in Yorkshire

1139 Stephen arrests the bishops of Salisbury, Lincoln and Ely, who virtually govern England
Matilda lands in England to lead her supporters
Stephen cedes Northumberland to the Scots

1141 Battle of Lincoln: Matilda's forces capture Stephen
Stephen's supporters defeat Matilda's army at Winchester, and capture Robert of Gloucester
Stephen and Robert exchanged

1142 Matilda escapes from Oxford castle as Stephen captures it

1143 First translation into Latin of the *Koran* by Robert of Chester

1144 Geoffrey of Anjou captures Rouen, and controls Normandy
Robert of Chester translates an Arabic book on chemistry into Latin
William of Norwich, 12-year-old apprentice, is found murdered: the Jews are blamed

1147 English crusaders interrupt their journey to the Holy Land to help Alfonso of Portugal take Lisbon
Death of Robert, Earl of Gloucester

Henry of Anjou

Matilda, arriving in England to assert her rights, soon put people's backs up with her domineering ways. The civil war raged for years, with barons changing sides as fortunes seemed to be waxing or waning.

However, a new strong man was at hand: Henry, son of Matilda and Geoffrey of Anjou. By the time he was 20 Henry had made himself master of Normandy, and was winning victories in England. A compromise was reached: Stephen kept his crown, but acknowledged Henry as his heir. A year later, Stephen was dead, and Henry of Anjou was king.

Henry II was red-haired, thick-set, full of life and energy. He appeared bluff and good humoured, and never calmer than when danger threatened. Underneath he had an iron will, and a talent for business and organization. He also had a violent temper, inherited from his father's family.

Henry's marriage had startled Europe. For his bride was Eleanor of Aquitaine, ruler in her own right of a considerable area in France. Eleanor had been married for 15 years to Louis VII of France, but, complaining that he was 'more monk than king', persuaded the Pope to grant a divorce on the grounds that the pair were too closely related. Two months later she married Henry, who was 12 years her junior.

In his own right Henry already ruled over Normandy, Anjou, Touraine and Maine. Together, he and his wife controlled more than half France.

Opposite: The Norman chapel at Ludlow castle in Shropshire, owned by the Lacy family. The Norman kings allowed barons to hold large estates in the marches which lay between England and Wales, and to keep enough armed men to police the area.

King David I of Scotland was the son of the Saxon Princess Margaret, and through his wife claimed the earldom of Northumberland, as well as the earldom of Huntingdon in southern England for which he did homage to the English king. He had sworn allegiance to Matilda who called for his help. David hoped to gain Northumberland but was defeated at the battle of the Standard; from now on, the breach between England and Scotland was clearly marked.

1147 Faversham abbey, Kent, founded
Henry, son of Matilda, invades England unsuccessfully
1148 Matilda leaves England
1149 Henry returns to England; knighted by David I of Scotland
1150 Henry invested as Duke of Normandy during the lifetime of his father, Geoffrey of Anjou
The Black Book of Carmarthen (collection of Welsh poems)
Theobald, Archbishop of Canterbury, refuses to recognize Stephen's son as heir to English throne
1151 Geoffrey of Anjou dies; son Henry succeeds him
The game of chess first reported in England
1152 Marriage of Louis VII of France and Eleanor of Aquitaine dissolved by the Church on the grounds that they are too closely related
Eleanor marries Henry of Anjou
Synod at Kells: Pope acknowledged as supreme head of the Church in Ireland
John of Salisbury completes his history of western Europe
1153 Henry of Anjou lands in England; begins new campaign
Treaty of Wallingford: Stephen agrees Henry shall be his heir
Death of David I of Scotland; succeeded by grandson Malcolm IV (to 1165)
Robert FitzHarding begins the keep of Berkeley castle (still held by his descendants)
1154 Nicholas Breakspear elected as Pope Adrian IV (only English Pope)
Death of Stephen. Henry II king of England (to 1189)

45

The Plantagenets

The Plantagenets ruled England for almost 250 years. These were years of strife and violence, which saw the beginnings of democracy in England, and the birth of Parliament. It was Plantagenet kings who fought the Hundred Years' War against the French, winning most of the battles but ultimately losing the war and most of England's French possessions.

The name 'Plantagenet' was a nickname for the founder of the family, Geoffrey of Anjou, who wore a sprig of broom, *planta genista*, as a badge. But it does not appear to have been used by the royal family until the mid 1400s. However, it is a convenient name for the kings of this time, though some historians prefer to call Henry II and his sons 'Angevins', men from Anjou.

Scotland saw a period of comparative stability, with three long reigns, but then disputes over the succession to the Crown allowed the English King Edward I to claim supreme power in Scotland, and even to nominate its king. The Scots were not for long deprived of their independence: the exploits of Sir William Wallace and Robert Bruce roused their enthusiasm and kept Scotland a separate nation for several hundred years. During this time, too, there began the 'Auld Alliance' between Scotland and France, both traditional enemies of England. In Wales, the princes gradually lost their fight to keep their country a separate nation. As for Ireland, the only English Pope, Adrian IV, 'granted' it to Henry II of England, beginning a long contest which has still not been resolved.

SCOTTISH KINGS

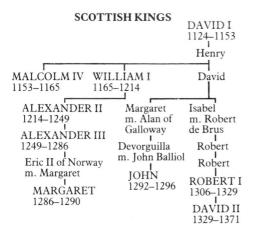

DAVID I
1124–1153

Henry

MALCOLM IV 1153–1165 WILLIAM I 1165–1214 David

ALEXANDER II 1214–1249

Margaret m. Alan of Galloway

Isabel m. Robert de Brus

ALEXANDER III 1249–1286

Devorguilla m. John Balliol

Robert

Eric II of Norway m. Margaret

JOHN 1292–1296

Robert

MARGARET 1286–1290

ROBERT I 1306–1329

DAVID II 1329–1371

THE PLANTAGENETS

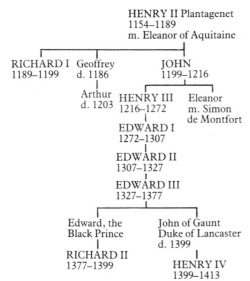

HENRY II Plantagenet
1154–1189
m. Eleanor of Aquitaine

RICHARD I 1189–1199 Geoffrey d. 1186 JOHN 1199–1216

Arthur d. 1203 HENRY III 1216–1272 Eleanor m. Simon de Montfort

EDWARD I 1272–1307

EDWARD II 1307–1327

EDWARD III 1327–1377

Edward, the Black Prince

John of Gaunt Duke of Lancaster d. 1399

RICHARD II 1377–1399

HENRY IV 1399–1413

At Edward I's Parliament in 1275 King Alexander III of Scotland sat on his right and Llewelyn of Wales on his left; Edward was overlord of both countries. The Plantagenet kings saw England shift from feudal control towards parliamentary power.

ELSEWHERE IN THE WORLD

1156 Civil war ravages Japan
1174 Saladin conquers Syria
1182 Jews are expelled from France
1190 Holy Roman Emperor Frederick Barbarossa drowns on the way to Holy Land
1197 Civil war in Germany
1210 Mongol leader Genghis Khan begins invasion of China
1215 Dominican Order founded
1218 Genghis Khan captures Persia
1228 Sixth Crusade: Jerusalem taken
1240 Kingdom of Mali conquers ancient Empire of Ghana
     Mongols capture Moscow and Kiev
1254-73 Great Interregnum: civil war for crown of Holy Roman Empire
1275 Marco Polo enters the service of Kublai Khan in China
1281 Mongols fail to conquer Japan
1291 Muslims capture Acre: end of the Crusades
1312 Order of Knights Templars ended
1320 Turks found Tughluk Dynasty in Delhi
1325 Traditional date for the founding of Tenochtitlán (Mexico City) by the Aztecs
1328 Philip VI, the first Valois king of France
1335 Pope Benedict XII reforms life in monasteries
1347 Black Death (bubonic plague) from eastern Asia reaches Cyprus
1348 Black Death sweeps Europe
1349 Jews persecuted in Germany
1351 Black Death ravages Russia
1358 French peasants revolt
1363 Mongol leader Tamerlane begins conquest of Asia
1368 Ming Dynasty in China (to 1644)
1378 The Great Schism: rival popes elected

The Invasion of Ireland

England's involvement in Ireland began in the reign of Henry II. The Irish had never evolved a strong central government but were ruled by a number of clan chiefs calling themselves kings; from time to time one of these would claim the title of *Ard-Rí* – High King.

In 1166 the cruel King of Leinster, Dermot MacMurrough, was driven out of Ireland by his enemies. He fled to Aquitaine, where he asked Henry II of England for help. With Henry's agreement he recruited a force of Welsh and Norman warriors, led by Richard de Clare, Earl of Pembroke. The Earl was known as 'Strongbow'. He married MacMurrough's daughter, and in 1171 succeeded his father-in-law as king of Leinster.

Despite this, and some military successes, Strongbow was less confident than his nickname suggests. He offered his lands to his overlord, Henry II, who landed in Ireland and received the submission of the Irish chiefs as well as the Welsh and Norman lords.

The Welsh Resistance

The Norman conquest of Wales was carried out by the powerful barons known as the Lords Marchers, because they guarded the marches, or frontiers, between England and Wales. By the time Henry II came to the throne much of southern Wales was more or less under their control, but the wilder country in the north remained largely independent.

The situation was complicated by the fact that the Welsh fought one another as well as the Normans, and the Normans also squabbled among themselves as well as fighting the Welsh.

Attempts to build up a strong Welsh kingdom were hampered by the practice of *gavelkind*, a form of inheritance in which a man's lands were divided equally among his sons. In this way conquests were immediately dissipated.

Among the most powerful of the princes in Henry's time was Owain Gwynedd, ruler of Gwynedd in North Wales. He twice defeated Henry's armies. It was in North Wales at this time that archers developed the longbow, in its heyday the most formidable of weapons.

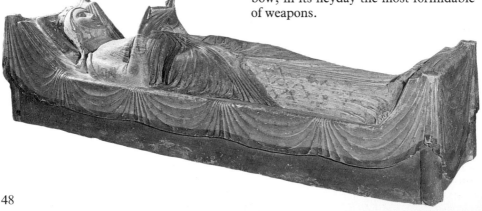

The Scottish Kings

At the time the first Plantagenets came to the throne in England, an 11-year-old boy had just become king of Scotland. He was Malcolm IV, great-grandson of Malcolm Canmore, and he was known as 'Malcolm the Maiden' because he was so young.

Malcolm struggled bravely against ill-health. He campaigned in Galloway against rebels, and in France under the banner of Henry II, to whom he owed allegiance as holder of the English earldom of Huntingdon. At 25 he died, and the throne passed to his tougher brother William, whose character is reflected in his nickname of 'the Lion'.

William ruled for 49 years, the longest reign of any Scots king. For 15 of those years he was the vassal of Henry II, who had captured him in battle, but he was able to buy Scotland's freedom from Richard I, who needed money to go on crusade.

William's son and grandson, Alexander II and Alexander III, also had long reigns (35 and 37 years), which were a time of comparative peace for Scotland. Then came a bitter dispute over the throne, settled finally by the victories of Robert I, the Bruce.

This effigy of Eleanor is in the abbey of Fontevrault in Anjou. She was a proud and forceful woman; Henry was persistently unfaithful to her (he had a number of bastards) and she fought bitterly with him. She supported their sons in rebellion against their father, and so spent some years in confinement. After Henry's death she supported Richard against John, but when Richard died she upheld John's claim against that of her grandson Arthur.

1154 Henry II king of England (to 1189)
Henry appoints Thomas Becket Lord Chancellor
1155 Papal Bull, *Laudabiliter*, permits Henry II to conquer Ireland
1157 Henry makes Malcolm IV of Scotland give up Northumberland, Cumberland and Westmorland
1158 Henry invades North Wales
Henry's brother Geoffrey dies; he inherits Brittany
1159 The King collects scutage (tax in lieu of military service)
1162 Thomas Becket appointed archbishop of Canterbury
Henry raises Danegeld for the last time, as a source of revenue
1163 Becket defies Henry over punishment of clergy in secular courts
Oxford University established
1164 Becket goes into exile
1165 Henry invades South Wales; defeated by Owain, King of Gwynedd
Malcolm IV dies: succeeded by his brother, William I, the Lion (to 1214)
1166 Rory O'Connor, Ard-Rí, banishes Dermot MacMurrough, King of Leinster who asks Henry for help
Constitutions of Clarendon: clerks condemned by the Church to be punished by lay courts
1169 Norman force invades Ireland in support of Dermot of Leinster
1170 Henry and Becket are reconciled
Richard, Earl of Pembroke ('Strongbow') leads Normans to capture Waterford and Dublin
Owain, King of Gwynedd, dies
Henry II has his son Henry crowned king to ensure succession
Becket defies Henry again, and is murdered in Canterbury cathedral

The Turbulent Priest

In the Middle Ages people believed implicitly in God, the saints and the Devil, and the Christian Church had enormous power over their minds and hearts.

It was against this background of reverence for the Church and its leaders that Henry II clashed with his one-time friend Thomas Becket. Becket was an ecclesiastical lawyer and, like most scholars of the day, a cleric, though only in minor orders. For eight years he served Henry as chancellor, the chief minister of England.

Henry, already in conflict with the Church on matters of law and finance, persuaded Becket to accept the post of archbishop of Canterbury. He thought that as archbishop and chancellor Becket would help keep the Church in check. Becket accepted reluctantly.

Overnight, the new Archbishop changed his way of life completely. He resigned the chancellorship and gave up his former good living and magnificent clothes. He now wore the black robes of a monk, and instead of using his talents to curb the Church he threw himself heart and soul into defending its rights and possessions.

Becket and Henry were soon in bitter conflict. The main issue was the King's insistence that clerics convicted of felonies should be punished by the royal courts. Becket was forced to agree to the Constitutions of Clarendon, recognizing this and other matters of contention, and escaped to exile in France. After six years the two men were reconciled and Becket returned, only to excommunicate some of his enemies in the Church itself. Hearing this Henry cried: 'Who will avenge me of this turbulent priest?'

Four knights took Henry at his word and hurried to Canterbury. As darkness fell they slew Becket at the foot of the altar steps in Canterbury cathedral. The deed aroused horror throughout Europe. Becket was revered as a martyr and a saint. Henry had to do penance – he was whipped by monks in front of Becket's tomb – and had to acknowledge defeat in his conflict with the Church. Two points on which he had clashed with Becket remained the Church's privilege until the Reformation: the right of the Church to have its own courts of law, and to appeal to Rome against any secular judgment.

Thomas Becket, Archbishop of Canterbury, is murdered at the altar of his own cathedral. Henry II had thought to have Thomas's complete allegiance when he appointed him archbishop; but his former crony proved loyal to his Church rather than his King.

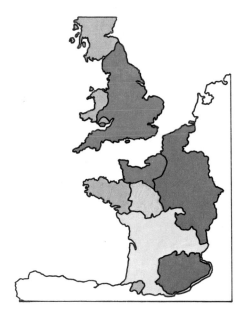

Henry II inherited England and Normandy (orange) from his mother Matilda. From his father Geoffrey of Anjou came Anjou (green). Eleanor of Aquitaine brought him the duchy of Aquitaine (yellow), covering almost a quarter of present-day France. Henry now ruled western France (apart from Brittany) from the English Channel to the Pyrenees; and in 1158 he inherited Brittany from his brother. The English king's extensive possessions in France gave him a dominating role in western Europe. Henry II had planned to divide his lands between his three eldest sons, Henry, Richard and Geoffrey, but the early deaths of Henry and Geoffrey and Richard's refusal to divide his inheritance with his youngest brother John kept it together.

1171 Strongbow becomes king of Leinster. Henry II lands in Ireland; princes submit to him
1172 Synod of Cashel: Irish Church reformed along English lines
Henry absolved of murder of Becket
1173 Henry II's four legitimate sons and their mother rebel in France
Barons in England join revolt
Becket canonized
Henry II crushes revolt in his French lands; Queen Eleanor imprisoned
1174 Henry does penance at Canterbury for Becket's murder
William of Scotland invades Northumberland and is captured
Henry II crushes English revolt and makes peace with his sons
Treaty of Falaise: William of Scotland freed after paying homage to Henry
Choir of Canterbury cathedral destroyed by fire
1175 Henry allows his son Richard to govern Aquitaine
1176 Assize of Northampton: Henry II establishes judicial rules
Eisteddfod held at Cardigan
1177 Henry makes his youngest son, John, Lord of Ireland
1178 Henry II establishes permanent central court of justice
1179 Grand Assize of Windsor curbs power of feudal courts
1180 Wells cathedral begun
1181 First Carthusian monastery in England founded at Witham, Somerset
1182 Glastonbury abbey burned
1183 Henry 'the Young King' dies
1184 Rebuilding of Canterbury cathedral completed
1185 Queen Eleanor freed

The Crusades

Palestine, the Holy Land of the Bible, was overrun by the Muslims in 638. At first they were tolerant of Christians on pilgrimage, but in the 11th century pilgrims were increasingly attacked. In 1095 Pope Urban II called on Christian warriors to unite to free the Holy Land. The emblem of the warriors was a cross, and from this came the name for the expedition, a crusade.

The first crusade freed much of the area from the Saracens as these Muslims are known. But the Muslims, for whom Jerusalem was also a holy city, reconquered it. There were many later and ultimately unsuccessful crusades to combat them.

Richard of Cornwall makes a treaty with the Saracens in 1240. Richard was the younger and cleverer son of King John. Like him, many kings and great nobles 'took the Cross' and journeyed to the Holy Land.

Henry II's Sons

Henry II had four self-willed and unruly sons: Henry, Richard, Geoffrey and John. Henry was known as 'the Young King' because his father had him crowned during his own lifetime (a way of safeguarding the succession).

Henry gave each of his three elder sons lands from his French possessions: 'the Young King' had Normandy, Maine and Anjou, Richard had Aquitaine, and Geoffrey had Brittany. John received no territories to rule, and contemporaries nicknamed him 'Lackland'. But the boys had no real power, and encouraged by their mother they rebelled against Henry repeatedly. 'The Young King' and Geoffrey both died before their father. Henry II was fighting a revolt by Richard when he learned that his beloved John had joined his enemies. Saying 'Shame, shame on a conquered king,' he gave up the struggle and died.

A 13th-century tile illustrating Richard I on crusade. A companion picture shows his great opponent, the Muslim leader Saladin. Richard defeated Saladin and came within sight of Jerusalem, but realized he could never capture it and made peace. He was a popular hero, but spent little time in England and left it badly in debt.

Richard the Lionheart

Richard I was impetuous and violent, and his bravery earned him the name *Coeur de Lion*, the Lionheart. He spent only a few months of his 10-year reign in England, and was an ardent crusader. Captured by his enemy, the Emperor Henry VI, he was rescued only when his long-suffering subjects paid an enormous ransom. They nevertheless welcomed him warmly in London, but almost at once he left for Normandy which had been attacked by the French king. He spent the remaining part of his reign defending his French lands, and was mortally wounded by an archer while besieging the castle of Chaluz.

1186 Henry II makes peace with Philip II of France; they agree to go on the Third Crusade
Pope Innocent III raises 'Saladin Tithes' in England and France to pay for Third Crusade
1188 Richard, third son of Henry II, does homage to Philip II of France
1189 Philip and Richard force Henry II to acknowledge Richard as heir
Death of Henry II: Richard I succeeds him (to 1199)
Massacre of Jews at Richard's coronation
1190 Richard departs on crusade
1191 Richard I conquers Cyprus, and marries Berengaria of Navarre
English crusaders reach Palestine; Richard captures Acre
Civil war in England between Richard's brother John and William Longchamp, the Justiciar
Walter de Coutances takes over as Justiciar
1192 Treaty between Richard and Saladin ends Third Crusade
Leopold of Austria captures Richard as he travels to England
1193 John claims the throne
Richard is handed over to Emperor Henry VI of Germany
1194 Richard is freed and returns to England; John flees to France
Coroners' courts set up
Richard campaigns in France
1196 Richard and Philip of France make peace
1198 Richard defeats Philip at Gisors
1199 Richard killed at siege of Chaluz; John succeeds him (to 1216)
1200 Peace with France
Llewelyn the Great of Gwynedd seizes Anglesey
1201 John grants a charter to the Jews
1202 Renewed war with France

The Great Charter

King John was a tough, energetic little man. Like many other Plantagenets, he was given to violent rages, and he was cruel behind a façade of geniality. One of his first acts was to organize the murder of his nephew, Arthur. This young prince, as son of John's older brother Geoffrey, had a good claim to the throne. Arthur's murder and John's tactlessness soon alienated the barons of Anjou and Poitou. Before long John had lost most of his French lands.

John soon set his English barons against him as well, taxing them harshly and abusing feudal rights. At last the barons rebelled, not individually but as a united body. They demanded that the King should confirm their ancient rights. In June 1215 the barons met the King in a meadow called Runnymede, beside the river Thames. There John put his seal to a document that has become famous as *Magna Carta* – the Great Charter. Although it was concerned mainly with the barons' rights, it contained some clauses that are the basis of modern democracy.

Magna Carta was in force for only a few weeks before John persuaded the Pope to annul it. But a month after John's death the following year it was reissued in a revised form, and reissued twice more in 1216 and 1225, the last version becoming the law of the land. After this it was reissued or reconfirmed a number of times, particularly when crises in government arose.

A 14th-century picture of King John enthroned. Among his disastrous quarrels was that with Pope Innocent III over the election of a new archbishop of Canterbury. The Pope wanted Cardinal Stephen Langton; John wanted John Grey, Bishop of Norwich. The King began to take Church money, and the Pope placed the whole country under an interdict, which for six years banned everybody from going to church or even having Christian burial.

Louis VII of France invades England at the invitation of the rebel barons who were exasperated by John's intransigence. John's death ended the rebellion and Louis withdrew. This illustration comes from the Chronicles of Matthew Paris, a monk at the abbey of St Albans who wrote in the mid-13th century.

The Terms of the Charter

Most of the 63 clauses in *Magna Carta* pledged the King to uphold the feudal system of the country, which was to the benefit of the barons. Those which have been of importance in later years include:

In all important matters the king must seek the barons' advice;

No special taxes could be raised without the barons' consent;

No freeman should be imprisoned or exiled, or deprived of property, except by the law of the land;

And – one of the most important – 'to none will we sell, to none will we deny or delay right of justice'.

The effect of the Charter was that the King could continue to rule, but must keep to the laws of the land, and could be compelled to do so.

1203 Murder of Arthur of Brittany, John's nephew
1204 Philip II of France conquers Normandy from John
John licenses Donnybrook Fair, Dublin (closed 1855)
1205 Dispute over new archbishop of Canterbury: John nominates John Grey, Bishop of Norwich
1206 Pope Innocent III rejects John Grey's nomination, supports election of Stephen Langton
Two-year truce in France
1207 John rejects Langton
Port of Liverpool founded
1208 Pope puts England under interdict
Llewelyn the Great of North Wales seizes Powys
1209 London Bridge completed (stands until 1832)
Scholars leave Oxford for Cambridge
1211-12 John campaigns in Wales
1213 Philip II accepts Pope's mandate to conquer England
John accepts Langton; interdict is lifted
English ships destroy French fleet preparing for invasion
1214 French defeat English and allies at battle of Bouvines
Alexander II king of Scotland (to 1249)
Barons threaten revolt
John takes crusader vows, and Pope excommunicates the barons
1215 John agrees to Magna Carta
Pope annuls Magna Carta; civil war resumed
1216 Louis of France invades England
John dies: succeeded by son Henry III, aged nine (to 1272)
William Marshal becomes regent
Magna Carta reissued
1217 French leave England

Llewelyn the Great

One of the leading princes of Wales was Llewelyn the Great, Prince of Gwynedd in North Wales. He spent most of his youth in England, and returned to Wales to depose his uncle, Dafydd, in 1194. Dafydd had usurped power while Llewelyn was very young.

Llewelyn made himself master of North Wales, and was acknowledged as leader of the Welsh by the people of South Wales, too. He married an illegitimate daughter of King John of England. This did not stop John invading Wales in an attempt to curb Llewelyn's growing power, but John was distracted by his troubles with his barons.

In the early part of the reign of John's son, the boy-King Henry III, Llewelyn was driven back from South Wales by the regent, William Marshal, Earl of Pembroke. However, Llewelyn was able to stabilize his territory to include present-day Gwynedd, Clwyd, Powys and the northern part of Dyfed.

Llewelyn tried to avoid a division of his lands on the old Welsh pattern at his death, and contrived that they should pass to his younger (and legitimate) son, Dafydd.

Salisbury cathedral was begun in 1220 and completed but for the tower and spire by 1258. It is a magnificent example of the Early English phase of Gothic architecture.

The Great Seal of Alexander II of Scotland. He made himself overlord of Argyll and planned the conquest of the western isles which were in Norse hands, but died suddenly before he could take them.

Below: The fight at Monmouth between William Marshal and Baldwin of Guines – an illustration from the Chronicles of Matthew Paris. William, a poor knight who made his fortune in the French wars, married the heiress Isobel of Pembroke who brought him estates in England, Wales, Ireland and Normandy. He supported Henry II against Richard I, Richard against John, and John against the barons, and became regent for Henry III.

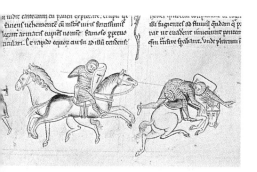

1219 Henry III's guardian William Marshal dies; succeeded by justiciar Hubert de Burgh
1220 Henry has second coronation
Salisbury cathedral begun
1221 Dominican friars reach England
1223 Pope Honorius III declares Henry III 'competent to rule'
1224 The King recovers 1115 royal castles held by the barons
Louis VIII of France declares war, and seizes Poitou
Franciscan Friars arrive in England
1225 Henry reissues Magna Carta and Charter of the Forests, in return for grant of general tax
English win back Gascony
1227 Henry III declares himself to be of full age to rule; Hubert de Burgh still retains power
1228 Death of Stephen Langton
Llewelyn the Great besieges Montgomery; Henry relieves city
1229 Llewelyn nominates his son Dafydd as his successor
Carmelite Friars arrive in England
Henry tries to take an army to France to recover his lands, but Hubert fails to provide shipping
1230 Henry's French campaign fails
1231 England and France make a truce
1232 Henry dismisses Hubert de Burgh
Peter des Roches, Bishop of Winchester, adviser to the King
1233 Revolt of Richard Marshal, Earl of Pembroke, allied with Llewelyn. Richard defeats royal forces near Monmouth, sacks Shrewsbury
Coal mining in Newcastle reported
1234 Henry makes peace with Richard
Richard murdered in Ireland
Under pressure, Henry dismisses Peter des Roches

Henry III

Henry III was a pious, sensitive man, but completely without any ability to govern. He could not live within his income, and when thwarted he had a nasty temper and a sharp tongue. In his youth the country was well governed for him by Hubert de Burgh, the justiciar. When he grew up Henry came under the influence of foreign advisers: first Peter des Roches from Poitou, who was bishop of Winchester, and his nephew (or perhaps son) Peter des Rivaux; and after Henry's marriage to Eleanor of Provence, her many uncles from Savoy. The principal adviser was Peter of Savoy, to whom Henry gave an estate near London, by the Thames: the Savoy Hotel and Theatre stand on its site.

First Act of Parliament

The term 'parliament' for the royal council of the English kings was coming into use in the reign of Henry III. The first Act of Parliament recorded was the Statute of Merton, which gained its name because the council met at Merton Priory, in Surrey. Its main provisions were to allow landlords to enclose common land for their own use, provided that freemen had enough pasture for their animals; and to declare that children born before marriage were illegitimate.

This map, from the Chronicles of Matthew Paris, shows England, Scotland and Wales in the mid-13th century.

1235 Henry III's sister Isabella marries Holy Roman Emperor Frederick II
1236 Henry marries Eleanor of Provence. Statute of Merton, the first Act of Parliament
1237 Barons insist on nominating three of Henry's counsellors
Treaty of York: Scots renounce claim to Northumberland, Cumberland and Westmorland
1238 Simon de Montfort, Earl of Leicester, marries Henry's sister Eleanor
Scholars from Oxford set up short-lived universities at Salisbury and Northampton
1240 Llewelyn the Great dies; succeeded by son Dafydd (to 1246)
1241 Henry III leads expedition to Wales
Arrival of Peter of Savoy, uncle of Queen Eleanor, as royal adviser
1242 Henry is defeated in war against Louis IX of France. Barons refuse to pay for French war
1243 Treaty of Bordeaux; five-year Anglo-French truce
1244 First contest for Dunmow Flitch
1245 Present structure of Westminster abbey is begun
Peter of Savoy receives estates in London that still bear his name
1246 Welsh prince Dafydd dies; succeeded by Llewelyn ap Gruffydd (to 1282) and his brother Owain
1247 Bethlehem Priory, London, founded; later 'Bedlam' lunatic asylum
Peace of Woodstock: Henry recognizes Llewelyn and Owain
1248 Henry appoints Simon de Montfort seneschal of Gascony
1249 Alexander II of Scotland dies; son Alexander III succeeds (to 1286)
Collegiate system in Oxford begins – University College founded
1250 First evidence of game of cricket

Simon de Montfort

A Frenchman became one of the champions of English liberties in Henry III's reign. He was Simon de Montfort, and he came to England in 1229 to claim the earldom of Leicester, which he inherited through his grandmother. He quickly became a favourite of the King, whose sister Eleanor he married.

Henry's inept and spendthrift ways provoked the barons, and with de Montfort as their leader they forced the King to agree to the Provisions of Oxford, in return for the financial help he badly needed. These laid down that the King was to rule with the advice of a council of barons.

Henry lost no time in persuading the Pope to absolve him from his oath, and won over many barons who disliked de Montfort's high-handed ways. De Montfort, who had gone abroad, returned to lead a rebellion which restored the Provisions of Oxford. Louis IX of France was then asked to act as arbitrator, and decided in Henry's favour. At this de Montfort resorted to arms, and defeated and captured Henry at the battle of Lewes, on the Sussex downs.

De Montfort ruled England, in the King's name, for a year. Then war broke out again, and Henry's son Edward defeated and killed de Montfort at the battle of Evesham.

Simon de Montfort is remembered for the Parliament he convened in 1265, which two knights from every shire and two burgesses from every town were summoned to attend. This was the beginning of the House of Commons.

Simon de Montfort, as shown in a window in Chartres cathedral. He was of French birth and education, but played a leading part in English history, leading the barons against Henry III and calling a parliament which included knights from the shires and burgesses from towns as well as great lords and bishops.

Llewelyn the Last

After the death of Dafydd the throne of Gwynedd passed to his nephews Owain and Llewelyn, sons of his bastard brother Gruffydd. Threatened by claims from Henry III and others to rule Wales, the brothers united and fought with such determination that by the Peace of Woodstock (1247) Henry recognized them as rightful rulers, though subject to paying homage to the English king.

Later, Llewelyn gained the ascendancy, and declared himself 'Prince of Wales'. But a rebellion against Henry's son, Edward I, cost Llewelyn his life in battle, and earned him the byname by which he is remembered in history: Llewelyn the Last.

This drawing, another from the Chronicles of Matthew Paris, shows Llewelyn ap Gruffydd attempting to escape from the Tower of London in 1244. Henry III was eventually forced to acknowledge him as 'Prince of Wales'.

1251 Simon de Montfort suppresses rebellion in Gascony
1253 Linen first made in England
1254 Treaty with the Pope: Henry III's son Edmund to become king of Sicily (when conquered)
Edward, son of Henry III, weds Eleanor of Castile
Llewelyn ap Gruffydd makes himself sole Welsh ruler
1257 Richard of Cornwall (Henry's brother) is elected 'king of the Romans' (ruler of Germany)
Llewelyn assumes the title 'Prince of Wales'
1258 Provisions of Oxford: barons take control of Henry III's government
Pope Alexander IV cancels grant of Sicily to Edmund
1259 Peace treaty between Henry III and Llewelyn ap Gruffydd
Provisions of Westminster: plan by the barons for legal reforms
1261 Pope absolves Henry III from oath to observe the Provisions of Oxford; Henry dismisses officials
1262 Llewelyn attacks England
1263 Simon de Montfort returns to England as leader of the barons; Henry accepts the barons' terms
Battle of Largs: Alexander III of Scotland defeats Norwegian attack on the Hebrides
1264 Battle of Lewes: de Montfort defeats and captures Henry III
Merton College, Oxford, receives its statutes
1265 De Montfort's Parliament: first to summon representatives of shires and towns. Battle of Evesham: de Montfort killed
1266 Norway drops claim to Hebrides
1267 Henry recognizes Llewelyn as 'Prince of Wales', but as his vassal

Above: Harlech was one of
eight royal castles built in Wales
between 1277 and 1330.
Edward I began his devastating
campaign to bring Wales under
his rule in 1277; it took him only
seven years.

Left: Edward I pays homage to
Philip I of France for his land in
Gascony in the south-west – the
meagre remnant of England's
once extensive French
possessions.

Edward the Lawgiver

Edward I, who was 33 when he came to the throne, was a complete contrast to his muddle-headed father. He was brisk, capable, an experienced general and a born leader of men. His love of order led him to reform the government of the land, and the many laws passed in his reign have earned him the nickname of 'the Lawgiver'.

Among his early laws were the Statute of Gloucester, which strictly defined the rights of barons to hold their own local courts of justice; the Statute of Mortmain, which forbade gifts of land to the Church; and three Statutes of Westminster all of which dealt with local government and the ownership and inheritance of land.

An important law was the Statute of Wales, which effectively marked the end of Wales as a separate country. Its introduction stated: 'Now God, by His grace, all obstacles whatever coming to an end, has converted it totally and in its entirety within our own dominion.' But it left Welsh common law, language and customs intact.

Time Immemorial

Besides correcting malpractices in local government, the first Statute of Westminster (1275) also set a limit to the time of legal memory: precedents and customs before this time cannot be cited. The date chosen was July 6th, 1189, the beginning of the reign of Richard I. It is described as time immemorial – 'from time whereof the memory of man runneth not to the contrary'.

1269 Rebuilt Westminster abbey church dedicated
Prince Edward goes on crusade
First toll roads in England

1270 Aedh O'Connor defeats Normans at Athankip, on the Shannon

1272 Edward sails for home from Palestine
Henry III dies: Edward I, though absent, is proclaimed king (to 1307)

1273 Burning of sea-coal banned in London because of pollution

1274 Edward I returns and is crowned
Llewelyn ap Gruffydd refuses to take oath of allegiance to Edward

1275 Edward holds his first Parliament
First Statute of Westminster corrects local government abuses
Wool duties granted to the Crown

1277 Edward I begins campaign in Wales against Llewelyn, who submits with Treaty of Conway
Oldest extant monumental brass: to Sir John D'Abernon, at Stoke d'Abernon, Surrey

1278 Statute of Gloucester: inquiry into local courts
In London, 278 Jews are hanged for clipping coin; guilty Christians escape with fines

1279 Statute of Mortmain forbids gifts of lands to the Church

1282 Llewelyn's brother David begins a revolt against the English
Edward marches into Wales: Llewelyn killed in battle

1283 Welsh revolt collapses: David is executed
Edward begins building castles in Wales (Caernarvon, Harlech)

1284 Statute of Wales (or Rhuddlan): Welsh government organized
Peterhouse, first Cambridge University college, founded

Edward I's much-loved wife Eleanor of Castile died at Harby in Nottinghamshire in 1290. At each of the 12 places where her body rested on its last journey to London, Edward erected a memorial cross. This one, at Hardingstone, is one of only three that remain.

The Kings and the Jews

After the Jews were dispersed from Palestine in AD 135 they settled in many countries of Europe, Asia and Africa. Having no land to cultivate, they turned to trade, and many of them took up usury (lending money at high rates of interest) which profitable pursuit was forbidden to Christians.

Jews were unpopular both for their usury and for the fact that they were blamed for the crucifixion of Christ. Many people tolerated them because of their value as a source of money when times were hard. Henry II even helped them to recover their loans through the courts, but he seized their estates when they died. John borrowed from them, and also had them tortured.

The Jews in England made a mistake when they acquired land, either by foreclosing on mortgages or by direct purchase. This added to the hatred with which they were regarded, and when Italian money-lenders from Florence and Siena came into the country, Edward I decided to expel almost all the Jews from England. Only skilled physicians were allowed to remain.

The Scottish Succession

When Alexander III of Scotland died he left the throne to his grand-daughter Margaret, aged three. She was known as the Maid of Norway, because her father was Eric II of Norway. But the little girl died on her way to Scotland, and for the next two years 13 people laid claim to the throne.

Eventually the Scots barons asked Edward I of England to choose a successor. He selected John Balliol – a descendant of William the Lion's younger brother David – who probably had

Above: John Balliol, who reigned in Scotland from 1292 to 1296. On his banner is the lion of Scotland; his own coat of arms is embroidered on his wife's dress.

the best claim. Edward treated Balliol as a puppet king, and at this the Scots barons rebelled. Edward invaded Scotland, burned Berwick and captured Balliol. For ten years Scotland was without a king, and Edward tried to rule it himself. He was defied by an outlaw knight, William Wallace, who led an uprising and made himself master of Scotland. His triumph was short-lived. Edward, who is known to history as 'the Hammer of the Scots', reconquered the country, captured Wallace and had him put to death.

1285 Second Statute of Westminster strengthens land-holding laws
1286 Alexander III of Scotland dies; succeeded by his grand-daughter Margaret 'the Maid of Norway' (to 1290)
1289 Treaty of Salisbury: Scots, English and Norwegians agree that Margaret and Edward I's son Edward should marry
1290 Treaty of Birgham guarantees liberties of Scotland
Margaret dies at sea
Jews expelled from England
Third Statute of Westminster further revises land laws
Eleanor of Castile dies
Edward I annexes the Isle of Man
1291 Thirteen claimants for Scottish throne: Scots ask Edward to decide
1292 Edward awards Scottish throne to John Balliol (to 1296)
Edward orders training for lawyers to be provided
1294 French seizure of Gascony leads to war with England
New revolt by the Welsh
1295 Welsh rebellion crushed
'The Auld Alliance': treaty between Scotland and France
The Harrowing of Hell, earliest surviving miracle play
1296 Edward invades Scotland, sacks Berwick, captures Dunbar
John Balliol abdicates: Edward declares himself king of Scotland, seizes Stone of Scone
Pope Boniface issues bull (edict) forbidding clergy to pay taxes
1297 Edward forces clergy to submit
Edward campaigns in France
Wallace leads revolt in Scotland
1298 Edward invades Scotland, defeats Wallace at Falkirk

The Prince of Wales

Having slain the princes of Wales, Edward I announced to the Welsh lords that he would give them a prince who had been born in Wales and could speak no English. To their surprise the new prince was his son Edward, born a few weeks earlier at Caernarvon castle. The young Edward was formally created Prince of Wales when he was 17.

By tradition, the eldest son of the reigning monarch is created Prince of Wales. There have been 21 altogether, including Prince Charles. Only 13 succeeded to the throne out of the previous 20. Two, Richard II and George III, became Prince of Wales as grandsons of the reigning monarch, their fathers

having died. Out of the nearly 700 years since Edward of Caernarvon first held the title, there have been 374 years when there was no Prince of Wales.

The first Prince of Wales was the fourth son of Edward I, his brothers having died in infancy. He was fond of rowing and swimming, but he was much under the influence of his men friends. When he was King, these favourites influenced his decisions in matters of state, to the fury of the barons. The first was Piers Gaveston, whom a group of lords seized and beheaded on Blacklow Hill, near Warwick. Later, Edward came under the spell of the Despensers, a father and son both named Hugh.

The French king's daughter Isabella was married to Edward II at Boulogne in 1308, when she was only 12. In 1326, sickened by his passion for Hugh Despenser, she led a rebellion against him with her lover the Marcher lord Roger Mortimer.

Robert I (the Bruce), King of Scotland, won the independence of his country and ensured an undisputed succession.

The Bruce and the Red

Within months of William Wallace's death the two chief claimants to the Scottish throne met in a church at Dumfries. They were Robert Bruce and John Comyn, known as the Red. Bruce came out of the church, saying 'I doubt me I have killed the Red Comyn!' His followers completed the murder. With such a bloody deed the great champion of Scotland began his career. He was crowned at Scone soon after, but an English army was quickly on the scene, and Bruce suffered two heavy defeats.

After a spell in hiding Bruce returned to the fray. At Bannockburn, near Stirling, Bruce finally defeated an English army twice as strong as his own, and made his throne safe.

1301 Edward I makes his young son Edward Prince of Wales
Edward begins new campaign in Scotland
1302 In *Unam Sanctam* Pope Boniface declares papal authority supreme
1303 *Carta Mercatoria* gives foreign merchants freedom of trade
1304 Scots submit to Edward
1305 William Wallace executed as a traitor to Edward I
1306 Robert Bruce, claimant to the Scottish throne, kills his rival, John Comyn
Robert Bruce crowned (to 1329)
English defeat Bruce, who goes into exile in Ireland
Edward makes the use of coal punishable by death (because of its noxious fumes)
1307 Bruce returns, defeats English
Death of Edward I; succeeded by son Edward II (till 1327)
Edward creates his favourite, Piers Gaveston, Earl of Cornwall
Bruce defeats the Earl of Buchan
1308 Edward II marries Isabella of France
Barons force Edward to banish Gaveston
1309 Edward accepts reforms, and recalls Gaveston
1310 Appointment of Lords Ordainers, committee of reform
1311 Gaveston again banished
Privy Seal office established
1312 Gaveston returns and is killed
Edward makes peace with barons
1313 Scots recover Isle of Man
John Balliol dies
1314 Scots defeat English at battle of Bannockburn
1315 Edward Bruce invades Ireland
1316 Edward II appoints Earl of Lancaster as his chief councillor

Above: Edward II allowed his passions for favourites to interfere with his obligations as a king. Deposed by his rebellious barons, he agreed, half fainting and with groans and tears, to abdicate in favour of his 14-year-old son Edward III.

The Death of Edward II

Edward II's feeble rule and unpleasant ways of life turned not only his barons but also his wife against him. She and her lover, Roger Mortimer, raised a rebellion and captured Edward. They and the barons compelled Edward to abdicate and hand over power to his 14-year-old son, Edward. Eight months later the deposed King was cruelly murdered at Berkeley Castle, on the banks of the Severn.

.Below: In both the early university towns of Oxford and Cambridge there were conflicts between 'Town and Gown' – the local citizens and the students. Mob Quad at Merton (below) gets its name from a famous early riot. The quad (short for 'quadrangular' courtyard) is the oldest in Oxford.

The Universities

The oldest universities in Europe were those of Bologna and Paris, and it was English students from Paris who, according to tradition, established the first British university at Oxford. They set up schools in the town in disused convent buildings some time in the mid-1100s. About a hundred years later the first colleges were formed: Merton, University and Balliol colleges all dispute which is the oldest. Cambridge is said to have been founded by a group of scholars migrating from Oxford after trouble with the townspeople.

Three Scottish universities, St Andrews, Glasgow and Aberdeen, were founded in the 1400s, with Edinburgh in the 1500s, along with Trinity College Dublin. These were the only British universities until the 1800s.

The Declaration of Arbroath

At the abbey of Arbroath, in Angus, an assembly of Scottish lords made a resounding declaration of independence. It was addressed to Pope John XXII, who had ordered Robert Bruce and his principal bishops to appear before him. It called on the Pope to intervene in Scotland's quarrel with England, and persuade the King of England to 'leave us Scots in peace, who . . . covet nothing but our own'.

The 53 lords who put their seals on the Declaration of Arbroath affirmed their loyalty to Robert Bruce, but threatened that if he knuckled under to the English they would 'drive him out as our enemy'. Soon after, Edward II agreed on a 13-year truce.

1318 Edward Bruce killed in Ireland

1319 Scots defeat English at Myton

1320 Declaration of Arbroath: Scots lords tell Pope of loyalty to Robert I (the Bruce)

1321 Barons led by Thomas of Lancaster make Edward banish his favourites, the Despensers

1322 Edward II recalls the Despensers
Edward defeats Lancaster at Boroughbridge and executes him

1323 Edward and Robert agree truce

1324 French invade Gascony

1325 Edward II sends his wife, Isabella, to make peace with France; she becomes the mistress of the exiled Roger Mortimer

1326 Isabella and Mortimer land in Essex to raise rebellion; they capture Edward
Despensers caught and executed
Edward's 14-year-old son Edward declared 'keeper of the Realm'; Mortimer is regent

1327 Edward II deposed and murdered; Edward III king (to 1377)
England regains Gascony

1328 Edward III marries Philippa of Hainault
Edward makes peace with Scotland

1329 Robert I of Scotland dies; succeeded by 5-year-old son David II (to 1371)

1330 Edward III arrests Mortimer, who is hanged for treason, and begins personal rule

1332 Edward Balliol, son of John, tries to seize throne of Scotland; defeated, he flees to England

1333 England takes the Isle of Man from Scotland
Battle of Halidon Hill: Edward III defeats the Scots and takes Berwick; Edward Balliol restored

Wadicourt

Crécy

spears
longbows
Genoese
crossbows

English   French

The Hundred Years' War

The Hundred Years' War between England and France was a series of wars, interspersed with truces. It began when Charles IV of France died without a direct heir, and Edward III of England had a slim claim to the throne through his mother. Philip of Valois, who took the French throne, was also anxious to regain Gascony, the last major English territory in France.

Two other factors influenced the start of the war: Edward loved adventure, and he knew, too, that if his equally adventurous and restless barons were involved in an overseas campaign they were less likely to start trouble at home. Finally, there was the wool trade with the weavers of Flanders. The Flemings depended on English wool, and Eng-

English and French dispositions at the battle of Crécy.

land's sales of wool were its only source of income apart from farming. But the aristocratic rulers of Flanders were pro-French and attempted to curb the wool trade.

In the early years of the war the English won two significant battles. The naval battle of Sluys gave them control of the English Channel, and made an English invasion of France relatively easy; while when the invasion began Edward scored a major land victory at Crécy, on the banks of the Somme. This battle was won by Edward's longbowmen, whose arrowstorm mowed down the French knights.

The Order of the Garter

Edward III founded the Order of the Garter as a purely military order of chivalry, designed to carry on the medieval ideals of knighthood. A legend which cannot be confirmed says that at court one day the Countess of Salisbury accidentally dropped her garter. The King picked it up, and rebuked his sniggering courtiers with the quip in old French, *Honi soit qui mal y pense* (evil be to him who thinks evil). This is now the motto of the Order.

Edward III makes peace with John of France at the Treaty of Brétigny which brought to an end the first part of the Hundred Years' War, after the English victories at Crécy and Poitiers on land and Sluys at sea. The Treaty was signed in May 1360 but never ratified, being replaced by that of Calais in October.

1334	David II of Scotland flees to France
	Oxford dons try to set up a university at Stamford, Lincs.
1335	Edward III campaigns in Scotland
1336	Parliament grants taxes to pay for Scottish campaigns
	Trade with Flanders is halted
	French attack Isle of Wight and Channel Islands
1337	William Merlee of Oxford attempts first scientific weather forecasts
	Philip VI of France seizes Gascony: start of Hundred Years' War
	Edward III claims French Crown
1338	French fleet sacks Portsmouth
	Edward III lands at Antwerp: makes alliance with German Emperor
	Flemish weavers make trade treaty with England
1339	Edward III invades France
	Balliol leaves Scotland
1340	English naval victory at Sluys wins control of English Channel
	Parliament appoints auditors of the King's expenditure
1341	David II returns to Scotland
1342	Scots complete expulsion of English and capture Roxburgh
	Edward campaigns in Brittany
1343	France and England make truce
1344	Parliament demands that money be spent as stipulated
	The gold noble (6s 8d) first coined in England
1346	Edward defeats French at Crécy
	Scots invade England: David II defeated and captured at battle of Neville's Cross
1347	Edward captures Calais
1348	Black Death reaches England
	Edward founds the Order of the Garter

71

The Black Death

The greatest disaster in its history struck Europe during the 1300s. In only 20 years the Black Death (probably bubonic plague) killed about one-third of Europe's population.

The Black Death reached England at Melcombe Regis, the port of Weymouth. Within a few weeks it had spread to Bristol and London, and within a year almost every part of England and Wales had been affected. The death toll is estimated at 2,500,000 – half the country's population.

The Black Death halted Edward III's campaign against Scotland, but the Scots' rejoicing at this was soon dashed when the plague struck there, too. Scotland and Ireland, however, suffered less severely than England. The immediate effect of the Black Death was a shortage of labour, and a rise in wages which amounted to about 50 per cent for craftsmen and agricultural workers, and 100 per cent for women farm workers.

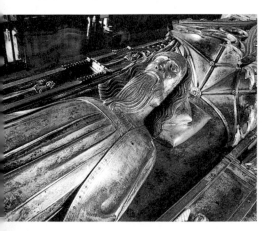

The Black Prince

Edward III's eldest son, Edward, Prince of Wales, was as fine a warrior as his father, and he distinguished himself by his bravery at the battle of Crécy when he was only 16. Here he won the three plumes and the motto 'Ich dien' (I serve) used by Princes of Wales ever since. He is known to history as 'the Black Prince', from the colour of his armour, but was not apparently so named during his lifetime.

Ten years after Crécy Edward won his greatest victory as a commander at Poitiers, where he captured the French King, John II. This monarch was ransomed for 3,000,000 gold crowns and the duchy of Aquitaine. Edward was ill for the last few years of his life, dying in 1376.

Racial Disharmony

When Lionel, Duke of Clarence was sent to govern Ireland in 1361 he found the Anglo-Irish becoming less English, and not inclined to fight their Irish neighbours. So he summoned a parliament at Kilkenny which passed 35 Acts, the Statutes of Kilkenny.

The Statutes forbade the English to marry with the Irish; the Irish language was banned in English-held territories; Irish laws and customs were also banned. This divisive act remained in force for two centuries.

The tomb of Edward III in Westminster abbey. The face may have been modelled from a death mask. His last years were lonely and inglorious; much of France was lost and he let his mistress, Alice Perrers, and his third son, John of Gaunt, take power.

The tomb of the Black Prince in Canterbury cathedral. He was a brilliant general but his eight-year rule of Aquitaine showed him a poor statesman – tactless, overbearing and recklessly extravagant. The last years of his life were tragic; illness made him bedridden and unable to control his armies, forcing him to retire to England. Despite this, he was a legend even in his own time.

1350 Black Death reaches Scotland
Extension of Windsor castle begins (finished 1356)

1351 Battle of the Thirty between 30 English and 30 Bretons
Statute of Labourers curbs wages
First Statute of Provisors bans papal appointments in England
Groat (fourpence) first minted

1353 Edward III transfers the wool staple (market) from Bruges to England
First Statute of Praemunire bars appeals to the Pope

1355 Edward III campaigns in Picardy
Black Prince sacks Carcassonne
Scots take Berwick-upon-Tweed

1356 Edward III recaptures Berwick
Edward Balliol gives up throne of Scotland to Edward III
Black Prince defeats and captures John II of France at Poitiers

1357 Treaty of Bordeaux between England and France
Treaty of Berwick: 10-year truce between England and Scotland; David II ransomed and freed

1360 Treaty of Brétigny: John II released for huge ransom; France cedes Aquitaine, Ponthieu and Calais.

1362 Wool staple moved to Calais
William Langland writes allegorical poem *Piers Plowman*

1363 Statute of Apparel prevents people wearing dress above their station in life

1364 Hostage for payment of John II's ransom escapes: John returns to captivity, and dies

1365 Parliament repudiates subjection of England to the Papacy

1366 Statutes of Kilkenny: Irish parliament forbids the English overlords to marry Irish people

Richard II

The boy-king who succeeded Edward III was only 10 years old. He had a poor inheritance. In his last years Edward was senile, and the cost of his wars left the Crown deeply in debt.

Richard II was too young to rule, so the government of the country was in the hands of his uncle, John, Duke of Lancaster, popularly known as John of Gaunt (Ghent, his birthplace). The young King first came to popular attention when he helped to quell the Peasants' Revolt.

Richard was a lover of art and literature, and not of the warlike occupations of his father, the Black Prince. His closest friend was Robert de Vere, Earl of Oxford, who was not a wise counsellor.

The Peasants' Revolt

The shortage of labour which followed the Black Death brought a great deal of unrest. Farm workers sought more money: landlords and government tried to keep wages fixed. Finally the imposition of a poll tax of one shilling a head sparked off open rebellion. It was

Ancient Allies

Portugal is England's oldest ally, thanks to the Treaty of London of 1373, which was confirmed by the Treaty of Windsor 13 years later. This alliance has never been broken. In 1372 John of Gaunt had married King Pedro of Portugal's daughter Constance of Castile, and the alliance was strengthened in 1387 when Pedro's son John I married Philippa of Lancaster, daughter of John of Gaunt by his first wife.

stirred up by agitators such as John Ball, a priest, and was led by Wat Tyler, a blacksmith, and Jack Straw (possibly a nickname).

More than 100,000 peasants from Kent and Essex marched on London, where they killed foreign merchants and burned John of Gaunt's palace, the Savoy. Richard II, still only 14 years old, faced a mob at Mile End and promised 'You shall have from me all you seek'. Tyler and his men of Kent remained in arms while the rest dispersed. A few days later, in the King's presence, Tyler was killed by the Lord Mayor of London, William Walworth. The revolt rippled on for a while, but died out. About 150 rebels were executed; the poll tax was quietly dropped.

The boy-king Richard II confronts the rebellious peasants. The promises he gave were soon broken.

1367 Black Prince invades Castile on behalf of Pedro the Cruel
1369 France again at war with England: Edward again claims Crown
Queen Philippa dies: Edward under influence of his unscrupulous mistress, Alice Perrers
1370 Black Prince sacks Limoges
1371 Merton College library founded: oldest in England
David II of Scotland dies; succeeded by Robert II (Stewart)
1372 John of Gaunt claims Castile as Pedro's son-in-law
Edward III makes last effort to invade France: English fleet destroyed in battle off La Rochelle
1373 Treaty of London: England and Portugal make perpetual alliance
Parliament gives Edward right to charge tunnage and poundage, customs duties
1375 Peace with France: England left with only Calais, Brest, Bordeaux and Bayonne
Robin Hood appears in ballads
1376 The 'Good Parliament': first to elect a Speaker (Sir Thomas Hungerford)
The Black Prince dies
Preacher John Wyclif says the Church should not own property
1377 'Bad Parliament' grants poll tax
Edward III dies: succeeded by 10-year-old grandson Richard II (to 1399); council of regency rules
French sack Isle of Wight
1378 English gain Cherbourg
1380 Wyclif translates the Bible
1381 Six-year truce with France
Short-lived Peasants' Revolt
1382 Richard marries Anne of Bohemia
William of Wykeham, Bishop of Winchester, founds Winchester College (oldest public school)

The Struggle for Power

Richard II remained under guardianship far longer than other monarchs of his time. When he was 20 he tried to escape from the rule of his uncles, but Parliament, probably unimpressed by the King's frivolous friends, kept him under restraint. John of Gaunt had gone off to Spain to pursue a claim (through his wife) to the throne of Castile. In this power-vacuum Parliament appointed a council to rule the kingdom. Its members became known as the Lords Appellant.

Richard asked five judges for their view, and they declared that the actions of the Lords Appellant and Parliament were illegal. This provoked a short civil war, in which an army led by the King's favourite, the Earl of Oxford, was defeated. The Lords Appellant considered deposing and killing Richard, but were restrained by John of Gaunt's son, the forceful Henry of Bolingbroke.

There the restraint ended. At what is called 'the Merciless Parliament' Richard's supporters were declared guilty of treason and put to death. A year later Richard, now 23, pointed out that he was of full age and assumed power. For eight years he ruled in peace. But he was biding his time.

In 1397 Richard revenged himself on the Lords Appellant. The Earl of Arundel was beheaded. The Duke of Gloucester, Richard's uncle, was murdered. Two others, Henry of Bolingbroke and the Duke of Norfolk, who had quarrelled, were banished. Soon after, John of Gaunt died, and Richard seized his estates. This was too much for Bolingbroke. He returned from exile, swiftly gathered a large body of supporters and took Richard prisoner. By general consent he was deposed, and Bolingbroke succeeded as Henry IV.

An illustration to Chaucer's 'Knight's Tale' from his stories of pilgrims on their way to Canterbury. He worked from Latin models, for an aristocratic but generally illiterate audience; the East Midlands dialect of Middle English that he used was the forerunner of the standard English of today.

John Wyclif has been called the 'Morning Star of the Reformation'. He attacked the Church for its worldliness and for its power in secular matters, and initiated the first translation of the Bible into English.

Geoffrey Chaucer

A quiet, enigmatic figure at the court of Edward III and Richard II was the poet Geoffrey Chaucer. He held a series of civil service posts, but was employed as an ambassador, going on secret missions for the King. He was favoured by John of Gaunt, whose mistress, and later third wife, was Chaucer's sister-in-law, Katherine Swynford. Chaucer wrote his poems for the royal court, and they circulated to a slightly wider audience. Their popularity is shown by the fact that they were copied and recopied many times.

1384-5 Scots raid England; English invade Scotland
1386 Treaty of Windsor confirms Anglo-Portuguese alliance
Barons compel Richard II to replace senior ministers
Salisbury cathedral clock, oldest in England, made
John of Gaunt begins campaign for Crown of Castile
1387 Lords Appellant (including Duke of Gloucester, Earls of Arundel and Warwick), impeach ministers
Earl of Oxford, Richard's crony, defeated by Henry of Bolingbroke, son of John of Gaunt, at Radcot Bridge, Oxon.
Geoffrey Chaucer begins work on *The Canterbury Tales*
1388 The 'Merciless Parliament' convicts Richard's ministers; Lords Appellant control government
Earl of Douglas killed defeating Henry Percy ('Hotspur') at Otterburn ('Chevy Chase')
1389 Richard II assumes personal rule
1390 Robert II of Scotland dies: succeeded by Robert III (to 1406)
1393 Great Statute of Praemunire reasserts supremacy of State in Church affairs
1394 Queen Anne dies
1395 Irish chiefs submit to Richard
1396 Treaty with France: Richard marries Isabella of France
1397 Richard has Lords Appellant tried and executed or banished
Children of John of Gaunt and Katherine Swynford legitimized
1398 Richard exiles Henry Bolingbroke
1399 John of Gaunt dies; Richard seizes his estates
Henry returns, raises rebellion and seizes the throne as Henry IV; Richard is imprisoned

Lancaster and York

The Plantagenets were a fierce and quarrelsome family, and never more so than when disputing the right to the throne. Edward III had five sons who reached adulthood. The two eldest, Edward the Black Prince and Lionel, Duke of Clarence, died before their father. Edward's only son, Richard II, had no children, and Lionel left only a daughter, Philippa. Philippa's grandson, Edmund, Earl of March, was a nine-year-old orphan when Richard II abdicated. This left the way clear for Henry IV, as the son of Edward III's third son, John of Gaunt, Duke of Lancaster, to seize the throne. The accession of Henry IV brought only a temporary respite in the civil strife which ravaged England.

The simple-mindedness, and at times downright insanity, of his grandson Henry VI revived all the disputes over the Crown. A strong claim was put forward by Richard, Duke of York, grandson of Edward III's fourth son, Edmund. Richard's mother was Anne Mortimer, great grand-daughter of the Duke of Clarence, so York combined the claims of the descendants of two of Edward III's sons, Clarence and York. The ensuing struggle for the Crown is known as the Wars of the Roses, from the badges of the two conflicting families, Lancaster and York. In the end Henry Tudor, son of Margaret Beaufort and great-great-grandson of John of Gaunt, was almost the last representative of the House of Lancaster. He won the throne.

Scotland saw its throne pass to the Stewarts, a gallant and ill-fated family. Wales lost its independence and was gradually integrated with England, while the long struggle by the English to conquer Ireland continued.

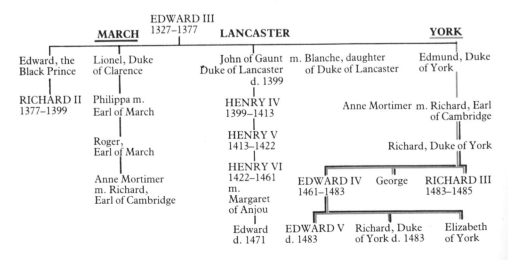

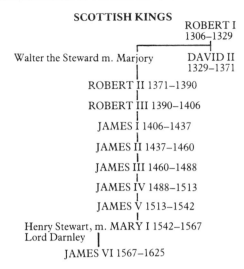

SCOTTISH KINGS

ROBERT I
1306–1329

Walter the Steward m. Marjory   DAVID II
1329–1371

ROBERT II 1371–1390

ROBERT III 1390–1406

JAMES I 1406–1437

JAMES II 1437–1460

JAMES III 1460–1488

JAMES IV 1488–1513

JAMES V 1513–1542

Henry Stewart, m. MARY I 1542–1567
Lord Darnley

JAMES VI 1567–1625

The Stewarts

David II of Scotland died childless, and the throne went to his nephew, Robert the Steward. Robert was the son of David's half-sister Marjory, who had married Walter FitzAlan, the sixth High Steward of Scotland (an important administrative post). The name FitzAlan had by this time been almost forgotten, and it was as Stewart, the old Scots form of the word, that the family came to be known. The spelling Stuart was adopted in the 17th century.

The Stewarts were in many ways an unlucky family. Nearly all of the rulers came to the throne young, and the land had to be ruled by nobles in their name. Five of them died violent deaths. Yet it was a Stewart, James VI, who united the thrones of England and Scotland as James I of England in 1603, and the Stewarts (Stuarts) reigned until 1714. The present Queen is descended from a daughter of James I and VI.

ELSEWHERE IN THE WORLD

1399 Tamerlane captures Damascus and Baghdad

1410 Battle of Tannenberg: Poles defeat the Teutonic Knights

1414-17 Council of Constance: Great Schism ends, Martin V Pope

1429 Jeanne d'Arc raises siege of Orléans: Charles VII crowned king of France at Rheims

1431 Khmer Empire ends: Angkor abandoned
Jeanne d'Arc burned as a witch

1434 Cosimo de Medici rules Florence

c1440 Johannes Gutenberg invents printing from movable type

1453 Turks capture Constantinople: end of the Byzantine Empire

1461 Turks finally conquer Greece

1462 Ivan III duke of Moscow (to 1505)
Castile takes Gibraltar from Arabs

1466 Peace of Thorn: Poland gains much of Prussia

1467 Civil war in Japan (to 1590)
Charles the Bold, Duke of Burgundy

1468 Songhai Empire in Western Africa founded

1469 Prince Ferdinand of Aragon marries Princess Isabella of Castile

1471 Portuguese take Tangier from Moors

1472 Portuguese discover Fernando Po, off West Africa

1474-77 War between Burgundy and the Swiss: Charles the Bold killed
Isabella becomes queen of Castile

1478 Spanish Inquisition established
Lorenzo de Medici ruler of Florence (to 1492)
Ivan III conquers Novgorod

1479 Ferdinand becomes king of Aragon: most of Spain united

1482 Portuguese settle on Gold Coast

1485 Hungary conquers Lower Austria

Owain Glyndwr

The last independent prince of Wales was Owain Glyndwr, who ruled lands in North Wales. A feud with his neighbour, Lord Grey de Ruthyn, led to rebellion. Grey intercepted a summons to Owain to campaign for Henry IV in Scotland; so the King declared Owain's lands forfeit, and gave them to Grey.

Owain raised an army and the Welsh, resentful of privileges given to Englishmen living among them, backed him in what became a national rebellion. Henry IV was preoccupied with uprisings in England, and Owain had considerable success. For some years he virtually ruled Wales. But a successful campaign led by the future Henry V broke the rebellion by 1409.

The Lollards

In the late 1300s a religious movement started in England which attacked many of the beliefs and practices of the Church of Rome. Its followers were known as Lollards, from a Flemish word meaning 'mutterer'. They originally followed the teachings of John Wyclif, but later became more extreme. Devout followers of the Church regarded them with horror as heretics, and as opponents of the established order of government.

To combat Lollardy, Henry IV's Parliament passed the cruel law *De Heretico Comburendo*, which said that convicted heretics who refused to recant, or recanted and relapsed, should suffer death by burning.

Opposite: James I of Scotland. He was kidnapped by the English and during his years in captivity he learned much about government. On his return to Scotland he tried to introduce some English ways, and in particular to widen the scope of the Scottish Parliament. His firm government was popular with some of his subjects but his stern dealings with great Scottish nobles led to his murder.

Left: The Great Seal of Owain Glyndwr. He was educated at Oxford, studied law in London, spent some time at Richard II's court and campaigned as squire to Henry IV.

IACOBVS I D·GRATIA
REX·SCOTORVM

The Captive King

The last years of the reign of Robert III of Scotland were dominated by his ambitious brother the Duke of Albany, who was governor of the land. Albany was suspected of murdering Robert's heir, David. To safeguard his second son, James, the King decided to send him to France by sea.

English sailors intercepted the ship and James, who was 10, was taken prisoner to London, where he remained a captive until 1424. Robert died of grief at the news, and James was proclaimed king, while Albany continued to rule the land in his name.

In captivity James read and studied, and wrote a long allegorical poem *The Kingis Quair* (The King's Book). He also became a musician and an athlete.

1399 Henry Bolingbroke seizes the throne as Henry IV (to 1413)
1400 Conspiracy by Earls of Huntingdon, Kent and Salisbury to kill Henry IV fails
Richard II dies in captivity
Henry IV campaigns in Scotland
Owain Glyndwr rebels; Henry marches to fight him
1401 Henry fails to crush Glyndwr
Statute *De Heretico Comburendo*: relapsed heretics to burn; first sufferer William Sawtrey
Henry IV marries Joan of Navarre
1402 Glyndwr captures Grey and Edmund Mortimer. Scottish invasion halted at battle of Homildon Hill
1403 Glyndwr captures Carmarthen
Revolt by the Percies: Henry IV kills Henry Percy ('Hotspur') at Shrewsbury, retakes Carmarthen
French forces sack Plymouth
1404 Tax on land revenues
Glyndwr controls Wales, takes title of 'Prince of Wales'
1405 Archbishop Richard Scrope rebels: fails and is executed
French land in Wales to help Glyndwr
1406 Prince James of Scotland captured by English on way to France
Robert III of Scotland dies; succeeded by captive James I (to 1420); Robert, Duke of Albany, regent
1407 Bethlehem Hospital (Bedlam) becomes hospital for the insane
1408 Henry Percy, Earl of Northumberland, invades from Scotland and is killed at Bramham Moor
1409 Glyndwr's rebellion collapses
1410 St Andrews University founded
1411 Henry, Prince of Wales, tries to control government: dismissed by Henry IV

The Agincourt Campaign

During the declining years of Henry IV much of the government devolved on his warlike son Henry, though the ailing King stoutly resisted a suggestion that he should abdicate. When Henry V came to the throne on his father's death he began by declaring a general pardon for his enemies, and then revived Edward III's old claim to the throne of France. That throne was occupied by Charles VI, who had been subject to fits of madness for the past 20 years. The dukes of Burgundy and Orléans were warring rivals for power in France. Henry allied himself with the Burgundians, the weaker party, and set out to conquer the country. The prospect of an overseas war did much to unite the warring factions in England.

Henry began by capturing the town of Harfleur at the mouth of the Seine. From there he set out with about 5000

Opposite: The effigies of Henry IV and his wife Joan of Navarre.

men, 4000 of them archers, to march east to Calais.

The English found their way barred by a French army more than three times as strong. Attempts to negotiate a clear road to safety failed, and Henry resolved on battle. The French unwisely chose a narrow front between two woods, which gave them no room to manoeuvre. Once again the English longbow won the day. This was the battle of Agincourt, settled in three hours with the loss of 10,000 Frenchmen and no more than 1500 English. Henry returned to England a hero.

The battle of Agincourt; the English strength lay in their combination of longbow archers and dismounted men at arms. Their casualties were about 1500 – the French some 10,000.

Victory and Death

Two years after Agincourt Henry V led a much larger expedition to France. Within three years he was master of Normandy. His ally, the Duke of Burgundy, was murdered by hotheaded supporters of Charles VI's heir, the Dauphin. This united the Dauphin's opponents, and as a result Henry V was acknowledged as regent of France during the mad King's lifetime, and his heir. To cement the agreement Henry married the King's daughter, Catherine of Valois.

Henry's triumph was short-lived. Two years later he died of fever on a further campaign, leaving the throne to his baby son, Henry VI, who was nine months old.

1413 Henry V king of England (to 1422)
1414 Campaign against Lollards: leader Sir John Oldcastle is excommunicated
Henry demands throne of France
1415 Conspiracy to put Edmund Mortimer, Earl of March, on throne: Lord Scrope and Earl of Cambridge executed, Mortimer pardoned
Invasion of France: Henry captures Harfleur
Battle of Agincourt: English win
Henry founds monastery at Twickenham (last before Reformation)
1417 Henry invades Normandy, aided by Duke John of Burgundy
Oldcastle burned as a heretic
1418 First existing letters of the Paston family (published 1787)
1419 Henry V completes conquest of Normandy
Duke of Burgundy assassinated
1420 Treaty of Troyes: Henry to be regent of France during life of Charles VI, and succeed him
Henry V marries Charles's daughter Catherine
Scottish regent Albany dies; succeeded by son Murdoch (to 1425)
1421 Henry's brother Thomas, Duke of Clarence, killed at Beaugé
1422 Henry V captures Meaux
Henry V dies suddenly; succeeded by infant son Henry VI (to 1461). Henry VI's uncles become regents: Humphrey of Gloucester in England; John of Bedford in France
Charles VI of France dies: succeeded by Henry VI, but his son Charles (VII) claims throne
1423 Anglo-Burgundian army defeats French and Scots at Cravant

The Loss of France

Two months after becoming king of England, the baby Henry VI was proclaimed king of France on the death of his mad grandfather, Charles VI. His father's brother Duke Humphrey of Gloucester was made regent in England. Another uncle, Duke John of Bedford, a skilled and experienced general, ruled France on his behalf. The French claimant to the throne, the Dauphin Charles, controlled the country south of the river Loire, but England's hold on the northern region seemed secure.

In 1428 the demoralized French forces were given unexpected inspiration. Jeanne d'Arc, a simple peasant girl, heard voices and saw visions which commanded her to liberate her country. She led the French to relieve the besieged city of Orléans and then to further victories. Under her command the Dauphin Charles marched to Rheims, where he was crowned king of France.

Jeanne's voices now went silent, and she wanted to return home. But she was captured by the Burgundians, still half-heartedly allied to England. They sold Jeanne to the English who had her tried for witchcraft and heresy, condemned and burned. An English soldier saw her die and said: 'We are lost – we have burned a saint.'

In 1435 the valiant Duke of Bedford died, and in the same year the Burgundians finally broke their alliance with the English, and made a treaty with France. Charles reorganized his army. The French learned that the hitherto invincible English archers could be

Opposite: The coronation of Henry VI as king of France by his uncle Cardinal Beaufort was held in Paris in 1431. This attempt to counteract the coronation of the Dauphin brought no success; Henry's reign saw the loss of almost all English land in France.

Left: Jeanne d'Arc, known to the English as Joan of Arc, kneels before the King of France. She claimed to be guided by the voices of Saint Michael, Saint Catherine and Saint Margaret which urged her to help the Dauphin Charles to claim his throne. Jeanne is shown in the male armour which she wore from the start of her campaign to her death.

defeated by surprise attacks, while improved French artillery pounded to ruins once impregnable English fortresses. By 1453 the English had been almost completely driven out of France; the Hundred Years' War was over.

Strong Man of Scotland

James I of Scotland was released by the regents of Henry VI after 18 years in captivity. He took back to Scotland an English bride, Joan Beaufort, granddaughter of John of Gaunt. He found the land badly governed by his cousin Murdoch, son of the late regent, Albany; within a year he had Murdoch and his sons executed for treason.

Within four years James had reorganized the Scottish government, strengthened Parliament, reformed the law courts and curbed the more rebellious of the Highland chiefs. Three of these chiefs he hanged; the rest he released after a short spell in prison.

1424 James I of Scotland is released, marries Joan Beaufort, and is crowned in Scotland
'Lords of the Articles' committee does main work of Scottish Parliament
1425 James I has regent Murdoch, Duke of Albany, executed
Le Mans surrenders to English
Riot in London between supporters of Humphrey of Gloucester and Henry Beaufort, Bishop of Winchester
1426 Gloucester and Beaufort reconciled at 'Parliament of Bats'
1427 French defeat English at Montargis
1428 English begin siege of Orléans
James I calls for election of representatives of sheriffdoms to Scottish Parliament
Jeanne d'Arc hears 'voices'
1429 Battle of the Herrings: English defeat French attack on supplies
Jeanne d'Arc leads French to relieve Orléans
English defeated at Patay
1430 Burgundian troops take Jeanne d'Arc, and hand her to English
Statute says shire-knights eligible for Parliament must hold freehold land worth 40s (£2) a year
1431 Humphrey of Gloucester crushes Lollard uprising in Abingdon
Henry VI crowned king of France
Jeanne d'Arc burned as a heretic
1433 Tattershall Castle, Lincolnshire, built with a million bricks
1435 John of Bedford, regent of France, dies; succeeded by Richard, Duke of York
French capture Dieppe
1436 French capture Paris
Scots defeat English near Berwick
First attempts to drain the Fens

The Scholar King

Henry VI's long minority saw much strife between powerful nobles vying for power. When he came of age the situation did not improve; he was a gentle, pious and scholarly man dominated by those around him. When the Duke of Suffolk arranged Henry's marriage to the forceful French Princess Margaret of Anjou, he signed a secret treaty ceding Maine to France. The English were furious when they found out. When the Hundred Years' War ended in ignominious defeat for England it was said that the Lancastrian line, which had seized the throne by force, was unlucky for the country.

During the Middle Ages one of England's principle sources of wealth was wool, the main export before 1350. After that date less wool was exported; instead woollen cloth was sold abroad, especially to Flanders. This picture shows merchants unloading a cargo of wool.

Who were the Beauforts?

The Beauforts were the descendants of John of Gaunt and his mistress, Katherine Swynford. For a time they were very powerful, but although they were made legitimate when Gaunt married Catherine, they were barred from the throne.

The second Beaufort son, Henry, became bishop of Winchester and a cardinal; he was the richest man in the kingdom. He vied for power with Humphrey of Gloucester during Henry VI's minority, and influenced the feeble King when he came of age. Henry Beaufort's nephew John, Duke of Somerset commanded Henry V's forces in France. After John's death his brother Edmund led the English forces in the last defeats of the Hundred Years' War, and was a possible heir to the throne. Edmund's sister Joan married James I of Scotland.

Several of the Beauforts died without children and others were killed in the Wars of the Roses, leaving Duke John's daughter Margaret as the Lancastrian heiress. She married Edmund Tudor and was the mother of Henry VII.

The Queen and the Yeoman

Queen Catherine, widow of Henry V, secretly married one of Henry VI's squires, a Welsh yeoman named Owen Tudor. They had three sons: Edmund, who was made earl of Richmond; Jasper, created earl·of Pembroke; and Owen, who became a monk. Edmund married Margaret Beaufort, heiress of John of Gaunt: their son in due course became Henry VII.

1437 Richard, Duke of York, captures Pontoise; replaced as regent of France by Earl of Warwick
Murder of James I of Scotland: succeeded by son, James II, aged six (to 1460): Earl of Douglas is regent
Henry VI declared of age, but the Council of State holds power
1438 Truce between England and Scotland
1439 Congress of Calais: fruitless bid for Anglo-French peace
Cardinal Beaufort, great-uncle of Henry VI, controls the government
Regent Douglas dies
England makes truce with Burgundy
1440 English recapture Harfleur from the French
Richard of York again becomes regent in France
Douglas's sons murdered by order of councillors after dining with James II: Stewart-Douglas feud
1441 Henry VI founds King's College, Cambridge
Humphrey of Gloucester's wife Eleanor condemned for sorcery
1442 French retake most of Gascony
1443 John Beaufort, Duke of Somerset, campaigns in Gascony and raids Anjou
1444 William de la Pole, Earl of Suffolk, negotiates truce with France
1445 Henry VI marries Margaret of Anjou
1447 Parliament called at Bury St Edmunds, Suffolk: Humphrey of Gloucester arrested: he dies in captivity
1448 English surrender Le Mans
England and Scotland at war

Henry VI founded Eton College and King's College, Cambridge (above) – fitting memorials to this pious and scholarly man. His subjects realized that he was weak and ill-advised, and though his unpopular regime led to his deposition, Henry himself was regarded by many as a saint.

York or Lancaster?

For some years after he married, Henry VI had no heir. There were two obvious candidates for the succession. Richard, Duke of York was descended in the male line from Edward III's youngest son, Edmund, and through his mother from Edward's second son, Lionel. He had a better claim to the throne than the King himself. The other candidate was the Lancastrian Edmund Beaufort, Duke of Somerset. Like Henry he was descended from Edward III's third son, John of Gaunt, but like all Beauforts he was barred from the throne. He was a favourite of Henry and Margaret.

York, an honest and competent man, did not press his claim. But in 1453 King Henry went mad; his wife gave birth to a son, Edward; and Somerset was blamed for defeats in France and was sent to the Tower. Law and order had almost broken down and unruly bands of soldiers, returned from fighting in France, roamed the countryside. York, the obvious choice, was made Lord Protector.

As suddenly as he went mad, King Henry recovered. York was dismissed and Somerset was released; Queen Margaret controlled the King. York still did not openly claim the Crown, but he decided to fight against Margaret's open enmity. His army met that of Margaret, Henry and Somerset at St Albans. Somerset and many of his supporters were killed, and York briefly became Protector again. After a few years of uneasy peace fighting broke out once more and this time the Lancastrians won. York and many of his followers were killed.

So began the Wars of the Roses, named (centuries later) after the emblems of the warring houses: the red rose of Lancaster, and the white rose of York.

1449 English sack Fougères, Brittany: war with France resumes
Richard of York becomes Lord Lieutenant of Ireland; Edmund, Duke of Somerset takes French command
James II of Scotland marries Mary of Gueldres; assumes power
1450 Duke of Suffolk accused of selling the realm to France, and is murdered on way to exile
Jack Cade's Rebellion: 30,000 rebels from Kent and Sussex control London for a few days
English lose control of Normandy
1451 French capture Bordeaux and Bayonne, leaving England only Calais
Glasgow University founded
1452 James II murders William, Earl of Douglas
Richard of York tries to seize power and fails
1453 French victory at Châtillon ends Hundred Years' War
Henry VI becomes insane: York is regent
1454 Henry recovers; his infant son Edward becomes Prince of Wales
1455 Wars of the Roses begin. Battle of St Albans: Yorkist victory. Henry VI captured
York becomes Lord Protector
1456 Queen Margaret dismisses York
1459 Civil war renewed: Lancastrian victory at battles of Bloreheath and Ludford
1460 Battle of Northampton: Yorkists capture Henry VI again. He agrees that York shall succeed him
James II of Scotland killed by exploding cannon at Roxburgh: succeeded by James III, aged eight (to 1488)

The Wars of the Roses

After the death of the Duke of York in 1460 the Yorkist leadership passed to his son, Edward, who was only 19. The war became dominated by one of the most powerful nobles, Edward's cousin Richard Neville, Earl of Warwick. His generalship and political skill gave him the nickname of 'the Kingmaker'.

The civil war now became vicious in the extreme, with each side exacting vengeance for the killing of its own supporters. After several battles, Edward of York entered London and was

Henry VI and his strong-willed Queen, Margaret of Anjou. The agreement to cede Anjou and Maine to France, made by the Duke of Suffolk when he was negotiating the marriage, infuriated the English when it became known. Margaret soon gained control over her husband. Her enmity towards Richard of York, whom she saw as a threat to the succession of her son Prince Edward, was one of the causes of the Wars of the Roses. Edward was eventually killed at Tewkesbury in 1471, after which Henry VI – now permanently witless – was executed by order of Edward IV.

proclaimed king as Edward IV. Soon after, the battle of Towton crushed the Lancastrians. Despite this, the Lancastrian cause was kept alive by the will of Queen Margaret.

Edward IV's marriage to Elizabeth Woodville brought her family to prominence and angered Warwick, who had hoped to arrange a French marriage. He rebelled and captured Edward – who already had Henry VI captive in the Tower. Warwick and Edward were reconciled but only briefly, and Warwick had to flee to France. There, as a price for French help, he allied with his old enemy Queen Margaret.

Warwick returned to England and won massive support; Edward in turn had to flee. Warwick restored poor King Henry to the throne. His second reign lasted only a few months. Edward returned to England with troops from Burgundy. At the battle of Barnet Warwick was killed, and at Tewkesbury a few weeks later the Lancastrians were finally crushed. Edward was king and master of the realm. This time he made no mistake: Henry VI was put to death in the Tower.

1460 Richard of York puts his claim to the throne before Parliament
Battle of Wakefield: Lancastrian victory. Richard of York killed
1461 Battle of Mortimer's Cross: Edward, Duke of York (son of Richard) defeats Lancastrians
Second battle of St Albans: Margaret rescues Henry VI, defeats Earl of Warwick
York assumes the Crown as Edward IV (to 1483)
Battle of Towton: Lancastrians defeated. Henry flees to Scotland
1462 Margaret raises army in Europe, lands in the North
Warwick crushes Lancastrians
1463 Edward again defeats Lancastrians: Margaret flees to France
1464 Edward crushes more Lancastrian rebellions; many nobles killed. Yorkists capture Henry
Edward IV marries Elizabeth Woodville
1466 Lord Boyd kidnaps James III and becomes governor of Scotland
1467 Scots Parliament bans 'fute-ball and golfe'
1468 Edward's sister Margaret marries Charles the Bold of Burgundy
1469 Warwick changes sides, captures Edward, but lets him go free
1470 Warwick forced to flee to France: he and Queen Margaret unite
Warwick lands with an army, restores Henry VI to the throne
Edward flees to Flanders
1471 Edward lands in Yorkshire with Flemish troops: resumes Crown
Battle of Barnet: Warwick killed
Battle of Tewkesbury: Prince of Wales killed, Margaret captured
Henry VI murdered in the Tower
1472 Scotland gains Orkney and Shetland from Norway

Edward IV was unusually tall and handsome, and his love of pleasure made him popular. He was only 19 when he took the throne with the help of the Earl of Warwick; he proved no puppet but a shrewd and strong ruler. His early death left a child as king yet again, and England once more faced a struggle for power between leading nobles.

The Yorkist King

Edward IV was handsome and pleasure-loving, but he proved the strong and efficient ruler England so badly needed. He called Parliament only when he needed money, and for some time he contrived to manage on what income he had. Popular demand called for reconquering the lost lands in France. Edward obtained funds from Parliament for this but allowed the French to buy him off, giving him two sources of money. Edward was ruthless, too: he called another Parliament to condemn his treacherous brother George, Duke of Clarence. Clarence died in the Tower: by tradition, he was drowned in a butt of Malmsey wine.

Edward had two young sons and five daughters; his rule and succession seemed secure. Then at the age of 40 he was taken ill, and died within ten days.

Richard III

Edward V was only 12 years old when he became king. The government of the country was left to Edward IV's brother Richard, Duke of Gloucester, renowned for his loyalty to the late King, his generalship and his abilities as an administrator. But the Woodvilles – relatives of Edward's Queen, Elizabeth – and Lord Hastings, one of Edward IV's generals, opposed Richard.

Richard acted suddenly: he accused Hastings of treason, and had him executed within the hour. He took Edward V and his younger brother to the Tower 'for safety'; they were never seen again. Next, he informed Parliament that Edward IV's marriage to Elizabeth Woodville was 'no marriage' because Edward had earlier made a marriage pre-contract with someone else; the little princes were thus illegitimate. Parliament asked Richard to accept the Crown, and after apparent hesitation he accepted.

Whether Richard was sincere or not is not certain. But most people believed him to be a villain, and when Henry Tudor, the last Lancastrian claimant to the throne, met Richard in battle and killed him, he was generally welcomed.

William Caxton

William Caxton, the first English printer, was a successful merchant who spent
30 years at Bruges in Flanders. When
he retired he learned how to print, and
produced five books in Bruges. Then he
returned to England and set up a press
close by Westminster abbey. Altogether
he produced 90 books, 74 of them in
English and many his own translation.
His most famous books were editions of
Chaucer's *The Canterbury Tales* and Sir
Thomas Malory's *Le Morte Darthur*.

*A page including a woodcut of St Jerome
from* Legenda aurea, *printed in 1483 by
William Caxton at his press in Westminster.*

1473 Edward IV sets up Council of the
Marches to keep order in Wales
1474 Edward makes alliance with
Burgundy for partition of France
1475 William Caxton prints first book in
English at Bruges
Edward IV invades France, but is
bought off by Louis XI
1476 Caxton makes first printing in
England
James III of Scotland subdues
rebellion by John, Lord of the
Isles
1477 Caxton prints first book in Eng-
land at his press in Westminster
1478 Edward calls Parliament, which
condemns his brother, George,
Duke of Clarence, for allying with
Warwick against him
1479 James III arrests his brothers,
Duke of Albany and Earl of Mar;
Albany escapes, Mar dies
James invades England
1482 Edward recognizes Alexander,
Duke of Albany, as king of Scotland
English army invades Scotland
Scottish nobles imprison James
and hang his favourites
Albany becomes regent
1483 Edward IV dies; succeeded by son
Edward V, aged 12
Richard, Duke of Gloucester,
regent: he declares Edward V
illegitimate and takes the throne
as Richard III (to 1485)
Edward V and his brother disappear
1484 Heralds' College is founded
Richard makes peace with Scots
1485 Henry Tudor, Earl of Richmond,
invades England
Battle of Bosworth: Richard is
killed; Wars of the Roses end
Henry VII king (to 1509)

The Tudors

The beginning of the Tudor period in British history also marks the effective end of the Middle Ages. The old feudal ways of life were largely gone, with the old aristocracy who had perished in the Wars of the Roses. A new aristocracy was arising, drawn from the ranks of the growing middle classes.

The Tudor period was a time of expansion, both in thoughts and in deeds. The new ideas of the Renaissance were being spread by the equally new invention of printing. The Reformation, the movement which began in Germany in an attempt to correct some of the worst features of the Roman Catholic Church, came to England, at first as a political move, and later as a matter of faith. At the same time the twin discoveries of the New World and the eastward sea route to India opened up new opportunities for expansion, trade and the acquisition of wealth.

Scotland suffered years of violence, partly because four of her Stewart sovereigns came to the throne as children. The Tudors finally completed the merging of Wales and England, so that one set of laws and rights applied to both countries. They also tried to complete the conquest of Ireland, largely by settling English colonists in plantations there.

The Tudors

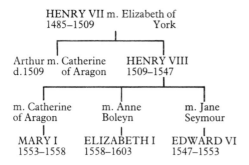

HENRY VII m. Elizabeth of
1485–1509   York

Arthur m. Catherine   HENRY VIII
d.1509   of Aragon   1509–1547

m. Catherine   m. Anne   m. Jane
of Aragon   Boleyn   Seymour

MARY I   ELIZABETH I   EDWARD VI
1553–1558   1558–1603   1547–1553

The Renaissance

The Renaissance is the modern name for the revival and spread of learning that took place from the 1400s onwards. It began in Italy, and spread over the rest of Europe. The works of the ancient Greek and Roman philosophers were found and studied. Artists developed new styles of painting, including the use of perspective. The speed with which the new ideas spread was due to the invention of printing in the 1440s.

The Renaissance came to England in the reign of Henry VII, who invited Italian scholars to come over. In England it found its greatest expression in literature: the Tudor period was a time of great poetry. It was also a time of major musical activity, especially the composition of Italian-style madrigals.

Henry VIII was 18 when he succeeded to the throne; a fine athlete, he loved sport and lavish pageantry. Here he jousts in front of Queen Catherine of Aragon at the tournament celebrating the birth of his son Henry, who died shortly afterwards.

ELSEWHERE IN THE WORLD

1492 Christopher Columbus discovers the West Indies

1493 Pope Alexander VI divides newly-found lands in the Americas between Spain and Portugal

1498 Vasco da Gama reaches India

1502-59 Series of wars between France and Spain over Italy

1507 America named after explorer Amerigo Vespucci

1513 Vasco Nuñez de Balboa discovers the Pacific Ocean

1517 Martin Luther begins the Reformation with his *95 Theses*

1519 Charles V, Holy Roman Emperor

1521 Diet of Worms: Luther condemned as a heretic
Hernán Cortés conquers Aztecs

1522 Magellan expedition: one ship completes voyage round world

1526 Barbar founds Mughal Empire in India

1532 Religious Peace of Nuremberg gives freedom of worship to Protestants
Francisco Pizarro conquers Peru

1533 Ivan IV, the Terrible, aged three, becomes ruler of Russia

1534 Ignatius Loyola founds the Society of Jesus (Jesuits)

1545 Council of Trent reforms the Roman Catholic Church

1548 Emperor Charles V annexes the Netherlands

1554-6 Turks conquer North Africa

1562-98 Religious wars in France

1568 Netherlands revolt against Spain

1571 Battle of Lepanto: Christian fleet defeats the Turks

1581 Dutch Republic founded

1582 Pope Gregory reforms calendar

1589 Henry IV king of France

1598 Edict of Nantes: French Protestants gain religious freedom

The Pretenders

Henry VII watched constantly for threats to his throne from the few remaining Yorkist supporters, often aided by foreign powers. France and Scotland were traditional enemies of England, and Richard III's younger sister, Margaret, was Duchess of Burgundy. She twice found youths prepared to pretend to be claimants to the throne.

The first was Lambert Simnel, the son of an Oxford joiner. Yorkists tried to pass him off as Edward, Earl of Warwick, son of the traitorous Duke of Clarence who was brother to Edward IV and Richard III. The real Warwick had been reported dead. In fact he was still alive; Henry produced him and paraded him through the streets of London. Simnel was captured and made a scullion in the royal kitchens. He lived for almost 40 years after his impersonation.

An Irish chief's last stand against English forces. When Henry VII came to the throne many of the great Anglo-Irish families were Yorkist supporters.

The second claimant was Perkin Warbeck, son of a Flemish tax-collector. Warbeck was supported in turn by the King of France, Duchess Margaret, the German emperor, and James IV of Scotland. He posed as Richard, Duke of York, who had been murdered with his brother Edward V in the Tower. Warbeck eventually landed in England and was caught. He was hanged for trying to escape and raise another rebellion. King Henry's stepfather Sir William Stanley was among those executed for supporting Warbeck.

Poynings' Law

To stop Irish support for Perkin Warbeck, Henry sent Sir Edward Poynings to Ireland as viceroy. Poynings called an Irish Parliament, which passed the Statute of Drogheda, also called Poynings' Law. This stated that no Irish Parliament should in future be called without the consent of the English king, and no Bill could be considered there without his permission. All laws passed in England should hold good in Ireland. This effectively ended home rule for Ireland for centuries.

A medallion struck to commemorate the marriage of Henry VII and Elizabeth of York, daughter of Edward IV, whose claim to the throne by birth was far stronger than that of Henry himself. This marriage conveniently removed one focus of Yorkist claims; other claimants were imprisoned or killed.

1485 Henry Tudor defeats Richard III, becomes king (to 1509)
Yeomen of the Guard founded
1486 Henry VII marries Elizabeth of York, daughter of Edward IV
Edward, Earl of Warwick, son of Duke of Clarence, imprisoned
1487 Lambert Simnel, pretending to be Earl of Warwick, proclaimed 'King Edward VI' in Dublin
Simnel captured in England
Henry sets up special court of his council (later called 'Court of Star Chamber') to deal with offences the Common Law had proved unable to suppress
1488 Scots rebels murder James III: son James IV king (to 1513)
1489 Statute calls for enclosures to stop depopulation of arable land
1490 Anglo-Dutch treaty signed
1491 Henry VII collects 'benevolences' to fund war with France
Perkin Warbeck is persuaded to impersonate Edward IV's son Richard of York
1492 Peace with France: Henry VII allows himself to be bought off
Warbeck finds support in Flanders
1494 Aberdeen University founded
Henry sends Sir Edward Poynings to Ireland to end Warbeck support. Statute of Drogheda (Poynings' Law) restates Henry's power
1495 Warbeck goes to Scotland
1496 James IV invades Northumberland in support of Warbeck
1497 Unsuccessful Cornish rebellion
John Cabot discovers Newfoundland for Henry VII
Warbeck captured in Devon
1498 Warbeck imprisoned in the Tower; Sir William Stanley executed for supporting him

Left: Henry VII, a portrait painted in 1505. His reign brought England 24 years of stable rule and increasing prosperity. His attention to detail – he signed almost every page of the royal accounts himself – made him one of England's most successful kings. His harsh taxation crippled the great nobles, and he took away their right to keep private armies. He ruled with a council which included some great nobles, but he relied more on minor nobles, clergy and landowners whom he repaid with land and titles. This pattern of a new nobility drawn from the gentry and merchant classes was to continue through the Tudor period.

Henry VII's Finances

Henry VII realized that he needed to have plenty of money if he was to be a powerful king. Otherwise he would have to depend on Parliament, or on borrowing money. So he set to work to build up wealth. He did not spend it lavishly, except when a display of pomp and circumstance was needed to impress other people.

Two of his ministers, Richard Empson and John Dudley, earned themselves universal hatred for the skill with which they collected taxes and penalties on Henry's behalf. Each in turn served as speaker of the House of Commons. Cardinal John Morton, who was Lord Chancellor until he died in 1500, devised 'Morton's fork', a cunning device for levying forced loans. A nobleman who spent freely obviously was wealthy and so could contribute generously, while one who did not spend had obviously saved plenty – and so could also contribute on a lavish scale.

When Henry VIII came to the throne he inherited a fortune, but in response to public outcry he had Empson and Dudley executed for treason.

Catherine of Aragon

Henry's eldest son, Prince Arthur, was married in 1501 to Catherine of Aragon, youngest daughter of the Spanish rulers Ferdinand and Isabella. The marriage was designed to strengthen an alliance between England and Spain, so when Arthur died suddenly six months later Henry made plans to marry Catherine to his younger son, Henry. This marriage was forbidden by the Church because the parties were too closely related, but Henry persuaded the Pope to allow it. The marriage took place after Henry VII's death in 1509.

This page of accounts from Henry VII's reign shows the King's initials against each entry. Henry began his reign in debt; he was such a shrewd businessman that he amassed a huge fortune.

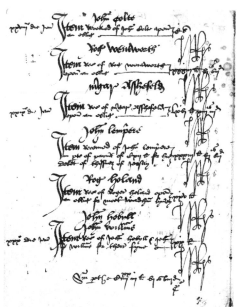

1499 Perkin Warbeck is tried for treason and executed
Treaty allows English cloth to be exported duty free to all parts of Burgundy except Flanders
1500 Wynken de Worde sets up a printing press in Fleet Street, London
1501 Arthur, heir to Henry VII, marries Catherine of Aragon
Palace of Holyroodhouse, Edinburgh, is built
1502 Death of Prince Arthur
1503 Henry's daughter Margaret marries James IV, King of Scots
Arthur's brother, Henry, betrothed to his widow, Catherine
First gold sovereigns minted
1504 Henry puts guilds under Crown supervision
First English shilling issued
Battle of Cnoc Tuagh: Lord Kildare, deputy governor of Ireland, defeats his rival Ulrich Burke
1505 Merchant Adventurers company gets a royal charter
1506 *Intercursus Malus*: new treaty gives English traders right to export cloth duty-free to Flanders
1507 Treaty between England and Venice bars Venetians from shipping goods between England and Flanders
1508 Walter Chapman and Andrew Myllar set up first Scottish printing press
1509 Henry VII dies; succeeded by son Henry VIII (to 1547)
Henry marries Catherine of Aragon
1510 English morality play *Everyman*
Parliament grants Henry VIII taxes tunnage and poundage for life
1511 Henry joins the Holy League with Spain and Pope against France

The wool trade still brought great wealth to much of England in the 14th and 15th centuries. The carving of a sheep is from the church at Lavenham in Suffolk, built like other great East Anglian churches on wool profits. There are more carvings of sheep on the porch and on the roof beams. The Guildhall at Lavenham, below, is one of the finest existing Tudor timber-framed buildings. It was built soon after the foundation of the Guild of Corpus Christi in 1529, and was one of three guildhalls in the little town.

Man of Power

The most powerful man in Ireland was Gerald Fitzgerald, Earl of Kildare, known to the Irish as *Garret Môr* – Garret the Great. In 1494 he was accused of treason and imprisoned in the Tower of London, suspected of supporting Henry VII's Yorkist rivals. But Henry realized that Garret Môr was Ireland's true leader. Saying: 'If Ireland cannot govern the earl, let the earl govern Ireland', he sent him back as deputy governor, a post Kildare held until his death in 1513.

Spurs and Flodden

In 1511 Pope Julius II asked Henry VIII, the King of Spain, and the Holy Roman Emperor to help him drive the French out of Italy. Henry agreed, seeing a chance of reconquering some of England's former territories in France. His first expedition was a failure, but in 1513 he led a second expedition in person, with the aid of Austrian mercenaries. At Guinegate he won a quick battle, known as the battle of Spurs because of the speed at which the French fled.

Meanwhile the Scots, traditional allies of France, invaded northern England. At Flodden Field, in Northumberland, the Scots faced an English army half its size but led by an experienced general, Thomas Howard, Earl of Surrey. English cannon and a murderous hail of English arrows won the day. The Scots lost their King James IV; 13 earls; and about 10,000 other men – the 'flowers of the forest' lamented by Scottish poets.

1512 Henry sends an unsuccessful expedition to capture Guienne
1513 Battle of Spurs: English defeat the French at Guinegate
Battle of Flodden: James IV of Scots killed; James V, aged two, succeeds (to 1542)
1514 Margaret, Queen Regent of Scotland, marries Archibald Douglas, Earl of Angus
Anglo-French truce: Henry's sister Mary marries Louis XII
Thomas Wolsey becomes archbishop of York
Trinity House, London, founded
1515 Duke of Albany becomes Protector of James V: Margaret flees to England
Wolsey becomes Chancellor
Hampton Court Palace begun
1516 Birth of the future Mary I
Sir Thomas More writes *Utopia*
1517 Evil May Day riots: London apprentices attack foreign traders
Wolsey is made papal legate
Albany goes to France, and is not allowed to return home
1518 Peace of London between France and England
Royal College of Physicians founded
1519 Henry VII's chapel at Westminster abbey completed
1520 Field of Cloth of Gold: Henry meets Francis I of France
Holy Roman Emperor Charles V visits Henry: Treaty of Calais
'Cleanse the Causeway'; Douglasses and Hamiltons fight in Edinburgh
1521 Pope Leo X gives Henry title of 'Defender of the Faith'
Albany returns to Scotland
1523 Thomas More becomes Speaker of the House of Commons

Union with Wales

In 1536 Henry VIII decided that Wales should be united with England. Until then Wales had been regarded as a separate principality, a dependency of England. By the Act of Union it became part of England; Welsh people enjoyed the same constitutional rights as English people, instead of being treated as a conquered race, kept down by military force. Another Act in 1543 extended to Wales the right to send members to the Parliament at Westminster.

The Welsh shires were created by the Tudors, and English law was extended to Wales, with English as the language of the law courts. It was at this time that Monmouthshire became part of England. It stayed that way until 1974, when it was reunited with Wales under its original name of Gwent.

Securing the Succession

In 1527 Henry VIII decided to tackle a serious problem: he had no male heir, only a daughter, Mary. No queen had ever ruled England, and the Wars of the Roses showed the damage that could be caused if there was a dispute over the succession. So Henry decided to divorce Catherine, who could bear no more children, and find a wife who could give him a son.

Henry ordered Wolsey to ask the Pope to grant a divorce. The Pope refused, and Wolsey fell from power. Henry decided to separate the Church in England from the authority of the Pope, a move carried out by a series of Acts of Parliament. Meanwhile Henry had married a lady of the court, Anne Boleyn. In 1533 the clergy were persuaded to declare Henry's marriage with Catherine invalid (using the original argument that he could not marry his brother's widow) and his marriage with Anne legal.

Anne soon produced a child, but it was another girl: Elizabeth. Henry was disappointed, and turned from Anne, a tempestuous, ambitious woman, to a quiet girl, Jane Seymour. In 1536 a charge of adultery was brought against Anne. It may or may not have been true, but she was accused of treason, tried and beheaded. Henry then married Jane, who produced the longed-for son, Edward, and died 12 days later.

Below: Cardinal Wolsey was Henry VIII's Lord Chancellor (chief minister), as well as archbishop of Canterbury. A highly skilled administrator, he ruled the country for 17 years. His origins were humble – his father probably reared cattle – but when he was in power Wolsey was notorious for extravagance and ostentation. He built a splendid palace at Hampton Court near London and commissioned a tomb of unrivalled magnificence for himself. Henry, infuriated by his failure to persuade the Pope to sanction Henry's divorce, dismissed him; he was stripped of offices and honours and arrested for treason, but died on his way to trial.

1525	Peace between England and France
	William Tyndale translates New Testament into English
1526	Peace between England and Scotland
1527	Henry VIII asks the Pope to annul his marriage to Catherine of Aragon
1529	Wolsey is stripped of power
	Sir Thomas More becomes Lord Chancellor
1530	Death of Wolsey
1531	Clan Donald and the Macleans rebel: pacified by James V
	Clergy agree to acknowledge Henry as their 'supreme lord'
1532	More resigns as Chancellor
1533	Henry marries Anne Boleyn
	Statute of Appeals forbids appeals to Rome
	Thomas Cranmer becomes archbishop of Canterbury; he declares Henry's marriage with Catherine void, that with Anne legal
	The Pope excommunicates Henry
1534	Act of Supremacy: break with Rome
	Brief rebellion of Lord Offaly, 'Silken Thomas', in Ireland
1535	More executed for treason
	Thomas Cromwell made Vicar-General
	Miles Coverdale makes first translation of whole Bible into English
1536	Catherine of Aragon dies
	Anne Boleyn executed; Henry marries Jane Seymour
	Small monasteries dissolved
	Pilgrimage of Grace: northern revolt against religious changes
	Cromwell made Lord Privy Seal
	Act of Union unites Wales with England

King of Ireland

Having made himself Supreme Head of the Church in England, Henry VIII decided to extend his powers to Ireland, where the English had a large holding covering most of Leinster and Meath. In 1541, at the instigation of a new Lord Deputy, Sir Anthony St Leger, an Irish Parliament was called in Dublin. It conferred on Henry the title of king of Ireland. At the same time more than 40 Irish chiefs and Anglo-Irish nobles were persuaded to surrender their lands to the King and receive them back as vassals – the terms on which English barons held their lands.

Henry's Later Marriages

Henry VIII married three times more. His chief minister, Thomas Cromwell, negotiated a marriage with a German princess, Anne of Cleves, to ally England with the princes of northern Germany. But when Anne arrived she was so plain that Henry described her as 'the Flanders mare'. The marriage was soon dissolved, and Henry married Catherine Howard, a young noblewoman. She was unfaithful to him, and paid for this by being beheaded. Henry's last marriage was to a widow, Catherine Parr, who knew how to manage him, and outlived him.

*The 'Henry Grace à Dieu' or 'Great Harry'
marked a completely new approach to the
design of fighting ships; she carried
broadside batteries of cannon instead of
acting as a troop carrier. She was built in
1514 to carry 186 guns, as part of Henry VIII's
programme of naval expansion. This picture
shows her after rebuilding in 1539-40 to
carry 122 guns. She was so top-heavy that
she could only sail short voyages, in sight of
land and in calm weather. Another of
Henry's warships, the 'Mary Rose', sank off
Spithead in 1545 in calm weather, when the
lower decks became swamped. But from
shipbuilding experiments like these the
English developed the fighting ships that
saved them from the Spanish Armada.*

Cardinal Beaton

James V of Scotland died in 1542,
leaving a week-old girl, Mary, Queen of
Scots, to succeed him. Henry VIII
wanted to arrange a marriage between
Mary and his own son, Edward. But a
pro-French, anti-Protestant group in
Scotland, led by Cardinal David
Beaton, Archbishop of St Andrews,
refused. Beaton had a Reformation
preacher, George Wishart, burned at
the stake for heresy, but was himself
assassinated in revenge.

The Monasteries

English monasteries were in decline in
the 1500s, and many of them were
badly run. In 1536 Henry ordered
nearly 400 of the smaller ones to be
dissolved, and took over their funds.
The monks were pensioned off. This
move was so successful that in 1539
Henry dissolved the larger monasteries.
He gained more wealth, but the charity
and care which the monks had given
poorer people was a great loss.

1537 Pilgrimage of Grace suppressed
Jane Seymour gives birth to a
son, Edward, and dies
1538 James V marries Mary of Guise
1539 Dissolution of larger monasteries
Statute of Six Articles
1540 Henry marries Anne of Cleves,
but soon divorces her and marries Catherine Howard
Cromwell executed for treason
War with France
Henry establishes regius profes-
sorships at Oxford and Cambridge
1541 Henry takes the title of king of
Ireland
Wales gets representation in the
English Parliament
1542 Catherine Howard executed
England and Scotland at war
Scots lose battle of Solway Moss
James V dies; daughter Mary
succeeds (to 1567)
1543 Henry marries Catherine Parr
1544 English army invades Scotland,
occupies Edinburgh
1545 Scots win battle of Ancram Moor
1546 Peace with France
Cardinal Beaton, Scottish statesman, assassinated
1547 First book printed in Welsh: *Yn y
Lhyvyr hwnn* (Scripture extracts)
Henry VIII dies; succeeded by
Edward VI, aged nine; Duke of
Somerset appointed protector
Repeal of the Six Articles
1548 Heresy laws abolished in England
1549 First Prayer Book in English;
made compulsory by Act of Uniformity
Clergy allowed to marry
1550 Fall of Somerset; succeeded by
Duke of Northumberland
Images and altars ordered to be
destroyed

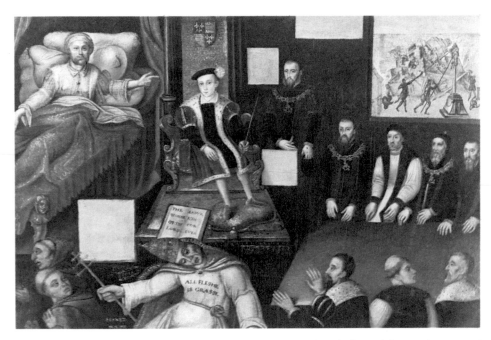

The Reformation

Although Henry VIII broke with the Pope, he supported the doctrines of the Church of Rome. But during the reign of his son Edward VI England moved steadily towards Protestantism, in the movement known as the Reformation. Edward was only 9 when he came to the throne, and the government was in the hands of his uncle, Jane Seymour's brother Edward, Duke of Somerset.

Under Somerset the laws against heresy were abolished, images and altars were removed from the churches, and an English-language Prayer Book was introduced. By an Act of Uniformity the use of this Prayer Book was made compulsory. The clergy, until now celibate, were allowed to marry.

Above: This painting celebrates the renewal of the Reformation under Edward VI, who is shown by the bed of his dying father. Next to Edward stands Somerset, the Lord Protector; beside him sit the Duke of Northumberland and Archbishop Thomas Cranmer. The Bible is open at Edward's feet; beneath it is the stricken Pope.

Opposite: Lady Jane Grey, granddaughter of Henry VIII's sister Mary, was heir to the throne after Henry's daughters Mary (a bigoted Catholic) and Elizabeth. She was married to the son of the Duke of Northumberland, Edward VI's chief minister. When Edward died, Northumberland had Jane proclaimed queen in an attempt to save the Protestant succession and his own power. But Northumberland was disliked; the people rallied to Mary and after only nine days Queen Jane's reign was over. She was beheaded in 1554.

'Bloody Mary'

Mary I was a sour and unhappy woman, prematurely aged at 37. Her great wish was to undo the Reformation and restore England to the faith of Rome. Her marriage to the even more bigoted Philip II of Spain hardened her resolve.

The opposition to Rome could only be crushed by harsh ways. Mary reigned for five years: in that time 300 Protestants were put to death, including Archbishop Cranmer, who had been responsible for the Book of Common Prayer. Others who died included Northumberland, his son, and the gentle Lady Jane Grey. Small wonder that the Queen acquired the nickname 'Bloody Mary'.

1553 Edward VI dies; Lady Jane Grey is proclaimed queen. After nine days, Jane is deposed: Mary Tudor queen (to 1558)
Duke of Northumberland executed
Navigator Richard Chancellor sets out to find North-East Passage
Sir Thomas Wyatt leads rebellion

1554 Wyatt, Lady Jane, and her husband executed
Mary marries Philip II of Spain
Chancellor reaches Moscow

1555 Catholic Restoration begins. Bishops Latimer and Ridley among many Protestants burned
John Knox returns from exile to Scotland

1556 Archbishop Cranmer burned
Cardinal Pole, papal legate, becomes archbishop
Earl of Sussex becomes Lord Lieutenant of Ireland, encourages English settlers there

1557-59 War with France

1558 French recapture Calais
Mary, Queen of Scots, marries Dauphin Francis of France
Mary I dies; succeeded by sister Elizabeth I (to 1603)
Acts of Supremacy and Uniformity re-enacted

1559 Francis becomes king of France: Mary, Queen of Scots assumes title queen of England

1560 Church of Scotland founded
Scottish regency set up
Reformation imposed in Ireland

1561 Mary returns to Scotland after husband's death

1562 Shane O'Neill rebels in Ireland
John Hawkins becomes the first English slave trader

1563 The 39 Articles enacted
Foxe's *Book of Martyrs* published

Mary, Queen of Scots

Mary, Queen of Scots became queen when just a week old on the death of her father, James V. She was brought up in France, her mother's country, and was married at the age of 16 to the Dauphin of France. When he became king, she became queen of France as well as Scotland. She was also the nearest heir to Elizabeth of England, and claimed that throne too.

After 18 months Mary's husband died and she returned to a Scotland she hardly knew. She was a Roman Catholic; the Scots were Protestants who disapproved of Mary's religion and foreign ways. She married her cousin, Henry Stewart, Lord Darnley, who was jealous and thoroughly unpleasant. When he murdered Mary's secretary, David Rizzio (suspected of being the Queen's lover), she determined on revenge. Soon after their son James was born, Darnley was strangled and the house where he was staying blew up. Suspicion fell on James Hepburn, Earl of Bothwell, and increased when Mary married Bothwell.

The Scots lords could not stomach Bothwell, and they forced Mary to abdicate in favour of her baby son, James VI. She fled to England, where Elizabeth made her a prisoner.

In England Mary became the focus for plot after plot by Catholics against the Protestant Elizabeth, who was finally forced in self-defence to agree to Mary's execution. Bothwell escaped to Denmark, where he was imprisoned for breach of promise, and died mad.

The manner of burning Anne Askew, John Lacels, John Adams, & Nicolas Beleman, with certane of y counsell sitting in Smithfield.

In 1563 John Foxe published a history of the Christian Church which concentrated on the persecution of English Protestants under Mary Tudor. Mary brought back England to the Roman Catholic Church and some 300 Protestant 'heretics' were burned in less than four years. Elizabeth restored the Protestant Church and Catholics in turn were persecuted; Foxe's book kept alive the memory of the Protestant Martyrs of Mary's time, and fed the English hatred of the Roman Church. This illustration from his book shows Protestants at the stake.

The beheading of Mary, Queen of Scots at Fotheringay. Elizabeth kept her cousin prisoner for 18 years before she became too great a risk as a focus for Catholic plots.

The Theatre

England's first theatre was built at Shoreditch, then a suburb of London. It was based on the enclosed courtyard of the big inns, where actors were accustomed to perform. The man who built it was the actor-manager James Burbage, whose more famous son Richard became a colleague of William Shakespeare.

Burbage's building was simply called 'The Theatre'. It was open to the sky, like the later Globe Theatre where Shakespeare acted. Other theatres, such as the Blackfriars and the Whitefriars, had roofs.

1564 War with France ends
1565 Mary, Queen of Scots marries her cousin Lord Darnley
Royal Exchange, London, founded
John Hawkins brings sweet potatoes and tobacco to England
1566 Darnley and others murder David Rizzio, Queen Mary's secretary
1567 Earl of Bothwell murders Darnley; Mary marries Bothwell
Shane O'Neill murdered
Mary abdicates; succeeded by son James VI, aged one (to 1625)
Earl of Moray regent; Mary held prisoner
1568 Mary escapes to England and becomes the prisoner of Elizabeth
1569 Rebellion in north of England; Durham cathedral sacked
1570 Regent Moray assassinated; succeeded by Earl of Lennox
1571 Regent Lennox killed in battle; succeeded by Earl of Mar
English Parliament bans exports of wool
1572 Duke of Norfolk and Earl of Northumberland executed for treason
Regent Mar dies; succeeded by Earl of Morton
Lord Burghley becomes England's Lord High Treasurer
Francis Drake attacks Spanish harbours in the Americas
1573 Sir Francis Walsingham becomes Elizabeth's Secretary of State
Hawkins becomes Treasurer of Navy Board: reforms the Navy
1575 English Parliament successfully claims freedom from arrest for its members
Elizabeth refuses Crown of the Netherlands
1576 James Burbage opens first theatre in London

The Armada

Under Elizabeth I England reverted quickly to Protestantism. For her brother-in-law, Philip II of Spain, it became a sacred duty to dethrone her and restore England to the old Roman faith. Elizabeth also angered Philip by supporting the Dutch in their war of independence against Spain, and her seamen were raiding Spanish colonies and treasure ships.

Philip planned an invasion: an Armada of 130 ships which was to sail up the English Channel, pick up soldiers from Dunkirk in France, where they were assembled, and land them on the English coast. The English got together an emergency fleet of experienced sailors, led by Lord Howard of Effingham, with Francis Drake, John Hawkins, and Martin Frobisher. The English fought a running battle up the Channel.
The Armada took shelter in Calais harbour, but Drake sent in fireships. To escape the danger of their whole fleet catching fire, the Spaniards hurriedly raised anchor and sailed out to another confused battle. Both sides had run short of shot, and with no further supplies available the Armada was forced to escape into the North Sea. It returned home after sailing right round the British Isles. The Armada lost 44 ships out of 128, and many of the rest had to be scrapped.

A detail from a painting showing the defeat of the Spanish Armada; English ships are flying the red-on-white cross of St George. The English ships were generally faster and more manoeuvrable than the great Spanish galleons, and their guns had a longer range.

1578 Regent Morton resigns: James assumes power, under influence of Roman Catholic Esmé Stewart
1580 Edmund Campion and Robert Parsons begin Jesuit mission to England
Francis Drake returns from circumnavigation of the world
1581 Earl of Morton executed for part in Darnley's murder
Campion executed for treason
1582 The Protestant Earls of Gowrie, Mar and Glencairn kidnap James VI; hold him at Ruthven castle
1583 Sir Humphrey Gilbert claims Newfoundland for England
Edinburgh University founded
James VI escapes from Ruthven
Throgmorton Plot: plan to kill the Queen, supported by Spain
1584 Sir Walter Raleigh tries to establish colony near Roanoake Island in North Carolina
1585 English army sent to help Dutch Republic against Spain
Navigator John Davis discovers Davis Strait and Baffin Island
1586 Drake sacks Santo Domingo and Cartagena in West Indies
Francis Walsingham uncovers Babington Plot, incriminating Mary, Queen of Scots
Mary tried and condemned for treason at Fotheringay castle
1587 Mary, Queen of Scots executed
Pope Sixtus VI proclaims Roman Catholic crusade against England
Drake partly destroys Spanish fleet at Cádiz
War with Spain breaks out
1588 Philip II launches 'Invincible Armada' against England: it is destroyed by English fleet
1589 The Rev. William Lee of Nottinghamshire invents stocking frame

111

Gloriana

Elizabeth I was a remarkable woman in an age of outstanding talent. She spoke five languages besides English: Greek, Latin, French, Italian and Spanish. She was a skilled performer on the virginals (a kind of harpsichord), a graceful dancer, and a fine archer. Temperamentally she varied from melancholy and merriment to a royal rage. She was a skilled politician, calculating and devious.

Above all, she loved England, and in return her people loved her. Her court celebrated her as 'Gloriana', and the ordinary people as 'Good Queen Bess'. Her enemies were mostly the Roman Catholics, who were badly treated and at times went in fear of their lives.

The court around Queen Elizabeth glittered like the Queen herself. Hers was an age when every gentleman aspired to be a poet or a musician, or both. For example, Sir Philip Sidney, the brave soldier who died at Zutphen, was a fine poet.

There were also professional writers and poets, patronized by the court if not of it. The outstanding name is that of William Shakespeare, but he was only one of many dramatic poets. Others had more than one occupation: Christopher Marlowe, slain in a tavern brawl, is thought to have been a secret agent; Edmund Spenser, whose The Faerie Queene delighted readers, helped in the plantation (settlement) of Ireland.

England led the way in the writing of music for keyboard instruments, and much of the traditional music of the Church was written at this time, by composers such as John Merbecke. The outstanding musicians were probably Thomas Tallis and his pupil William Byrd. Towards the end of Elizabeth's reign madrigals, and the habit of singing them, were introduced into England. Thomas Morley edited a collection of madrigals in honour of Elizabeth, called The Triumphs of Oriana, but it was not published until 1603, when the Queen was dead.

Expanding England

Spain and Portugal had led the way in the discovery of America and the development of the sea route to the East Indies and India. During Elizabeth's reign England began to catch up. It was a time of discovery and expansion, encouraged and partly financed by the Crown, but largely a matter of private enterprise.

Martin Frobisher tried hard to find the North-West Passage to India round the top of America; John Hawkins began the English slave trade to the Spanish colonies in America.

Sir Walter Raleigh spent a large fortune trying to establish a colony near Roanoake Island, North Carolina, and laid the foundations for the later colonization of Guiana. Sir Francis Drake explored the southern seas and sailed round the world. His was only the second expedition to do so. Drake and the others did their best to break the would-be Spanish and Portuguese monopoly of trade with India and the Americas, plundering the Spanish colonies and their treasure ships bearing looted gold and silver back to Europe.

Queen Elizabeth visits Parliament; she is in the House of Lords with members of the Commons standing in the foreground, at the bar of the House.

1590 First Shakespeare plays performed
1591 Trinity College, Dublin, founded
1592 Plague kills 15,000 Londoners
1593 Poet and playwright Christopher Marlowe killed in brawl
1594 Irish revolt: Hugh O'Donnell and Cormac MacBaron defeat English at Ford of the Biscuits, near Enniskillen
1595 Spaniards land in Cornwall, burn Mousehole and Penzance
Raleigh explores Orinoco River
1596 English expedition sacks Cádiz
Irish leaders ask Spain for help
Tomatoes brought to England
In *The Metamorphosis of Ajax* John Harington describes his new invention, the water-closet
1597 Hugh O'Neill, Earl of Tyrone, heads new rebellion in Ireland
1598 Battle of the Yellow Ford: Irish defeat the English
1599 Earl of Essex becomes Lord Lieutenant of Ireland; he concludes truce with Tyrone, goes home and is arrested
Lord Mountjoy succeeds Essex
James VI writes *Basilikon Doron*, about divine right of kings
1600 Essex loses position at court
East India Company founded
1601 Essex dabbles in plots, is tried for treason and executed
New Poor Law passed
Mountjoy crushes Irish rebellion
Act abolishes monopolies
1602 Spanish army lands in Ireland, but surrenders at Kinsale
1603 Elizabeth I dies; succeeded by James VI of Scotland as James I of England (to 1625)
Amnesty in Ireland
Main and Bye plots: Raleigh is jailed for involvement

The Stuarts

The family of Stewart had ruled Scotland for 232 troubled years before James VI became James I of England, and so united the two countries in his own person, though not yet in law. (From now on, the French spelling, Stuart, is commonly used.) Eventful as those years had been, they were not so dramatic as the following 111 years during which the Stuarts ruled over England, Wales, Scotland, and – in name at any rate – over Ireland.

In that time the combined nation underwent two revolutions, one full of battles and slaughter, the other almost bloodless. In the beginning the Stuarts claimed to rule by divine right; eventually it was made plain that they ruled by the consent and invitation of Parliament. By the end of the Stuart period England and Scotland were formally united, and even unruly Ireland was more firmly controlled by the English than it had ever been before.

Meanwhile, the British were expanding overseas. Many colonies, particularly in North America, were set up during the Stuart period. The religious tensions and dissensions at home drove people abroad to seek a land where they could worship God in their own way. The most famous such group was the Pilgrim Fathers, who founded the Plymouth Colony in 1620 and laid the foundations of the New England states. Elsewhere, British traders established settlements in southern Africa and India which would eventually develop into an empire.

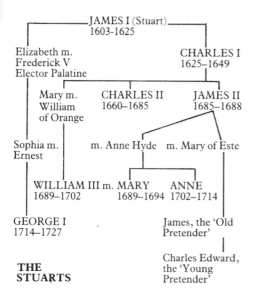

THE
STUARTS

James I and VI

The new king of England was, as he said himself, an 'old and experienced king', for he had ruled Scotland for 25 years. He believed in the divine right of kings to rule. He had manipulated the Scots Parliament more or less as he liked: the English Parliament was far less easy, insisting that the King could rule only by consent.

Although brought up a Calvinist, James was in favour of the Anglican Church and its ways: 'No bishop, no king', he once said. So he took steps to reassert the Act of Uniformity and make sure it was obeyed.

As a person, James was coarse-mannered, pedantic, inclined to lecture others, but kindly.

This Flemish painting shows the execution of King Charles I, whose portrait is inset on the left.

ELSEWHERE IN THE WORLD

1604 Russians begin settling Siberia
1606 Willem Jansz sights Australia
1608 French explorer Samuel de Champlain founds Quebec
1610 Galileo makes stellar observations using a telescope
Tea introduced into Europe
1614 French *Estates-General* called to curb nobles; last until 1799
1616 Willem Schouten rounds Cape Horn
1618 Defenestration of Prague: two Catholic officials pushed out of a window: Thirty Years' War starts
1619 Ferdinand II becomes Holy Roman Emperor (to 1637); Bohemians depose him for a time
Negro slaves arrive in Virginia
1624 Cardinal Richelieu chief minister in France (to 1642)
1638 Turks conquer Baghdad
1640 Portuguese rebel against Spain
1643 Louis XIV, king of France, aged 5: Cardinal Mazarin is chief minister
1644 Manchu Dynasty in China (to 1912)
1648 Thirty Years' War ends: Dutch and Swiss republics independent
1649 Serfdom established in Russia
1667-8 War of Devolution
1672 William III ruler of the Netherlands
1683 Turks besiege Vienna
1685 Edict of Nantes revoked: Protestant families flee from France
1689-97 War of League of Augsburg
1692 Salem witchcraft trials, New England
1700-21 Great Northern War between Russia and Sweden
1701-13 War of the Spanish Succession
1713 Pragmatic Sanction to ensure succession of Maria Theresa as ruler of Holy Roman Empire

Right: The Globe Theatre in London, where many of Shakespeare's plays were performed. Like other early theatres, it was built outside the City walls because the aldermen did not approve of playacting. The early theatres were built in the shape of inn yards; the courtyard or 'pit' was open, and around it were three rows of covered balconies. The stage was built out into the courtyard. Little is known of Shakespeare's life; he wrote and acted in the reigns of Elizabeth and James I.

Below: James I was well educated and wrote a number of treatises and poems; in his early years as king of Scotland he had successfully managed the unruly Scottish lords. He was welcomed by the English but his insistence on the absolute power of the monarch, flowing from the 'divine right' that God alone makes or deposes kings, brought him into conflict with Parliament.

THE HIGHE AND MIGHTIE PRINCE, Iames THE SIXT, BY THE GRACE OF GOD KINGE OF SCOTLANDE. R.E. *fēai*.

Lady Arabella

Lady Arabella Stewart was a first cousin of James I and VI, and near in the line of succession to the throne. For this reason Elizabeth I, and later James, were determined that Arabella should marry only someone they could trust. Arabella fell in love with William Seymour, later Duke of Somerset; he was a great-great-grandson of Henry VII and, by Henry VIII's will, he was the next heir to the British throne after Elizabeth.

James forbade this match, but the couple married secretly. They were imprisoned. An escape was planned: Seymour got away, but Arabella was recaptured and confined in the Tower, where she died, insane. Seymour later became a leading Royalist general in the Civil War.

The Authorized Version

When James came to the throne there were five English translations of the Bible in use, none of which was satisfactory. The King ordered a new translation. Fifty Churchmen and scholars were organized into six committees, and they completed the task within seven years. The result was the Authorized Version, or King James Bible, which is still the most popular English version after more than 350 years. The beauty of its language has been a lasting influence on all English-speaking peoples. It provided a major inspiration for the Puritan movement which overthrew the Stuarts.

The Gunpowder Plot

James I enforced laws against Roman Catholics severely: they had to go to Anglican churches, or be fined. A group of Catholics decided to start a revolution by blowing up the Houses of Parliament at a time when James was there. But one of the conspirators told a relative, one of the peers, of the plot. 'Retire yourself into the country . . . they shall receive a terrible blow this Parliament, and yet they shall not see who hurts them', he wrote. The authorities were warned and the cellars of Parliament were searched. In them were found several barrels of gunpowder, and Guy Fawkes, one of the conspirators. He and the other conspirators were caught, tortured to make them confess, tried and executed. The leader of the conspiracy was not in fact Fawkes but Robert Catesby; but Fawkes is still remembered as the villain.

1603 James VI of Scotland becomes James I of England (to 1625)
1604 James proclaims enforcement of Act of Uniformity
Act of Oblivion in Ireland
James's first Parliament rejects his plan to unite England and Scotland, but James is proclaimed 'king of Great Britain, France and Ireland'
New Church rules cause 300 Puritan clergy to resign
Peace with Spain
1605 Gunpowder Plot uncovered
Uniformity proclaimed in Ireland
1606 Guy Fawkes and other plotters are executed for treason
James levies taxes without consent of Parliament
1607 'Flight of the Earls' to Spain from Ireland
First permanent settlement in America at Jamestown, Virginia
1609 Plantations (settlements) plan for 200,000 ha. of confiscated Irish estates
1610 James's cousin Lady Arabella Stewart marries William Seymour: the couple are imprisoned
1611 James dissolves Parliament
Plantation of Ulster begins
Authorized Version of the Bible
Explorer Henry Hudson left to die by his crew
1612 Henry, Prince of Wales dies
1613 James's daughter Elizabeth marries Frederick V of the Palatinate
1614 'Addled Parliament' quarrels with James over finance
1615 Lady Arabella dies
George Villiers, James's favourite, becomes duke of Buckingham
English fleet defeats Dutch fleet off Bombay

King Charles I, Queen Henrietta Maria and their two eldest children. Both his sons, Charles (born in 1630) and James (born in 1633) became king – Charles with great success, James disastrously. His daughter Mary married William of Orange and was mother of William III of England; his daughter Henriette married the brother of King Louis XIV of France. Charles was devoted to his family.

Charles I's Finances

Charles I inherited a difficult financial situation. Parliament believed that 'the king should live of his own', meaning that revenues from customs duties and Crown lands should pay all government expenses, and also the expenses of the court. It was usual for Parliament to vote the customs duties – tunnage and poundage – for life to each new sovereign.

But both Elizabeth, in her last years, and James I found expenses rising faster than income. This was partly due to inflation, caused by the influx of gold and silver from America. James resorted to all sorts of methods to raise money, including creating the title of baronet and selling it to wealthy candidates.

Irritated at what it considered unlawful taxation, Parliament voted tunnage and poundage to Charles for one year only. As a result, Charles had a constant struggle to find money by other means, levying taxes without consent and making people pay forced loans.

Francis Bacon

Francis Bacon was one of the most gifted men of his day. He was a practising lawyer, and Member of Parliament. Eventually he was made Lord Chancellor, and was raised to the peerage as Baron Verulam, and later Viscount St Albans. As a judge he made many enemies, and they brought him down with an accusation of taking bribes.

Bacon admitted taking the bribes, but asserted that he had never allowed such gifts to sway his judgment, and had several times found against the persons giving him bribes. He was heavily fined and banned from the court, though soon pardoned. He spent his remaining years in writing, and it is as one of the greatest philosophers and an essayist that he is now remembered.

1616 Walter Raleigh released from Tower to lead new expedition
Navigator William Baffin discovers Baffin Bay
1617 Raleigh attacks Spanish colonies
1618 Francis Bacon becomes Lord Chancellor and Baron Verulam
Raleigh executed for treason
1619 Physician William Harvey announces discovery of blood circulation
1620 Pilgrim Fathers sail from Plymouth to colonize America
1621 Bacon made Viscount St Albans
James calls third Parliament: it votes money for English involvement in Thirty Years' War
Parliament impeaches Bacon
Great Protestation asserts the rights of Parliament; petition against popery
1623 Charles and Duke of Buckingham fail to negotiate Spanish marriage
First English settlement in New Hampshire
1624 James calls fourth Parliament: it condemns monopolies
Marriage arranged between Charles and Henriette Marie of France
1625 James dies: succeeded by Charles I (to 1649)
Charles marries French princess (known as Henrietta Maria)
Parliament votes tunnage and poundage for one year only
1626 Charles's second Parliament impeaches Buckingham, is dissolved
War with France
Charles collects taxes without Parliamentary approval
1627 Buckingham fails in expedition to La Rochelle
Charles levies forced loan

Above: The first permanent English colony in North America was built at Jamestown in Virginia, in 1607. The colonists hoped to find gold and to set up successful trading stations. But no gold was discovered, and all they could send back to England was timber. Food shortages and illness killed about two-thirds of the settlers in the first year, and the colony was harassed by Indians. Outstanding among the settlers was Captain John Smith, shown here, who explored the rivers of Virginia and mapped the area; he made friends and traded with some of the local Indian tribes. He encouraged the settlers to build a fortified town, and trade for food with the Indians until they learned to grow their own supplies.

Right: Other American colonies were set up by Englishmen persecuted for their faith who wanted to found a settlement where they could worship as they pleased. Among them were the Pilgrim Fathers, a group of Puritans who set out in 1620 in their ship 'Mayflower'. They established their settlement on the shore of Cape Cod Bay, in what is now Massachusetts; they named it Plymouth, after their last port of call in the Old World. It was the second permanent English settlement in America.

The Puritans

The Reformation of England proceeded only a little way in breaking with the beliefs of the Church of Rome. The Church of England retained bishops, ceremonial and vestments. But many people wanted a simpler, purer form of worship, with no bishops or elaborate ceremonies. They became known as *Puritans*.

Some Puritans travelled to America, where they could worship as they chose, but most remained in England, determined to fight oppression rather than evade it. They were the dominant influence in Parliament in the clash which was rapidly developing with Charles I.

King and Parliament

In the first four years of his reign Charles I called three Parliaments and disagreed with all of them. At the root of the problem were war, first with Spain, and then with France in support of the Huguenots (the French Protestants), and money. Parliament was all for the war, and voted funds for it – but at a price.

That price was embodied in the Petition of Right, moved by the House of Commons. It demanded an end to martial law, billeting of troops on people, imprisonment without trial, and forced loans and taxes levied without the consent of Parliament. The King had reluctantly to agree.

The quarrel between King and Parliament continued, because Charles continued to collect tunnage and poundage after the time limit Parliament had set. The Commons passed three resolutions condemning the actions of Charles and his ministers. When the Speaker, Sir John Finch, tried to announce that the King had adjourned the House, the Members of Parliament held him in his chair while the resolutions were put to the vote, and the doors were barred against Black Rod, the royal messenger from the House of Lords. To this day the Commons slam their door in Black Rod's face whenever he comes to summon them to hear the Queen's Speech at the opening of Parliament.

After this incident Charles did dissolve Parliament, and he ruled for 11 years without it. Like his father James I he firmly believed in the disastrous doctrine of the divine right of kings.

1628 Charles I calls his third Parliament: it grants five subsidies. MPs present Petition of Right, and a remonstrance against collection of tunnage and poundage; Charles prorogues Parliament
1629 Parliament reassembles: 'Three Resolutions' condemn Charles's actions. Commons bar door to King's officers
Charles dissolves Parliament
Cornelius Vermuyden drains land west of river Trent
1630 John Winthrop leads 1000 settlers to Massachusetts, founds Boston
1631 English mathematician William Oughtred introduces multiplication symbol '×'
1632 Lord Baltimore receives charter for Maryland colony
Sir Thomas Wentworth becomes Lord Deputy in Ireland
1633 William Laud appointed archbishop of Canterbury
1634 Wentworth calls Irish Parliament, imposes the 39 Articles there
1635 Charles exacts Ship Money from inland towns
1636 Charles rules that Scottish Church should be governed by bishops
1637 John Hampden tried and found guilty for refusing to pay Ship Money
Riot in Edinburgh over reading of the Liturgy
William Prynne condemned to mutilation for seditious writing
1638 National Covenant in Scotland challenges the King's prerogative
1639 First Bishops' War between England and Scotland; settled by Pacification of Berwick
Wentworth becomes Earl of Strafford and Lord Lieutenant
Second Bishops' War begins

The Civil War

The Civil War, or Great Rebellion as some people called it, was sparked off by religion. Charles tried to impose bishops on the Scottish Church, and the Presbyterians of Scotland refused. They signed a Covenant to resist, and raised an army. Charles made peace, but it did not last.

Charles had to summon Parliament to obtain money to pay for the expenses of his army, but dissolved it just after three weeks. Then the Scots invaded England, and Charles persuaded them to halt on payment of £850 a day. Desperate, he had to call Parliament again. This Parliament lasted for 20 years.

The Commons began by impeaching Strafford and Laud, the King's hated ministers, for treason, and to make sure of Strafford they passed an Act of Attainder and had him executed. They abolished two ancient courts – Star Chamber and High Commission – which Charles had used to raise money illegally.

Tempers got higher and higher: Members of the Commons, led by John Hampden and John Pym, insisted on reforms. Charles tried to arrest them and three other Members for treason. He failed, and soon fighting broke out.

Charles's main support was in the west; Parliament held the east, and London. Early battles were inconclusive, but in 1644 a Parliamentary army, which included a well-trained force (the 'Ironsides') led by Oliver Cromwell, a country gentleman, defeated a Royalist army at Marston Moor and won all the north of England.

Parliament reorganized its forces into a New Model Army, based on the 'Ironsides' of Cromwell. With that it crushed the King at the battle of

King Charles I was tried by Parliament and found guilty as a tyrant; he was sentenced to death by a majority of only one vote. He was executed at Whitehall, and impressed everyone with his dignity.

In 1649 Cromwell led an army to Ireland, where there was a strong Royalist force. In September he laid siege to the fortified town of Drogheda, storming it and killing almost the entire garrison. Cromwell's actions in Ireland included the dispossession of many landowners, and increased the Irish hatred and resentment of the English.

1640	'Short' Parliament: it refuses funds and Charles dissolves it Scots win victory: Charles agrees to truce and pays £850 a day 'Long' Parliament (to 1660) Strafford and Laud impeached
1641	Act of Attainder condemns Strafford: he is executed Triennial Act Court of Star Chamber and High Commission abolished Massacre of English in Ireland MPs set out grievances in Grand Remonstrance
1642	Charles tries to impeach five members of the Commons Civil War begins (to 1645) Drawn battle of Edge Hill
1643	Solemn League and Covenant: alliance between Scots and Parliament Royalists generally successful except in East Anglia
1644	Battle of Marston Moor: Oliver Cromwell defeats Royalists Second battle of Newbury: Royalist victory Marquis of Montrose wins Royalist victories in Scotland
1645	Laud attained and executed Self-Denying Ordinance discharges MPs from civil and military office Battle of Naseby, final defeat of Charles, ends the war; he surrenders to the Scots
1646	Charles and Parliament negotiate
1647	Scots surrender Charles to Parliament; Army, in conflict with Parliament, seizes Charles
1648	Scots try to help King: Cromwell defeats them at Preston Thomas Pride reduces Parliament to 60 members by expelling Presbyterians

Naseby, and the war was over. A Scottish Royalist army under the Marquess of Montrose was defeated at the same time.

Charles fell into the hands of the Scots, who handed him over to Parliament. Four years of negotiations followed, including a brief Second Civil War. Parliament came to the conclusion that it could not trust the King. He was tried for treason, found guilty by a special court, and beheaded.

The actual fighting involved a comparatively small part of the country and comparatively few people. But the impact of the Civil War was felt everywhere, not least because it split families in their allegiance.

The Souldiers in their passage to York turn unto reformers pull down Popish pictures, break down rayles, turn altars into Tables.

Above: Parliamentary troops wreck a church, from a contemporary woodcut. They considered pictures and statues to be 'popish'.

Left: The reverse of the second Great Seal used by the Commonwealth, showing the House of Commons in 1651. Two years later Cromwell, thinking that Parliament was becoming tyrannical itself, took some of his soldiers to the House and forced its members to leave. 'The Lord hath done with you' he said.

The Commonwealth

The execution of Charles I left England firmly in the hands of Parliament and its Army. For the next 11 years the country was a *Commonwealth*, a republic.

Charles's son was proclaimed as Charles II in Scotland, and the Irish also rallied to the Royalist cause. Cromwell took an army to Ireland, where he subdued the Royalists with great severity. Charles and an army of Scots marched into England, where they were routed by Cromwell at the battle of Worcester; Charles escaped to France.

Government was in the hands of the 'Rump', the few remaining Members of the Commons. The House of Lords was abolished. But the Members of the Rump were bigoted Puritans, and incompetent. Oliver Cromwell turned them out, and called a new Parliament, nominated by the Army and the independent Nonconformist Churches. It was nicknamed 'Barebone's Parliament', after one of its more bigoted Members, Praise-God Barebone. This Parliament also failed to provide a strong government, and Cromwell took up the post of Lord Protector.

The Protector called Parliaments, but for the most part he ruled as a dictator – although an unwilling one. He was considering calling a new Parliament when he died of malaria at the age of 59.

The Restoration

Oliver Cromwell nominated his son to succeed him. Richard Cromwell was a weak and mild man, and the Army, still the main power in the land, turned him out. His enemies named him 'Tumbledown Dick'. The 42 surviving Members of the Rump were recalled.

Amid all the chaos there was a strong revival of Royalist feeling in the country. Finally General George Monk, commander in Scotland, organized new elections, and a fresh Parliament recalled Charles II from exile to be king.

1649 Charles tried for treason and executed: Commonwealth set up
Irish rise in favour of Charles II: Cromwell suppresses them
1650 Montrose caught and executed
Charles II crowned in Scotland
1651 Cromwell defeats Charles at Worcester: Charles escapes
Navigation Act limits shipping
Act of Indemnity and Oblivion
1652-54 War with Dutch over shipping
1653 Cromwell turns out the 'Rump', calls a nominated Parliament
Cromwell Lord Protector
1654 Cromwell quarrels with Parliament
1655 Cromwell dissolves Parliament: rule of the major-generals
Anglican services banned
1656-59 War with Spain: England captures Dunkirk from Spaniards
1656 Cromwell excludes opponents from his third Parliament
1657 Cromwell refuses the Crown
1658 Cromwell dissolves Parliament
Death of Cromwell: succeeded by son Richard as Lord Protector
1659 New Parliament called; quarrels with the Army and is dissolved
'Rump' Parliament returns and persuades Richard to resign
1660 George Monk, commander in Scotland, marches to London
Monk rules as captain-general
Long Parliament recalled
Declaration of Breda: Charles II promises amnesty
Convention Parliament recalls King Charles II (to 1685): Army disbanded, Act of Indemnity passed
1661 Charles II's first Parliament
1662 Charles weds Portuguese princess Catherine of Braganza
Charles sells Dunkirk to France

125

Left: Charles II was an astute man who proved a highly successful king. During his 25-year reign he re-established the monarchy on a firm and popular footing, and on a sound financial basis. He was a tolerant ruler; his first act as king was to pardon his enemies. He was also skilful enough not to antagonize Parliament; after years in exile he was determined, as he put it, not to go on his travels again.

Below: In 1665 London was ravaged by the Great Plague, which killed 68,596 people out of a total city population of about 460,000. The following year came another disaster – the Great Fire of London. This began in a baker's house in Pudding Lane and quickly swept through the crowded wooden houses. It raged for several days, until houses were blown up to make gaps the fire could not cross. The King himself directed the firefighters and even laboured among them. The fire was not an unmixed disaster; filthy alleys were burned down and the plague halted, but many fine buildings were destroyed.

Religious Persecution

Ever since the Reformation the English had feared Roman Catholics, both on religious grounds and also as a threat to national sovereignty. After the rigours of the Civil War and Commonwealth they also feared the Puritans. Parliament therefore passed a group of Acts, together known as the 'Clarendon Code' after the King's chief minister, the Earl of Clarendon.

The Code compelled all clergymen and people holding office in local and national government to take Communion in accordance with the rites of the Anglican Church. Nonconformist prayer-meetings were limited to five people, and dissenting clergy were barred from coming nearer than 5 miles (8 kilometres) to a town.

The Dutch War

The English and Dutch were rivals in fishing and trade, and when the Dutch started settlements on the Hudson River of North America among the English colonies, the merchants appealed to Parliament and war was declared. It began with an English victory in a naval battle of 300 ships off Lowestoft. Later, when the English fleet was unable to put to sea because of lack of supplies, the Dutch were able to sail up the Medway, raid Chatham, and capture the flagship *Royal Charles*. Such success as the English ships had was due partly to the efforts of the Clerk of the Acts, a diligent civil servant named Samuel Pepys. He is famous to modern readers because of the detailed diary he kept for some years.

1664 British take New Amsterdam (now New York) from Dutch
Conventicle Act forbids meetings of more than five dissenters
Royal Marines formed

1665 War between England and the Netherlands (to 1667)
Five-Mile Act restricts movements of Nonconformist ministers
First issue of *The London Gazette* (then called *The Oxford Gazette*)
Great Plague kills 68,596 people in London

1666 French declare war on England
English privateers take Tobago
First cheddar cheeses made
Great Fire of London: 180 hectares destroyed
Scottish Covenanters rebel, but are defeated

1667 Dutch burn English fleet in the river Medway
Peace of Breda between Dutch, French and English

1669 Samuel Pepys, his sight failing, makes his last *Diary* entry

1670 First settlement in S. Carolina
Secret Treaty of Dover between Charles II and Louis XIV of France
James, Duke of York, professes Roman Catholicism
Hudson's Bay Company formed

1671 Ex-pirate Henry Morgan becomes deputy-governor of Jamaica

1672 England at war with Netherlands

1673 Test Act excludes Catholics and Nonconformists from office:
Duke of York gives up his posts
York marries Mary of Modena, a Catholic princess

1674 Peace with the Netherlands

1675 Foundation stone of new St Paul's cathedral laid
Greenwich Observatory founded

Henry Purcell was one of the greatest ever English composers. In 1677 he became composer for Charles II's string orchestra and in 1679 was appointed organist of Westminster abbey, succeeding the great John Blow. Three years later he became one of the organists of the Chapel Royal. He wrote music for the Church, the court, and for the stage and private entertainments. In his day there were no public operas in London, and his most famous work, the miniature opera 'Dido and Aeneas', was written for a girls' school in Chelsea. He died when he was only 36.

Whig and Tory

The terms Whig and Tory came into use in Charles II's reign as terms of abuse for political opponents. Whig was originally a name for Scottish cattle thieves; it was applied to people who wanted to exclude James from succession to the throne. Tory was the name for a group of Irish bandits, and was applied to people who opposed James's exclusion and supported the prerogatives of the Crown.

The late 17th century saw great interest in scientific discoveries and theories, and groups of men would meet regularly to discuss new developments and carry out experiments. In 1662 Charles II granted a charter to one such group and founded the Royal Society. Its members included Robert Boyle, the philosopher; the naturalist and chemist Robert Hooke, who demonstrated such things as the expansion of metals, vacuum effects and the first effective compound microscope; and (elected in 1671) Sir Isaac Newton, the great mathematician and physicist who became the Society's president in 1703. This engraving shows the bust of the royal founder and patron, supported by Lord Brouncker, the first president, and the earlier scientist Francis Bacon.

Coffee Houses

During the 1600s the new, exotic drink of coffee was introduced into England from the Middle East. In 1652 the first coffee house in the country was opened in London, and coffee houses quickly became popular as meeting places. In 1688 Edward Lloyd opened a coffee house in Tower Street, which was the rendezvous for people who would insure ships and their cargoes. Lloyd issued a publication called *Lloyd's News*, which gave details of shipping movements. From this coffee house sprang the modern Lloyds, the world's leading market for shipping and other insurance.

The Monmouth Rebellion

Charles II had no legitimate children, but by various mistresses he had 14 illegitimate sons and daughters. The most important of his sons was James, Duke of Monmouth.

Monmouth was a capable soldier, who suppressed a Covenanters' revolt in Scotland and commanded English troops during the war with the Dutch. He was handsome, easy-mannered and popular. After the accession of James II, Monmouth thought he could rally the Protestant cause and win the throne for himself. But he picked his time badly: James had not been king long enough to make himself unpopular, and the motley army Monmouth was able to raise was defeated· at the battle of Sedgemoor, in Somerset. Monmouth was executed for treason, and so were nearly 300 of his followers. A further 800 were sold as slaves to Barbados.

1677 William of Orange marries Mary, daughter of the Duke of York
1678 Titus Oates reveals a 'Popish Plot'; Sir Edmund Berry Godfrey, magistrate who received Oates' evidence, is found murdered
Disabling Act bars Roman Catholics from Parliament
John Bunyan publishes first part of *The Pilgrim's Progress*
Cavalier Parliament dissolved after 18 years
1679 Duke of York leaves England
New Parliament meets: plan to exclude York from the succession vetoed by House of Lords
Covenanters rebel in Scotland; crushed by Duke of Monmouth
1680 William Dockwra sets up penny post in London
1681 Charles grants Pennsylvania rights to Quaker William Penn
Parliament meets in Oxford, but is dissolved
First London street lights (oil)
1682 Edmund Halley observes his comet
1683 Rye House Plot to murder the royal brothers uncovered
Oates revealed as liar and fraud
Duke of York reinstated
1684 *Pilgrim's Progress*, Part II
Monmouth banished for plotting
1685 Charles II dies; succeeded by his brother James II (to 1688)
Duke of Argyll unsuccessfully rebels
Monmouth lands to claim the throne: defeated at Sedgemoor
The Bloody Assize: hundreds of rebels hanged or sold as slaves
1686 James introduces pro-Catholic measures
1687 Declaration of Liberty of Conscience by the King

The Glorious Revolution

The Revolution of 1688 was accomplished with little or no bloodshed, and so has gained the name of the 'Glorious Revolution'. James II's obvious attempts to favour Catholics so incensed the Protestants that seven leading noblemen, headed by the Earl of Shrewsbury, invited William of Orange to come and deliver the country from its unpopular ruler. They were prompted to this action by the birth of a son to James by his second wife, thus pushing into second place James's daughter Mary, William's wife.

As soon as William landed revolts broke out all over the country, and

A Dutch painting showing William III landing at Torbay with his Protestant army. William had a good claim to the throne in his own right; he was the son of Charles I's daughter Mary, who had married the Protestant Prince William of Orange. He, in turn, was married to James II's daughter Mary, whose mother was the Protestant Anne Hyde. The throne came to them as joint sovereigns, William III and Mary II.

James found he could not even rely on his army. He fled, but was captured on board ship and brought back to London. There he was felt to be an embarrassment, so he was allowed to escape again. This time he reached France.

130

James's attempt to raise an army in Ireland was frustrated when William defeated him at the battle of the Boyne. This battle is still celebrated annually by the Protestants of Ulster.

Window Tax

A way of raising revenue devised by the ministers of William and Mary was a tax on all windows over six in every house worth more than £5 a year. This tax, which was effectively a tax on light and air and thus injurious to health, was increased six times until 1832, when it was reduced. It was finally abolished in 1851. Old houses may sometimes be seen with windows bricked up to avoid this tax.

A medallion commemorating the marriage of William and Mary, which took place in 1677.

1688 James issues Second Declaration of Liberty of Conscience. Seven bishops protest: tried for sedition and acquitted
Son and heir born to James II
Seven English lords invite William of Orange to England
William lands at Torbay: James flees the country

1689 Convention Parliament elected: it declares James to have abdicated, offers throne to William III (to 1702) and Mary II (to 1694)
Declaration of Rights
War with France
Toleration Act gives Nonconformists freedom of worship
James lands in Ireland
Highlanders rise for James
First major English opera: Purcell's *Dido and Aeneas*

1690 New Parliament elected
Act of Grace gives indemnity to James's supporters
William defeats James at the battle of the Boyne: James flees

1691 William campaigns in Netherlands (to 1697)

1692 Massacre of Glencoe

1694 Bank of England founded
Triennial Bill: Parliament to be elected every three years
Death of Queen Mary II

1695 Window tax (to 1851)

1696 New English coinage introduced

1697 Treaty of Ryswick ends French war

1698 Thomas Savery invents a steam pump

1699 Billingsgate fish market set up

1700 First Eddystone lighthouse built

1701 Act of Settlement establishes Protestant succession
James II dies: France recognizes his son as 'James III'

The Act of Union

The political union of England and Scotland, which James I and VI had vainly tried to bring about when he became king of England in 1603, was finally accomplished in 1707.

The Scots did not accept the English Act of Settlement, which settled the Crown on the descendants of Sophia of Hanover and so guaranteed Protestant monarchs. There was an unspoken threat that Scotland might, when Queen Anne died, bring back the Catholic Stuarts by making James II's son, James Edward the 'Old Pretender', king of Scotland. This threat brought the English Parliament to favour the move towards union.

Scots had come to realize that their country was no longer able to be prosperous as an independent nation. Their Parliament held out for, and got, free trade with England, and cash to pay off huge debts acquired in a disastrous colonizing venture in Darien in Central America. The Scots also kept their own law courts, legal system and Presbyterian Kirk.

The resulting kingdom was called Great Britain. For some years after the union the people of North Britain, as the English tended to call Scotland, felt themselves at a disadvantage in an unequal partnership. The English majority in the combined Parliament meant that measures which favoured England at Scotland's expense were passed: for example a tax on linen, unimportant in the south but a major industry north of the Border.

Queen Anne, last of the Stuart monarchs, was the younger daughter of James II and his first wife Anne Hyde. She was married to Prince George of Denmark, of whom Charles II remarked that he had tried him drunk and tried him sober, and could find nothing in him. Their many children all died in infancy except for William, Duke of Gloucester, who lived only to the age of 11.

Opposite: In 1702 Britain was drawn into the War of the Spanish Succession; at issue was whether an Austrian or French prince should become king of Spain. British forces, led by the brilliant John Churchill (later Duke of Marlborough), backed the Austrian side, and won a series of victories against the French. The most famous was the battle of Blenheim, shown here, in 1704; Marlborough and Prince Eugène of Savoy inflicted a crushing defeat on the French. The War ended with a compromise; the French prince took the throne, on condition that Spain and France would never be united.

1702 William III dies; succeeded by sister-in-law Anne (to 1714)
War of the Spanish Succession (to 1714): Marlborough the principal allied general
First English daily newspaper, the *Daily Courant*

1703 Queen Anne's Bounty (fund to help poor clergymen) established

1704 English take Gibraltar from Spain
English win battle of Blenheim

1705 'Darley Arabian', ancestor of modern racehorses, is brought to England

1706 English win battle of Ramillies
First English evening newspaper, the *Evening Post*

1707 Union of England and Scotland as Great Britain

1708 English fleet foils attempt by James Edward, 'the Old Pretender' to land in Scotland
British win battle of Oudenarde
Robert Walpole becomes Secretary for War

1709 British win battle of Malplaquet
Abram Darby smelts iron with coke and coal for first time

1710 St Paul's cathedral finished
Marlborough falls from favour

1711 South Sea Company formed
Ascot Races established

1712 Thomas Newcomen's steam engine
Newspaper Stamp Act passed
Last execution for witchcraft in England

1713 Treaty of Utrecht ends war
South Sea Company takes over the National Debt

1714 Death of Sophia of Hanover, Anne's heir
Death of Queen Anne: succeeded by Elector of Hanover as George I (to 1727)

The Hanoverians

The Hanoverian kings ruled Britain for 123 years. They presided over the growth and loss of one empire, and the beginnings of another. More important, they lived in an age of revolutions, upheavals which shook the established order and laid the foundations of the modern world in which we live.

The first, and the most important, was the Industrial Revolution. It entailed no bloodshed, no changes of frontier or ruler. But it affected the lives of an ever-increasing number of people, and it is still going on. It involved the invention of machines to do work that had formerly been done by hand, and the harnessing of the power of steam (and later other forms of energy) to drive these machines, thus reducing the reliance on the muscle power of men and animals. Hardly less important was the Agricultural Revolution, which led to improved methods of growing crops, improvement of livestock by selective breeding, and the invention of new farm equipment and machinery.

The first of the political revolutions occurred in North America, where England's 13 colonies revolted against acts of the home government which they considered oppressive. It was followed by the French Revolution, in which years of domination by a small, wealthy, privileged class led to a bloodthirsty struggle. There was for a time a sympathetic alliance between the French and the Americans against their common enemy, Britain. (However, the revolutionaries of France were quick to suppress a revolt by Negro slaves in the French colony of Haiti.) In the first quarter of the 19th century the South American colonies of Spain and Portugal also won independence, while the Greeks freed themselves from Turkish dominance.

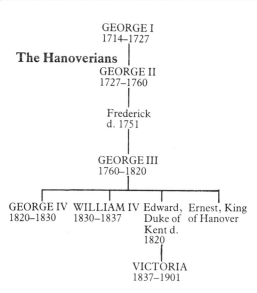

The Hanoverians

GEORGE I
1714–1727

GEORGE II
1727–1760

Frederick
d. 1751

GEORGE III
1760–1820

GEORGE IV   WILLIAM IV   Edward,   Ernest, King
1820–1830   1830–1837   Duke of   of Hanover
                                   Kent d.
                                   1820

VICTORIA
1837–1901

The Hanoverian Succession

The Hanoverian kings were descended from James I's daughter Elizabeth. She married the Elector Palatine Frederick V, who was chosen king of Bohemia in 1619, defeated in battle the next year and exiled. His brief reign brought Elizabeth the nickname 'the Winter Queen'. Their daughter Sophia married the Elector of Hanover. She was recognized as Queen Anne's heir but died a few months before her, so the throne passed to Sophia's son George.

British forces capture Quebec in Canada from the French, in 1759. The Hanoverian period saw Britain build up a substantial empire in North America and later in India; but tactless handling caused the loss of many of the New World colonies, which broke away to form the United States of America. The former French colonies in Canada, perhaps surprisingly, remained loyal to Britain.

ELSEWHERE IN THE WORLD

1714 Austria takes Spanish Netherlands
1733-5 War of Polish Succession
1740 Frederick II, the Great, king of Prussia (to 1786)
     Death of Emperor Charles VI: War of Austrian Succession (to 1748)
1756-63 Seven Years' War
1762 Catherine II, the Great, tsarina of Russia (to 1796)
1776 13 colonies in North America declare independence
1783 Montgolfier Brothers fly first successful hot-air balloon
1789 Start of French Revolution
     George Washington, first president of United States of America
1791 Slaves in French Haiti rebel
1792 France becomes a republic
1793 Execution of French king and queen: the Reign of Terror
1795-9 Directory rules France
1796 Napoleon conquers Italy
1799-1804 Consulate runs France
1800 French defeat Austrians
     Volta makes electric battery
1803 France sells Louisiana to US
1804 Napoleon I, emperor of the French (to 1814)
1806 End of Holy Roman Empire
1808-14 Peninsular War
1811-22 Spanish colonies in South America achieve independence
1812 Napoleon retreats from Moscow
1813 Napoleon loses battle of Leipzig
1814 Napoleon abdicates, goes to Elba
1815 Napoleon returns for the Hundred Days; defeated at battle of Waterloo and exiled to St Helena
1818 Chaka founds the Zulu Empire
1819 Spain cedes Florida to US
1830 Greece independent from Turkey
1835-7 Boers make the Great Trek in southern Africa

Above: The battle of Preston in 1715. Jacobite forces entered the Lancashire town in November, and proclaimed the Old Pretender king. They remained there for several days until George I's troops took the town.

The Jacobite Rebellions

People who sympathized with the Stuart cause were known as *Jacobites*, from the Latin name (*Jacobus*) of James II. In 1715 Scottish Jacobites raised a rebellion, supported by a small revolt in the north of England. The 'Fifteen', as it was later known, was fairly easily suppressed, and James Edward Stuart, the 'Old Pretender', arrived to find the rising over. He quickly went away again.

Thirty years later James's son, Charles Edward – the 'Young Pretender' or Bonnie Prince Charlie – arrived in Scotland to raise his standard on his father's behalf. Only a few of the clans rose to join him. The Pretender had some initial success, capturing Edinburgh, and marched south into England as far as Derby. The news of his arrival there caused a financial panic in London, but it was needless: Charles, finding no support in England, was already retreating. A few months later the clansmen were routed at the battle of Culloden, a fight lasting only half an hour. Charles escaped to France after many adventures. Stern reprisals against the Highlanders, including the banning of the kilt, followed.

Left: Charles Edward Stuart, the Young Pretender, gained astonishing affection and loyalty from his followers, who helped him escape from the English and hid him for many months. Many hoped that he would return to lead another rebellion but although he visited London in 1750 and perhaps again in 1754 his plots were futile. He died, drunken and ill-tempered, nursed by his only daughter, Charlotte Duchess of Albany, who never married.

The South Sea Bubble

The South Sea Company was a trading venture formed in 1711. In 1720 its considerable success led to speculation in its shares, and dozens of other but worthless companies were formed to attract speculators. Shares were being bought and sold for ten times their real value. Eventually the South Sea 'Bubble' burst: the shares found their true level, and hundreds of speculators were ruined. The South Sea Company continued trading until 1856.

Sir Robert Walpole, leader of the Whig party, was effectively England's first Prime Minister. George I spoke almost no English; he cared little for England and spent most of his time in Hanover. As a result the Cabinet system of government developed.

1714 Queen Anne dies; succeeded by Hanoverian George I (to 1727)
Marlborough is reinstated

1715 Impeachment of Earls of Bolingbroke and Oxford, and Duke of Ormonde, for Jacobitism
'The Fifteen': Jacobite rising. Scots Jacobites beaten at battle of Sherriffmuir, English at Preston. 'Old Pretender' James Edward lands in Scotland but leaves at once
Whig Robert Walpole becomes First Lord of the Treasury (effectively Prime Minister)

1716 Septennial Act: duration of Parliaments prolonged to seven years
Treaty of Westminster between Britain and Holy Roman Empire

1717 Triple Alliance between Britain, France and the Netherlands
'Old Pretender' leaves France
Walpole resigns

1718 The Empire joins to form the Quadruple Alliance
Britain at war with Spain

1719 Declaratory Act affirms the right of British Parliament to legislate for Ireland
Irish Parliament passes Toleration Act to help dissenters
James Figg becomes first boxing champion of England

1720 Heavy speculation in South Sea and other companies; 'South Sea Bubble' bursts: many investors ruined

1721 John Aislabie, Chancellor of the Exchequer, sent to Tower for fraud
Walpole is chief minister again

1722 Bookseller Thomas Guy founds Guy's Hospital, London

1723 Treaty between Britain and Prussia, cemented by royal marriages

The Agricultural Revolution

In 1730 Viscount Townshend resigned from the government and retired to his estates at Raynham in Norfolk. Here he started a revolution in agriculture, whereby farming methods that had been unchanged since the Middle Ages were radically altered.

Farmers were accustomed to leave each field fallow every third year. Townshend experimented by planting in rotation crops that in turn absorbed or put back different nutrients in the soil. One crop was turnips, from which came his nickname of 'Turnip' Townshend.

Townshend's methods were improved by another Norfolk peer, Thomas Coke, the Earl of Leicester.

The increased crop yields these methods produced made it easier to feed livestock in winter. Meanwhile a Leicestershire farmer, Robert Bakewell, improved the breeds of sheep, and paved the way for modern methods of stock breeding.

Earlier a Berkshire gentleman-farmer, Jethro Tull, invented a machine for sowing seed, hitherto done by hand. Tull's device, the first farm machine, drilled holes and put a seed in each.

Thomas Coke, Earl of Leicester, with some of his Southdown sheep. He increased his rent-roll almost ten times by introducing scientific methods of agriculture, and turned the sandy rabbit-warren of his estate at Holkham in Norfolk into an efficient model farm, visited by people from all over Britain and even Europe.

Gulliver is pinned down in Lilliput; an illustration to Dean Swift's 'Gulliver's Travels' in which he satirized the manners and politics of his time.

Elector George

George I was the great-grandson of James I. He was also, through his father, elector of Hanover. This title meant that he was not only the king of Hanover, one of the states of the Holy Roman Empire, but also one of the nine German princes who had the right to elect the Emperor whenever the imperial throne fell vacant.

George spoke no English: he and his ministers conversed in French. In his later years he relied increasingly on the First Lord of the Treasury, Robert Walpole, who is regarded as Britain's first Prime Minister.

1724 Lord Carteret becomes Lord Lieutenant of Ireland
1725 Treaty of Hanover between Britain and Prussia
Walpole is knighted
George I revives Order of the Bath
1726 John Harrison invents 'gridiron' (temperature proof) pendulum
1727 Death of George I: succeeded by son George II (to 1760)
Spaniards besiege Gibraltar
1728 Siege of Gibraltar ends
1729 Treaty of Seville, between Spain, France, Britain: Britain keeps Gibraltar
Scientist Stephen Gray discovers principle of electrical conduction
John and Charles Wesley start sect, later called Methodists
1730 Viscount Townshend begins experiments in agriculture
Edinburgh Royal Infirmary founded
1731 Treaty with Holy Roman Empire ends Ostend-based rival to East India Company
Spanish coastguards seize British ship *Rebecca*: her captain, Robert Jenkins, loses an ear
1732 Walpole is offered No. 10 Downing Street, London, as official residence; he is now called 'Prime Minister' as a term of abuse
James Oglethorpe receives charter to form colony of Georgia
1733 Walpole plans to introduce tax on wines and tobacco
National campaign against new taxes: Walpole withdraws them
John Kay patents his flying shuttle: start of Industrial Revolution in Britain
George II's wife, Caroline, has Serpentine lake made in London's Hyde Park

Frederick, Prince of Wales

One of the less endearing characteristics of the early Hanoverians was the dislike between fathers and sons. George I loathed his son, George II, and they supported rival political factions. George II in turn hated his son, Frederick, Prince of Wales (1707-1751). A bitter subject of dispute between Frederick and his father was the small allowance the King gave him. The Prince was far from being states-man-like, but does not seem to have deserved his mother's astounding re-mark: 'My dear first-born is the greatest ass and the greatest liar and the greatest *canaille* and the greatest beast in the whole world, and I heartily wish he were out of it.' Frederick died before his father; it was his son who became George III.

Opposite: John Wesley who, with his brother Charles and George Whitefield, founded the Methodist movement. They preached their message of faith, repentance and salvation in open fields, houses and barns all over the country. Wesley travelled some 8000 kilometres every year for about 50 years, preaching especially to poor people. Methodist chapels were built, many in places where there were few churches. Wesley himself was an Anglican but his preaching angered the leaders of the Church of England and their bishops refused to ordain Wesleyan preachers. In 1784 he finally broke with the Church, and ordained his own ministers. The 'method' by which he and his followers lived meant an active and selfless Christian life of thrift, abstinence and hard work.

Below: Laying the cornerstone of the first Methodist chapel, Wesley's New Room, Horsefair, Bristol, built in 1739.

The Early Novelists

Pamela; or Virtue Rewarded, which was published in 1740, is generally regarded as the first true English novel. This bawdy work was written by Samuel Richardson, printer to the House of Commons, and it set the pattern for future novels. Richardson went on to write *Clarissa Harlowe*, the first and one of the greatest tragic novels. Like *Pamela*, it was written as a series of letters. Richardson was followed by Henry Fielding, whose *Joseph Andrews* (1742) parodied *Pamela*; Tobias Smollett (*Roderick Random;* 1748); and Laurence Sterne (*The Life and Opinions of Tristram Shandy;* 1759-67).

Perhaps the most lasting of the early novels was Oliver Goldsmith's *The Vicar of Wakefield* (1766), still widely read.

1734 Jack Broughton, inventor of boxing gloves, wins championship of England from James Figg
1735 Frederick, Prince of Wales, heads opposition to Walpole
1736 John and Charles Wesley organize groups of Methodists
Porteous Riots in Edinburgh: Captain John Porteous hanged by a lynch mob for giving orders to fire on a rioting crowd
1737 Licensing Act for London theatres: all plays to be censored by the Lord Chamberlain
Death of Queen Caroline
1739 War of Jenkins's Ear (with Spain; lasts to 1748)
Admiral Edward Vernon ('Old Grog') storms Porto Bello, Darien
Foundling Hospital established in London
1740 War of the Austrian Succession: Britain on Austrian side (to 1748)
'Old Grog' makes first navy issue of rum diluted with water (called 'grog' after him)
Commodore George Anson sails to Chile and Peru, and around the world (returns 1744)
Edinburgh mob raids granaries
1741 Royal Military Academy established at Woolwich
1742 Walpole falls from power, becomes Earl of Orford; Whig ministry continues until 1762
George Frideric Handel's *Messiah* has first performance in Dublin
1743 Battle of Dettingen: George II leads troops into action – last British king to do so
1744 Robert Clive goes to India as a clerk
First major cricket match (All-England 40 & 70, Kent 53 & 58 for 1 wicket)

The Loyalty of the Clans

Whatever their faults, the Stuarts were able to inspire an immense loyalty in their followers. After the disaster of Culloden Moor in 1746, Charles Edward, the Young Pretender, was a wanted man, hunted through the Highlands. But although the Government put a price of £30,000 on his head – a tremendous fortune in those days – none of the clansmen of the Western Highlands betrayed him.

In five months' wanderings before a French ship picked him up, Charles was helped by many people, including Flora Macdonald, who enabled him to travel to Skye disguised as her 'Irish maid'. Flora was later arrested and jailed in the Tower, but was freed by an Act of Indemnity in 1747. She married, and emigrated to North Carolina. She returned to Scotland in 1779.

The 'Lost' 11 Days

The calendar as organized by Julius Caesar was fractionally longer than the solar year, and by the 16th century the two were out of step by 10 days. Pope Gregory XIII reformed the calendar in 1582 to bring the two into line. Most Roman Catholic countries adopted his reform at once, but the by now staunchly Protestant English refused to follow his reform.

In 1752 Parliament at last decided to line up with most of the rest of Europe. By now the difference was 11 days, so the change was made by going from September 2nd straight to September 14th. Many people protested at having, as they thought, 11 days of their lives taken away.

Earlier, New Year's Day, which had been March 25th since 1155, was decreed to be January 1st.

Opposite: King George II leads his army at the battle of Dettingen in 1743. He was the last British monarch to lead his troops in battle; a vain and pompous man he, like his father, left government to his ministers.

Below: The Mughal Emperor Shah Alam hands Robert Clive of the East India Company documents which grant him the right to collect revenue. Both French and British had set up trading stations in India; when war broke out between the two in Europe, India too became a battle ground. The British controlled shipping and could cut off French soldiers and supplies; under their brilliant general Clive they took over the French settlements. They made treaties with local rulers which gave them control over most of India.

1744 *God Save the King* first printed
1745 Battle of Fontenoy: Duke of Cumberland defeated by French
Middlesex Hospital founded
'Young Pretender', Charles Edward, lands in Scotland and raises army. Jacobites enter Edinburgh, win battle of Prestonpans.
Jacobite army reaches Derby
'Black Friday': financial panic on London Stock Exchange
Jacobites begin retreat
1746 Jacobites win battle of Falkirk
Culloden Moor: Cumberland crushes Jacobites in half an hour
'Young Pretender' escapes to France
Highland dress banned (until 1782)
1747 Carriage tax imposed
Anson defeats Canada-bound French fleet off Finisterre
1748 Treaty of Aix-la-Chapelle ends the War of the Austrian succession: Britain gains nothing
Holywell Music Room, Oxford, opens – oldest concert hall still in use
1749 Halifax, Nova Scotia founded
Consolidation Act reforms Navy
1750 First local cricket club formed at Hambledon, Hampshire
Jockey Club founded
'Young Pretender' visits London
Westminster Bridge completed
1751 Calendar change: Jan. 1 to be New Year's Day in England (previously March 25), as in Scotland
Frederick, Prince of Wales, dies
Clive takes Arcot from French
1752 Britain adopts Gregorian Calendar: 11 days dropped
Clive captures Trichinopoly
Manchester Royal Infirmary founded

In 1714 Parliament offered a prize of £20,000 for a time-keeping device that would be so accurate that navigators could use it to work out longitude. It should not vary by more than 2 minutes on a six-week voyage to the West Indies and back. John Harrison decided to work for the prize; his first three time-keepers seemed accurate enough, but war with Spain did not allow them to be tested. His fourth chronometer, above, varied by no more than five seconds on a voyage to the West Indies in 1761; it again passed the test in 1764 and in 1773 the prize was finally given to Harrison.

The Black Hole of Calcutta

During the Seven Years' War Siraj ud-Daula, the Nawab of Bengal, thought the time was ripe to eliminate both the French and the British from India. He began by capturing Calcutta from the British. He took 146 prisoners, who were herded into a room about 4.5 by 5.5 metres. It was extremely hot and badly ventilated. After a night in those conditions only 23 emerged alive. Modern Indian historians put the number of prisoners at 43, with 15 dead.

The British counterattacked. Clive with an army of 3000 defeated the Nawab at the battle of Plassey. Siraj ud-Daula was murdered by his own people, and Bengal passed under the protection of the British.

The Seven Years' War

The Seven Years' War was a world-wide conflict. It was fought between Britain and France for colonial possessions in America and India; and between Prussia, supported by Britain and Hanover, against an alliance of Austria, France, Russia and Sweden in Europe. Spain became involved as an ally of France.

The conflict in North America is often called the French and Indian Wars, and concerned border disputes between British and French colonies. The French had early successes, but were decisively beaten when a British force under James Wolfe captured the French city of Quebec in a night assault. Wolfe and the French commander, the Marquis de Montcalm, were killed.

In India the French began in a strong position, but vigorous campaigning by soldiers of the East India Company, commanded by one of its clerks, Robert Clive, gradually won the day.

As a result of the peace settlement, France lost all but a few small bases in India, and in America all Canada and possessions east of the Mississippi River. From Spain, Britain gained Florida.

The British conduct of the war was masterminded by William Pitt (later Earl of Chatham), known as Pitt the **Elder** to distinguish him from his son.

The British Museum

One man's private collection formed the basis of the British Museum – that of Sir Hans Sloane, an Irish-born physician of Scottish ancestry. Besides being a distinguished doctor, he was a man of wide-ranging interests. Sloane Square and other places in London are named after him.

Sloane left his collection to the nation on condition that the Government paid his executors £20,000. The collection included 50,000 books and manuscripts, 23,000 coins and medals, and 20,000 natural history specimens. Other collections already in public hands were added to form the Museum.

Dr Samuel Johnson, whose Dictionary was published in 1755. He was the first to try and explain the different meanings of each English word and to illustrate their use by quotations. Johnson also wrote and issued a periodical, 'The Rambler', setting out to instruct and delight his readers while his lives of the English poets are models of biography and of literary criticism. His life was recorded by James Boswell.

1753 Surveyor George Washington sent to tell French to quit Ohio
Newmarket races established
Naturalization of Jews allowed

1754 French and British war over boundaries in North America
Washington surrenders to French at Fort Necessity

1755 Royal and Ancient Golf Club, St Andrews, founded
French defeat British at Fort Duquesne (now Pittsburgh)
Samuel Johnson publishes his great *Dictionary*

1756 'Black Hole' of Calcutta: Britons imprisoned in tiny room; 123 die
Seven Years' War against France
Duke of Devonshire PM, with William Pitt as Secretary of State

1757 Clive defeats Nawab of Bengal at Plassey, and retakes Calcutta
Sankey Navigation, canal linking St Helens coalfield to Mersey
Duke of Newcastle PM

1758 George Washington takes Fort Duquesne
Clive is governor of Bengal

1759 Battle of Quebec: British conquer Canada
British Museum opens

1760 Death of George II: succeeded by grandson, George III (to 1820)
Clive leaves India; becomes MP
Botanical Gardens at Kew open

1761 Pitt resigns

1762 War against Spain declared
Tory Earl of Bute becomes PM

1763 Peace of Paris ends Seven Years' War: British proclamation provides government for Florida, Grenada and Quebec
Tory Ministry falls: Whigs take office under George Grenville
MP John Wilkes attacks King's Speech and is arrested

Captain James Cook is killed in a scuffle with natives on Hawaii, who had grown tired of English sailors asking them for food. In three voyages, Cook claimed New Zealand and the eastern coast of Australia for Britain and mapped the coasts, while artists and naturalists on his ship drew pictures and recorded the strange plants and animals they saw on the voyages.

Wilkes and Liberty

Freedom of speech and Parliamentary privilege were championed by the unlikely person of John Wilkes, a Member of Parliament and an agitator. Wilkes attacked the government of Lord Bute in a paper, *The North Briton*, and was sent to the Tower for seditious libel. A court declared that the general warrant under which he had been arrested was illegal, and he was freed.

Wilkes's enemies had him expelled from the House of Commons, and he was tried in his absence for libel and outlawed. With the watchword of 'Wilkes and Liberty!' he was re-elected, and again expelled. Again he was re-elected, and once more expelled. Wilkes then turned to local government, and became successively alderman, sheriff and Lord Mayor of London. In 1774 he was yet again elected to Parliament, and this time held his seat for 16 years.

The Industrial Revolution

The Industrial Revolution began in Great Britain because it was the one country in Europe which had all the factors necessary for it: a long period of settled government; growing trade and knowledge of science; and a desire for expansion.

Before the revolution, country people made most of their own clothes, furniture and tools. In towns craftsmen worked mostly independently. There were no factories: work was sent out to people in their own homes. This was particularly true in the textile trade, where the Industrial Revolution began.

In the 18th century inventions to improve textile working snowballed. First came John Kay's flying shuttle, which enabled weavers to produce wider cloth more quickly. To keep pace with the weavers came machines to spin thread faster: James Hargreaves's spinning jenny, Richard Arkwright's water frame and Samuel Crompton's spinning mule.

These big new machines were installed in riverside factories and driven by water-wheels, but before long James Watt's improvements to the steam engine meant that steam power replaced water power. People gathered to work in the new factories, and cities to house them were quickly built where conditions were usually very bad.

Meanwhile Abram Darby found out how to smelt iron using coal and coke instead of charcoal. Coal mining increased rapidly to keep pace with the demands of the iron foundries and the steam engines.

1764 Wilkes expelled from Commons
James Hargreaves invents the spinning jenny
Clive returns to India to govern Bengal

1765 Stamp Act: further taxes on American colonies; challenged in Virginia
Thomas Chatterton forges the 'Rowley Poems'

1766 Stamp Act repealed
Pitt, now Earl of Chatham, forms new government
John Byron takes the Falkland Islands for Britain
Theatre Royal, Bristol opens (oldest still in use)

1767 Christie's auction rooms founded
Robert Clive leaves India
Tea, glass, paper and dyestuffs taxed in American colonies

1768 James Cook begins first voyage of discovery
Royal Academy founded
Wilkes elected as MP again

1769 Richard Arkwright invents the spinning frame
Wilkes expelled from Commons

1770 Tory Lord North becomes PM
Parliament repeals all but tea tax in American colonies
Cook discovers Botany Bay
Spain and Britain nearly at war over Falklands

1771 Spain agrees to cede Falklands to Britain
First edition of *Encyclopaedia Britannica*, as a part-work

1772 Warren Hastings appointed governor of Bengal
Lord Chief Justice Lord Mansfield decides a slave is free on landing in England
Daniel Rutherford discovers nitrogen

Right: The first iron bridge, built at Coalbrookdale in Shropshire in 1779. The use of iron for building was widely practised during the 19th century.

Slavery

One of the most important changes in the 18th century was in people's attitudes to slavery. Until that time most people had regarded the fate and treatment of slaves with indifference. But in England a growing number of thinkers, including many Quakers, began to denounce slavery as inhuman.

The turning point came when Granville Sharp, a clergyman's son who worked as a clerk, fought in the courts to maintain that 'as soon as any slave sets his foot on English ground, he becomes free'. He selected the case of James Somerset, a slave from Virginia, to contest. The case was heard by the Lord Chief Justice, Lord Mansfield, who decided in favour of Somerset. At a stroke 14,000 Negroes who were held as slaves in England were set free.

Below: The New Lanark Mills near Glasgow were built in the 1780s. This great cotton-spinning factory was later managed and part-owned by the philanthropist Robert Owen, who reduced working hours and housed his workers. But most of the people who came to work in the new factories were not so lucky. As the Industrial Revolution took work from the countryside to the new industrial towns, many of the workers came to live there. They crowded into filthy slums, living and working in appallingly unhealthy conditions.

The American Revolution

The British colonies in North America largely looked after their own affairs and made their own laws. But Britain controlled their overseas trade, and limited what they could manufacture – though the laws on manufacturing were often quietly broken.

Trouble began when the British conquered the French colonies in North America, and decided they had to keep an army on the continent to ensure the safety of the colonies against French rebellion. The British government decided also to tax the colonists to pay for this army. Successive attempts to tax sugar and colonial imports of lead, paint, paper and tea met with fierce opposition, as did a stamp tax on all legal documents and newspapers. The colonists declared that they should not be taxed by a Parliament where they were not represented. All except the tea tax were lifted, but an attempt by the British to make sure that only British-imported tea was drunk led to the 'Boston Tea Party', in which a group of colonists threw a cargo of tea into Boston Harbor.

From then on the situation deteriorated rapidly, until the night when British troops marched into Concord, Massachusetts, to seize a colonial arms dump. Armed colonists and soldiers faced each other in the cold dawn light at Lexington, on the road to Concord. A shot was fired – nobody knows who did it – and the war had begun. In 1776 the colonists decided to declare independence, and later they were supported by French, Spanish and Dutch.

1773 Boston Tea Party; cargo of tea dumped in harbour

1774 Britain passes Coercive Acts to control colonies, and closes port of Boston
John Wilkes becomes Lord Mayor of London
Joseph Priestley discovers oxygen

1775 American War of Independence begins: British defeated at Lexington and Concord; British victory at Bunker Hill
James Watt perfects steam engine

1776 Adam Smith publishes *The Wealth of Nations*
British forces driven from Boston, but capture New York
St Leger horse race founded
13 American colonies declare independence

1777 British victory at Brandywine, American victory at Saratoga
John Howard begins prison reform

1778 Britain declares war on France

1779 Spain declares war on Britain
James Cook killed in Hawaii
First cast-iron bridge completed at Coalbrookdale
Samuel Crompton invents the spinning mule
The Oaks horse race founded

1780 Henry Grattan demands Home Rule for Ireland
Gordon Riots (anti-Catholic) in London
Britain declares war on Holland
The Derby horse race founded

1781 French prevent British from taking Cape of Good Hope
William Herschel discovers the planet Uranus
British surrender at Yorktown

Warren Hastings

Warren Hastings was the first British Governor General of India. He was a successful ruler, defending the East India Company's territories from attack by Indian princes and the French. Many Indian princes fought among themselves, and Hastings had to quell the civil wars and make alliances with friendly Indian rulers. To do all this with little help from home Hastings had to act in a sometimes ruthless manner, especially in raising money to pay for protecting the Indians.

Corruption was rife in India at the time, and though Hastings himself made only a moderate fortune, other 'nabobs', as wealthy English traders were known, were less scrupulous than he. When he returned to England his political enemies, headed by Edmund Burke, impeached him for corruption. He was cleared after a seven-year trial, but was financially crippled by paying for his defence.

The Canal Network

Most of the roads of 18th-century Britain were poor, and unsuitable for moving the heavy loads such as coal and iron required by the new industries. The easiest way to move such loads was by water, but this was only possible around the coast and along parts of some rivers. The solution was to dig canals, unknown in Britain since the Romans dug the first Fossdyke in Lincolnshire.

Britain's canal network was dug between 1757, when the 16-kilometre 'Sankey Navigation linked the St Helens coalfield to the Mersey, and 1847, when the Caledonian Canal in Scotland was completed. By that time the canals totalled about 6800 kilometres, but the more convenient railways were already taking away their traffic. The canals were dug by thousands of men, using picks and shovels and barrows. They were called *navvies*, short for navigators – a term still used today.

George Washington, who led the rebellious colonies in North America to independence. He worked as a surveyor when a young man, and fought against the French. In 1775 the Americans appointed him commander in chief of all their forces, and he proved an inspiring leader; he was also the one person who was trusted by nearly all the colonists. In 1789 he was inaugurated as the first president of the new United States.

Left: The settlement at Port Jackson, four years after its foundation in 1788 as the first of a number of British convict settlements in Australia. Earlier convicts had been transported to the American colonies, but this became impossible with American independence. Before long the convicts were followed by free settlers, who came to farm Australia's fertile lands. In 1851 the discovery of gold was announced, and as a result the continent's population doubled in the next ten years. Although many of the gold seekers were unsuccessful, they stayed on to farm.

1782 Spain captures Minorca from Britain
Whig ministry under Lord Rockingham
Wilkes wins support of Commons
Henry Grattan demands legislative freedom for Ireland
HMS *Royal George* capsizes at Spithead: 800 men drowned

1783 Britain grants Ireland right to pass her own laws
Duke of Portland heads a coalition
Peace of Versailles ends American War of Independence
Portland government defeated: William Pitt the Younger forms a ministry

1784 General Election: Pitt wins a large majority
India Act controls East India Company
First balloon ascent in England
Henry Cavendish discovers water is compound of oxygen and hydrogen

1785 Warren Hastings is recalled
First balloon crossing of the English Channel
Daily Universal Register (now called *The Times*) launched

1787 Sierra Leone founded as settlement for freed slaves
Edmund Burke impeaches Warren Hastings (trial 1788-95)

1788 Marylebone Cricket Club codifies cricket laws
Penal settlement established in Botany Bay, New South Wales
George III becomes insane

1789 Mutiny aboard HMS *Bounty*
George III recovers

1790 Wolfe Tone founds Society of United Irishmen
Firth-Clyde Canal completed
Pitt wins increased majority

The War With France

The French Revolution was regarded with fear by most British people, because they thought the movement might spread to Britain. The execution of the French King, Louis XVI, led Britain to form a coalition with Austria, Prussia, Spain, Portugal, Sardinia and the Netherlands against France.

The French had many victories on land, which were partly balanced by British victories at sea. The British seized Ceylon (Sri Lanka) and Cape Colony from the Dutch, who had been conquered by the French. When Spain became a French ally its fleet was defeated by Sir John Jervis off Cape St Vincent, and a Dutch fleet was beaten off Camperdown. When Russia tried to unite its fleet with those of Denmark and Sweden against Britain, Horatio Nelson and his more cautious commander-in-chief, Sir Hyde Parker, destroyed the Danish fleet off Copenhagen. Nelson had already destroyed a French fleet in the battle of the Nile, thus frustrating an attempt by Napoleon to make a permanent conquest of Egypt.

The Naval Mutinies

Although Britain depended on the navy for its safety, the sailors who served in its ships were treated abominably. Most were conscripted by the press gangs. Their pay was miserable: 7d (3p) a day for ordinary seamen, and 8½d (3½p) for able seamen. The food, supplied by villainous contractors, was almost uneatable. Discipline and punishment were severe, and conditions aboard ship appalling.

In 1797 the seamen of the fleet anchored at Spithead mutinied, asking for better pay and food, and the dismissal of about a hundred tyrannical officers. After some negotiation their demands were met. The fleet at the Nore, near Sheerness in the Thames, also mutinied, but their demands were more extreme. They did not get their way, and several of the ringleaders were hanged.

William Pitt (below) led the Tory government from 1783, when he became Chancellor of the Exchequer, First Lord of the Treasury and Prime Minister. He was only 24 years old. He remained in office until 1801 when he resigned, returning in 1804 until his death in 1806. He was the son of William Pitt, Earl of Chatham. At first most of the House was against him, but he had the support of the King and of the people, and at the next election they voted in his supporters. Pitt supported moderate parliamentary reform and a liberal trade and economic policy. In 1799 he introduced an income tax to help Britain pay for its wars with France. His early death from ill health took place not long after Britain's great naval victory at Trafalgar.

Charles James Fox, the brilliant Whig politician and orator, was Pitt's chief opponent. He was a man of great wit, charm and generosity, but he was a gambler and constantly in debt. His career in politics was blighted by his antagonism to George III.

The Rights of Man

One of the leading revolutionaries of the 18th century was the agitator and pamphleteer Thomas Paine. He won the friendship of Benjamin Franklin, and went to America. There he wrote many pamphlets and served in the Revolutionary forces. In 1787 he went to France, returning to England in 1791 to write *The Rights of Man*, a defence of the French Revolution.

Paine was promptly accused of treason, but before he could be tried he escaped to France. There he was made a French citizen, and served in the Convention. His outspokenness landed him in jail. He returned to America in 1802, and died there in 1809, aged 72.

1791 Britain increases navy
Ordnance Survey established
The Observer founded
Thomas Paine issues Part I of *The Rights of Man*
1792 William Murdock lights house in Cornwall by gas
William Tuke reforms treatment of lunatics at York Retreat
Mary Wollstonecraft writes *Vindication of the Rights of Women*
1793 France declares war on Britain
Britain seizes Corsica and French settlements in India
1794 Lord Howe defeats French fleet in the English Channel
Britain takes Seychelles, Martinique, St Lucia and Guadeloupe from France
1795 Lord Fitzwilliam, Lord Lieutenant, fails to carry through Catholic emancipation in Ireland
Dutch surrender Ceylon (Sri Lanka) to Britain
Hastings cleared of treason
Speenhamland System for poor relief begins
1796 Spain declares war on Britain
Ireland put under martial law
Edward Jenner vaccinates against smallpox
1797 Rebellion in Ulster quelled
Naval mutinies at the Nore and Spithead
1798 Irish rebellion quelled
Horatio Nelson wins naval battle of the Nile
Thomas Malthus writes *Essay on the Principle of Population*
1799 Income Tax first introduced
British army in Holland surrenders
1800 Britain captures Malta
Combination act forbids trades unions

Above: Linen-workers in County Down in Ireland, at the end of the 18th century. Over half the population in this area were Protestants, many descended from Protestant immigrant weavers from Scotland who had settled there in the early 17th century.

Union With Ireland

In 1801 the union of Britain with Ireland, a dream of English kings for hundreds of years, was finally brought about. The British Parliament was all for the union. The Irish Parliament hesitated, but it was a corrupt body, and when some of its Members were offered pensions, peerages and other inducements a majority was persuaded to vote for union, too. Only a few Irish Members, headed by Henry Grattan, fought to the last against it.

William Pitt, the British Prime Minister, had hoped to see a law passed to lift the ban on Roman Catholics holding office, including membership of Parliament. But here he was opposed by George III. This pleasant but obstinate monarch, hovering on the brink of insanity, believed that if he were to agree to such a step he would be breaking his Coronation oath to uphold the Church of England. To avoid driving the King over the brink into madness, Pitt gave way, and Catholic emancipation was delayed for almost 30 years. As a result, Ireland was at first represented in the Union Parliament only by its Protestant minority. And since Protestants and Catholics were, as now, at each others' throats, the situation in Ireland remained troubled.

The Young Hero

Despairing of Ireland's future, many Irishmen looked to France for help. Among them was a 24-year-old doctor's son, Robert Emmet. After visiting Napoleon in Paris Emmet believed the French would soon invade England, and decided to start a rebellion. But it was badly organized, and ended in complete chaos and betrayal by men who had been trusted. Emmet was hanged for treason outside the Church of St Mary's in Dublin, and has been revered as a hero by Irishmen ever since.

Below: Horatio Nelson led the British navy to an overwhelming victory over the French fleet at the battle of Trafalgar in 1805 but was shot in the moment of victory. In earlier battles he lost one eye and his right arm.

1801 Act of Union: Ireland becomes part of United Kingdom; present union flag adopted
Pitt resigns: Addington PM
Horatio Nelson wins naval victory off Copenhagen
British occupy Cairo
General Enclosure Act passed
Elgin Marbles brought from Athens
Iron tram-road laid from Croydon to Wandsworth, Surrey
Richard Trevithick builds a steam road carriage

1802 Peace between Britain and France
Health and Morals of Apprentices Act foreshadows Factory Acts
Thomas Telford begins building roads through the Highlands
John Dalton produces his atomic theory, and tables of atomic weights

1803 War with France is renewed
Irish patriot Robert Emmet rebels: is captured and executed
Caledonian Canal begun
Income Tax re-imposed

1804 Addington resigns: Pitt is PM
Spain declares war on Britain

1805 Battle of Trafalgar: Nelson dies defeating the French
Napoleon drops plans to invade Britain

1806 British occupy Cape of Good Hope
Pitt dies: Lord Grenville leads 'Ministry of all the Talents'
Sir Francis Beaufort designs his scale of wind force

1808 British army sent to Portugal: start of Peninsular War
British commander Sir John Moore killed at Corunna: succeeded by Arthur Wellesley
Dartmoor Prison opened

The Spanish Ulcer

The Peninsula War – so called because it took place in the Iberian Peninsula – was Britain's main contribution to the war against Napoleon. Spain was nominally ruled by Napoleon's brother Joseph, but its people, and the Portuguese, asked Britain's help. Napoleon called the Peninsular War the 'Spanish ulcer', because it drained away armies and money he needed for his conquests elsewhere.

The hero of the Peninsular War was Arthur Wellesley, who became, as his victories mounted up, successively a viscount, a marquis, and finally Duke of Wellington. After Napoleon abdicated in 1814 Wellington played a leading part at the Congress of Vienna, which tried to resettle Europe after the war. When Napoleon escaped and made himself emperor again in 1815 it was Wellington, aided by the Prussian Field Marshal von Blücher, who defeated him at the battle of Waterloo. The British exiled Napoleon to the lonely island of St Helena in the South Atlantic, where he died in 1821.

The Unnecessary War

The 'War of 1812' between Britain and the US need never have been fought. The Americans objected to British ships blockading Europe, and also stopping and searching American ships to look for British deserters. Britain, after many angry words, announced it would lift the blockade for American ships. But two days later, before word of this decision reached them, the Americans declared war.

Above: Sir Walter Scott (1771-1832), whose novels (many set in Scotland against a historical background) became enormously popular in the early 19th century.

Opposite, above: The novelist Jane Austen (1775-1817) described with wit and affection the lives of the upper middle class people of her time, in novels that are still much read today.

Right: George Gordon, Lord Byron (1788-1824), whose poems and exploits delightfully shocked the society of his time. He became a champion of liberty for oppressed peoples, and died of malaria while fighting for Greek independence.

The war included the burning of Washington DC. Britain's heaviest defeat, the battle of New Orleans, was fought 15 days after peace was signed in Europe.

1810 Arthur Wellesley (now Viscount Wellington) forces French to withdraw from Portugal
Durham miners strike

1811 US bans trade with Britain
George III goes permanently insane: son George is appointed Prince Regent
Luddites destroy machinery in Nottinghamshire and Yorkshire
Welsh Protestants leave the Anglican Church

1812 Wellington storms Ciudad Rodrigo. British capture Badajoz
PM Spencer Perceval assassinated at the Commons
US declares war on Britain
Wellington enters Madrid
Henry Bell's steamship *Comet* on the Clyde (maximum speed 7 knots)
Main streets of London lit by gas
Repeal of the Conventicle Act helps Protestant dissenters
Baptist Union formed

1813 US troops force Britain to abandon entire Niagara frontier
US warship *Chesapeake* captured
Wellington routs French at Vittoria: King Joseph Bonaparte of Spain flees to France
US naval victory on Lake Erie
British take Fort Niagara
Elizabeth Fry begins prison visits
William Hedley's *Puffing Billy*, smooth-wheeled locomotive

1814 Allies enter Paris
British burn Washington
Statute of Apprentices repealed
Treaty of Ghent ends war with US
Treaty of Paris ends war with France: Britain retains Malta
The Times printed by steam power
MCC first play cricket at Lord's

The Peterloo Massacre

Two of the burning issues of the early years of the 19th century were repeal of the corn laws, which kept corn and bread prices high, and the reform of Parliament. On August 16th 1819 a crowd of 80,000 gathered in St Peter's Fields, Manchester, to hear a speech by the radical agitator Henry Hunt (known as 'Orator' Hunt). The local magistrates decided to arrest Hunt and other leaders of the demonstration, but instead of doing so before the crowd gathered, they waited until the people were listening to Hunt, in an orderly manner, and then sent in the cavalry. In the ensuing scrimmage 11 people were killed and 400 injured. The incident became known as the Peterloo Massacre, an allusion to Waterloo.

'Prinny'

Although George IV was king for only 11 years, he had been ruler for nine years before that as Prince Regent for his insane father, George III. He was a complete contrast to his father. George III was a simple, kindly man, known to his subjects as 'Farmer George', and providing a moral example to his subjects through his virtuous ways of life. 'Prinny', as George IV was known, was clever, generous, a patron of the arts and a good linguist. But he was vain, a drunkard, a gambler and lazy, and faithless to both his friends and his many mistresses. His conduct disgusted even his close friend, George Brummell, known as 'Beau' Brummell because of the quiet elegance of his dress and his excellent taste.

Above: Arthur Wellesley, Duke of Wellington, served in the army in India and conducted the Peninsular War which drove the French from the Iberian peninsula. His ability to inspire his troops to hold a position against seemingly overwhelming odds earned him the nickname of the 'Iron Duke'. He commanded the Allied forces at the battle of Waterloo. After the war he turned to politics and was Prime Minister from 1828 to 1830, when he became unpopular for his resistance to reform. But he soon regained the affection of the British public, and when he died in 1852 he was buried in St Paul's cathedral.

Opposite: The Life Guards charge at the battle of Waterloo when Napoleon, returned from exile and at the head of a French army, was finally defeated by the British and Prussians.

1815 Apothecaries' Act stops unqualified doctors practising
Humphry Davy invents the miners' safety lamp
Battle of New Orleans: British defeated by Americans
Corn law prohibits corn imports
Battle of Waterloo: Napoleon defeated and sent to St Helena
Income Tax ends

1816 Poverty in England causes emigration to US and Canada

1817 March of the Blanketeers: Manchester protestors, each carrying a blanket, demand reform
The Scotsman newspaper founded

1818 Canadian-US border fixed at the 49th parallel
Vulcan: first all-iron sailing ship

1819 Britain gains Singapore
Peterloo Massacre: 11 killed when troops dispel mob in St Peter's Fields, Manchester
Working day for juveniles cut to 12 hours in England

1820 George III dies: succeeded by Prince Regent as George IV (to 1830)
First iron steamship launched

1821 *Manchester Guardian* founded

1822 Bottle Riots: Viceroy of Ireland attacked by Orangemen in Dublin
Royal Academy of Music founded

1823 Death penalty abolished for more than 100 crimes
Rugby football first played

1824 Combination Acts of 1799-1800, banning trades unions, repealed
RSPCA founded

1825 Stockton and Darlington Railway opens

1827 Robert Peel reforms criminal law

1828 Test Act repealed
Corn Law eases imports of corn

Parliamentary Reform

The Whigs – soon to be known as the Liberals – came to power in 1830, after almost 50 years in the political wilderness, and at once set about the long overdue question of Parliamentary reform. Parliamentary representation was chaotic and unfair. New industrial towns had grown up that had no Members while ancient constituencies returned Members with only a few electors. These 'Rotten Boroughs' as they were known included Old Sarum in Wiltshire, which had no houses, and Old Dunwich, in Suffolk, most of which was under the sea. Yet each returned two Members to Parliament, while Manchester and Birmingham were unrepresented.

The Act of 1832 sorted out most of these ridiculous seats, and local landowners lost their right to 'nominate' Members of Parliament. It also created

The early 19th century saw the start of the railway age in Britain. The first public railway was opened in 1825 and ran from Stockton to Darlington; the picture below shows part of a train of waggons at its opening. On the right is a cutting on the Liverpool to Manchester railway, opened five years later. With the coming of the railways, goods and people could be transported quickly, easily and relatively cheaply, and before long a vast network of railways linked all major towns in Britain.

455,000 new voters, twice as many as already existed, by giving the vote to town-dwellers occupying property worth at least £10 a year. This effectively meant merchants and shopkeepers and the growing middle classes.

Freedom for Roman Catholics
A few years before Parliament was reformed another injustice was righted. Roman Catholics, who had been barred from sitting in Parliament or holding public offices, were at last allowed to do so. The only posts barred to them were those of Lord High Chancellor or Lord-Lieutenant of Ireland, and no Roman Catholic could succeed to the throne. These restrictions still apply, except that there is no longer a Lord-Lieutenant of Ireland. Jews received a similar concession in 1858.

The Tolpuddle Martyrs
The Tolpuddle Martyrs were six labourers from Tolpuddle in Dorset who formed a trade union. Each took an oath of allegiance to the union, which was against the law. They were tried for this, found guilty, and sentenced to seven years' transportation to Botany Bay in Australia. But there was such an outcry that they were pardoned and brought back. Five of them emigrated to Canada.

1829 Roman Catholic Relief Act frees Catholics from discrimination
Metropolitan Police established
British ban *suttee* (suicide by widows) in Hindu India
Rainhill locomotive trials: George Stephenson's *Rocket* wins
First horse-drawn omnibus in London
First Oxford-Cambridge Boat Race
1830 George IV dies: succeeded by brother William IV (to 1837)
King's College, London, founded
Royal Geographical Society founded
1831 Reform battle begins: Lords reject Reform Bill
Electromagnetic induction discovered
Charles Darwin begins his voyage in HMS *Beagle*
James Clark Ross reaches North Magnetic Pole
1832 Reform Act passed
Geological Survey begins
Durham University founded
Book jackets first used
1833 Britain reaffirms sovereignty over Falkland Islands
Factory Acts: no under-nines to work in factories, nine-hour day for 9- to 13-year-olds
Slavery ends in British Empire
First State grant for education
1834 Tolpuddle Martyrs
Fire destroys Houses of Parliament
1835 Terms Liberal and Conservative begin to replace Whig and Tory
Local Government reformed
1836 Civil marriages become possible
London University founded
1837 Death of William IV: succeeded by niece, Victoria (to 1901)

The Age of Empire

The period from the accession of Queen Victoria to the outbreak of the First World War has been called the Age of Empires. During this time the British Empire reached its greatest extent, when it covered about one-fifth of the world's land area, and contained about a quarter of the world's then population. Because it was scattered right around the globe, it was called 'the Empire on which the Sun never sets'. British atlases traditionally showed the Empire in red.

Britain was not the only country to build an empire in the 19th century. There was an undignified scramble for colonies in Africa, and Britain, France, Germany and Italy all gained territories there. The German *Reich* – which means empire – was formed in 1871 by the amalgamation of all the German states except Austria and Hungary, which were also federated to form the Austro-Hungarian Empire. The Russian Empire expanded eastwards to its full present size; at one time it even included Alaska, which the Russians sold to the US for a price which worked out at 2 cents an acre (5 cents per hectare). In the Mediterranean region the Ottoman Empire, ruled by Turkey, declined.

The period was not without its share of revolutions: there was a spate of them in Europe in 1848, which became known as the 'Year of Revolutions'. A number of countries overthrew their monarchies and became republics.

The Victorian Age, the period to the death of Queen Victoria in 1901, was marked by its strict outward morality, its almost universal adherence to Christian worship, its enormous advances in science and technology, and above all by its firm belief that, however slowly, things were always improving in every way.

The Edwardian Period, the brief reign of Edward VII which followed, was a period of gradual freedom from the more restrictive aspects of the Victorian Age, but one which was overshadowed by the ever-growing threat of war.

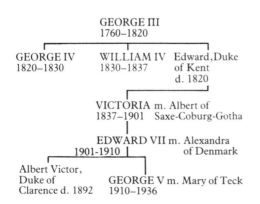

162

Above: The Victorian Era was a time of national pride in Britain's military glory, as shown by this poster depicting naval and military successes and commanders.

Opposite: When Queen Victoria came to the throne the monarchy was held in low esteem, frequently lampooned in the Press and despised for extravagance and immorality. Victoria, guided by her husband Prince Albert, revolutionized the image of the monarchy into one of high morality and hard work, giving the country a new set of ideals.

ELSEWHERE IN THE WORLD

1848 'Year of Revolutions' in Europe
Gold found in California
1852 Second French Empire
1854-6 Crimean War
1861 Italy unified
Civil War in US (to 1865)
1865 US President Lincoln assassinated
1867 Russia sells Alaska to US
1870-71 Franco-Prussian War
1871 German Empire proclaimed
1881 US President Garfield assassinated
1882 Triple Alliance between Germany, Austria and Italy
1886 Gold found in South Africa
1889 Brazil becomes a republic
1896 Gold found in the Yukon
1898 US-Spanish war of Cuba
US annexes Hawaii
1900 Germany starts arms race
1901 Russia occupies Manchuria
US President McKinley assassinated
1904-5 Russo-Japanese War
1905 Norway independent from Sweden
1906 San Francisco earthquake kills 700
1907 Triple Entente between Britain, France and Russia
1909 US explorer Robert Peary reaches the North Pole
1910 Japan annexes Korea
1911 Italy annexes Tripoli
Norwegian explorer Roald Amundsen reaches South Pole
China becomes a republic
1912 First Balkan War: Turkey defeated by Bulgaria, Greece, Montenegro and Serbia: Albania independent
1913 Second Balkan War: Bulgaria defeated by Greece, Romania, Serbia and Turkey

The Chartists

Chartism was a movement calling for political reform, its name being based on the People's Charter of 1838. Its main demands included votes for all males, voting by ballot, annual parliaments and payment for Members of Parliament. There were several outbreaks of Chartist agitation, including riots in 1839 when 24 people were killed at Newport and Birmingham. The movement eventually faded away because of indifferent leadership. But most demands were eventually met.

Time of Small Wars

Victoria's reign saw no conflicts on the scale of the Napoleonic Wars or the world wars, but there were plenty of small wars going on, many of them as Britain gradually expanded its empire.

There were three Afghan Wars, caused by Russian infiltration; the British were anxious to stop the Russians advancing into India.

The Opium War arose when the Chinese seized opium belonging to British merchants at Canton, in an effort to stop them trading in it. The British maintained that the Chinese had no right to do this. The war ended with a treaty in which China ceded Hong Kong to the British, who had taken it in the war.

In India there were always small wars going on to defend the East India Company's possessions, which over the years had come more and more under the control of the British government. After the Indian Mutiny of 1857 the British lands in India passed finally into government control.

Left: The Royal Family in 1846. Prince Albert was Victoria's first cousin; their marriage was outstandingly successful and when Albert died at the early age of 42 Victoria was devastated.

Below: Isambard Kingdom Brunel, a civil engineer who was remarkable for his versatility. He worked with his father, Sir Marc Brunel, on the first tunnel under the Thames between Rotherhithe and Wapping. A sudden flood injured him, and while he was convalescing he designed a suspension bridge over the Clifton gorge near Bristol. In 1833 he became chief engineer to the Great Western Railway company, at the age of 27. He built over 1600 kilometres (1000 miles) of railway, and many tunnels and bridges. He also built three ships: the 'Great Western', the first transatlantic steamship, in 1837; the 'Great Britain', the first large iron-hulled screw steamer, in 1843; and the 'Great Eastern', which laid the first successful transatlantic cable, in 1858. Other projects included a prefabricated hospital building for the Crimean War.

1837 Queen Victoria succeeds (to 1901)
Last use of pillory in England

1838 Manchester merchants form the Anti-Corn Law League
First Afghan War, to check Russian infiltration (to 1842)
Lord Durham sent to Canada to report after rebellion there
Working Men's Association sets up People's Charter, seeking reforms
National Gallery opened

1839 Parliament rejects Chartist petition: weeks of rioting follow
Anglo-Chinese opium war (to 1842)
W.H. Fox-Talbot invents light-sensitive photographic paper
Grand National first run at Aintree
Treadle bicycle invented

1840 Victoria marries Prince Albert of Saxe-Coburg-Gotha
Universal penny post introduced: first adhesive postage stamps
Electroplating invented
Treaty of Waitingi with Maoris gives Britain New Zealand

1841 *Punch* begins publication

1842 Mines Act bans women and children under 10 from working underground
US-Canada boundary defined
Edwin Chadwick heads commission on sanitary condition of the labouring population

1843 British forces conquer Sind, India
Maori War: revolt against British
Thames Tunnel is opened
474 clergy leave Scottish General Assembly to form United Free Church of Scotland
Steamship *Great Britain* launched
William Wordsworth appointed Poet Laureate
News of the World first published

The Factory Acts

Before the Industrial Revolution people tended to work at home in family units. When factories were set up the families went to work in them together, but in appalling conditions. The average age at which children began work was 8, but many started at 4, and one child was working in the lace trade at the age of 2. The working day was sometimes as long as 18 hours. In the mines, children were working in wet and darkness and foul air. Conditions were no better for their elders.

Beginning in 1833 a series of 40 Factory Acts was passed by Parliament to improve conditions. One of the most important was that of 1847, which cut working hours for women and children to 10 a day. This, and many other measures of a similar nature, were inspired by the seventh Earl of Shaftesbury. He is commemorated by a statue

For centuries Europeans trading with China had to pay for goods in gold and silver, since they produced nothing the Chinese wanted. But in the late 18th century the British began to trade with them in opium from India. The Emperor tried to stop this trade and in the war that followed the British seized many Chinese ports; this picture shows them seizing the town of Chinkiang. By the Treaty of Nanking in 1842 the British gained the island of Hong Kong and five ports were opened to foreign trade. From now on Britain gained more and more control over the coastal cities of China, and British gunboats even patrolled the great inland waterways.

in Piccadilly Circus, London, popularly called 'Eros' but intended to symbolize Christian charity. Shaftesbury was also a patron of the Ragged Schools, an early attempt to provide education for poor children. It was estimated that half the children in England and Wales could not read, though Scots children were better educated.

The Great Famine

Although Ireland grew large quantities of wheat and other crops most of this food was exported to the enrichment of absentee landlords, many living in Britain. About half of Ireland's 8 million people lived almost entirely on potatoes. Blight ruined the potato crop in 1845 and again in 1846, causing terrible suffering. Repeal of the Corn Laws, to allow the import of cheap corn from America, came too late to save many people. The Great Famine killed almost a million Irish, while 2 million more emigrated to America. The famine added to the bitter hatred for the British, which has persisted to this day.

Starving Irish peasants at the workhouse gates, 1846.

1844 Factory Act; Female workers limited to 12-hour day, 8- to 13-year-olds to 6½ hours
Ragged School Union co-ordinates schools for poor children
Rochdale Pioneers found the first Co-operative Society
First public baths and washhouses opened in Liverpool
YMCA founded
Leading Irish statesman Daniel O'Connell sentenced for sedition: House of Lords reverses verdict

1845 Maoris again rebel against the British in New Zealand
Export duties repealed, import duties ended or cut
Blight wrecks Irish potato crop
Robert William Thomson invents a pneumatic tyre

1846 Conservative PM Sir Robert Peel repeals the Corn Laws
Potato failure leads to severe famine in Ireland
Daily News founded, with Charles Dickens as editor

1847 Factory Act: 10-hour day for children aged 13 to 18 and women
Sir James Simpson uses chloroform as an anaesthetic
United Presbyterian Church of Scotland formed

1848 'Year of Revolutions' in Europe stimulates renewed Chartist demonstrations and petition to Parliament
Irish group led by Smith O'Brien rebel in Tipperary; suppressed
Irish famine ends, but thousands emigrate to America
Public Health Act improves sanitation

1849 Bedford College for Women, London, established
Rebellion in Montreal

Fighting Disease

The cholera epidemic of 1854, which killed 52,293 people, was the third such epidemic of the century. It spurred people to fight the disease by improving sanitation in the bigger cities, where the worst mortality occurred.

In London the work was entrusted to the engineer Sir Joseph Bazalgette. His task was to provide a system of sewers which would not only drain off surface water, but also take household sewage: at that time householders had to use cess-pits, emptied perhaps once a year, and were forbidden to discharge into the sewers.

Bazalgette constructed five major sewers, into which a network of smaller ones flowed. One of the main sewers runs under the Embankment, which was built for that purpose. Beside it runs the District Underground Railway. Balzagette's sewers, thanks to careful design and maintenance, have remained in use for over a century.

Fighting Pain

Surgery was carried out without anaesthetics until the mid-1800s. The first experiments with anaesthesia were made in the US, but an important step forward came when the Scottish physician Sir James Simpson developed the use of chloroform to ease the pains of childbirth. The new painkiller was given great support when Queen Victoria used it for the birth of her eighth child, Prince Leopold.

Charles Dickens (1812-70) wrote a large number of immensely popular novels, many appearing in instalments. He was deeply concerned by the problems of poor people; these are movingly described in many of his books, and he also took an active part in schemes to help the poor.

Opposite: The Great Exhibition was the brainchild of Prince Albert, who designed it as a festival of work and peace. The government refused to finance it, but the private guarantors Albert had to find were not out of pocket: the exhibition was visited by 6 million people and made a handsome profit. A huge steel and glass hall, like a giant greenhouse, was built to house the exhibition, and erected in only seven weeks. It was designed by the gardener-architect Sir Joseph Paxton, and people promptly called it the 'Crystal Palace'. After the exhibition it was removed to Sydenham as a museum, and exhibition and concert hall. It was destroyed by fire in 1936.

1850   Anglo-Kaffir War in Africa
Tenant Right League founded in Ireland
Britain buys Gold Coast forts from Denmark
Local authorities empowered to start public libraries
1851   Window Tax abolished
The Great Exhibition
Yacht *America* wins the Queen's Cup race round Isle of Wight (now called America's Cup)
First double-decker bus
First cable laid under the Channel
1852   British annex part of Burma
Britain gives New Zealand a new constitution
1853   William Gladstone's first budget cuts or ends duties on foodstuffs
Peace in Burma
Advertisement Tax repealed
Queen Victoria has chloroform for birth of eighth child
Smallpox vaccination compulsory
1854   Crimean War: Britain, France, Turkey, Sardinia against Russia
Siege of Sevastopol
Florence Nightingale pioneers modern nursing
Cholera epidemic kills 52,293
Millwall Docks, London, opened
1855   Fall of Sevastopol
Newspaper stamp duty abolished
Establishment of responsible government in most of Australia
Chemist Alexander Parkes invents xylonite (early form of celluloid)
Dried milk powder invented
Daily Telegraph first published
London sewers modernized
YWCA founded
Missionary David Livingstone finds the Victoria Falls

The Crimean War

The Crimean War was basically a fight between Russia and Turkey. The Russians felt that the Muslim Turks had failed to deal fairly with Christians in their Balkan territories, or in the question of access to the 'Holy Places' in Palestine. They also wanted access through the Bosporus and Dardanelles for their warships. Two years' negotiations broke down, and the countries went to war. British and French fleets entered the Black Sea to protect Turkish coasts, and Britain and France were quickly drawn in on Turkey's side. Sardinia later joined the conflict against Russia.

The allies landed in the Crimea and besieged the Russian fortress of Sevastopol. The allies won three battles against the Russians, at the Alma River, Balaclava, and Inkerman. Disease and bad weather took a fearful toll of both sides. Eventually Sevastopol fell, and soon afterwards peace was made. The Turks guaranteed the rights of Christian subjects, and Russia ceded some small amounts of territory.

The Indian Mutiny

There were several causes for the Indian Mutiny. The army of Bengal was composed of Indian troops with British officers. Discipline was poor, and the westernization of India which was being imposed – which included the abolition of old customs such as *suttee* (widows lying on their husbands' funeral pyres) and infanticide – was not universally popular.

The flashpoint was the issue of cartridges greased with animal fat. The *sepoys* (Indian soldiers) had to bite the ends off the cartridges, and so taste the fat: this contravened both the Hindu and Muslim religions. On 10th May 1857 sepoys at Meerut, 65 kilometres north of Delhi, shot their British officers and then captured Delhi. The mutiny spread quickly through the Bengal army.

The course of the mutiny was marked by the massacre of British prisoners by the mutineers, and the bloody revenge taken by the British, and the Sikhs who supported them, when suppressing the revolt.

The result of the mutiny was that the British government took control of India from the commercially-minded directors of the East India Company. and thoroughly reorganized the Indian army.

The battle of Balaclava on October 25th 1854. In appalling confusion, 670 men of the Light Brigade attacked the main Russian artillery positions instead of an isolated outpost. The Crimean War became notorious for the inefficiency of its commanders, made public by the war correspondent W.H. Russell of The Times.

1856 Victoria Cross instituted
Treaty of Paris ends Crimean War
William H. Perkins makes first aniline dye (mauve)
Big Ben cast at Whitechapel
War with Persia (to 1857)

1857 Anglo-Chinese War (to 1858)
Indian Mutiny begins: Massacre of Cawnpore (Kanpur), relief of Lucknow
Matrimonial Causes Act: divorce courts set up in England and Wales
Albert created Prince Consort
National Portrait Gallery opens
Charles Hallé founds Hallé Orchestra in Manchester

1858 Indian Mutiny ends
Government takes over control of India from East India Company
Jews allowed to sit in Parliament and hold office
Charles Darwin and Alfred Russel Wallace announce theory of evolution of species

1859 Samuel Smiles publishes *Self Help* – manual on how to succeed in life
Scottish National Gallery opened

1860 Second Maori War in New Zealand
Last bare-knuckle boxing match in England: 42-round draw
First modern Welsh Eisteddfod
British Open Golf Championship begins
Bronze coinage replaces copper

1861 *Trent* affair: US warship seizes Confederate emissaries on British ship. Clash narrowly avoided
Prince Consort dies of typhoid
Paper duties repealed
Isabella Beeton: *Book of Household Management*
Daily weather forecasts begin

The First Dominion

Having lost one North American empire, Britain was anxious not to lose another. When trouble was brewing in Canada, Lord Durham was sent as a special high commissioner to examine the situation. He reported that the best way to keep Canada was to give the colonists self-government.

At first only Upper and Lower Canada (now Ontario and Quebec) were united, but after a few years in which more and more power was devolved to the colonists, New Brunswick and Nova Scotia agreed to join in an almost completely independent country, the Dominion of Canada. It was the first of the great self-governing Dominions which were to help turn the British Empire into the present-day Commonwealth of Nations.

Florence Nightingale at work in the wards of Scutari Hospital. The daughter of wealthy parents, she trained as a nurse against their wishes, and early in the Crimean War took 38 nurses to Scutari where she organized a barrack hospital. She was an exceptionally good administrator and brought down the death rate in Scutari hospitals from 42 per cent to 2.2 per cent.

Safer Surgery

With the development of anaesthesia, surgery could be painless as well as skilled. But a high proportion of patients died from infected wounds and gangrene. When the French scientist Louis Pasteur proved that infection was caused by organisms in the air, the English surgeon Joseph Lister began experiments in treating wounds with chemicals to destroy the organisms. He began the practice of antiseptic surgery which has saved millions of lives.

The Climbing Boys

Charles Kingsley's delightful fantasy *The Water Babies*, described as a fairytale, exposed one cruel practice of the 19th century. Sweeps used to send little boys up chimneys to clean them, which they found easier (for themselves) than using a long brush. The book appeared in 1863, and the next year Parliament passed an Act against this ill-treatment of children. Magistrates and local authorities still connived at the practice, which was finally stamped out by a further, stiffer Act in 1875.

Charles Darwin (1809-1882) sailed as naturalist on a surveying expedition to South America and Australasia from 1832 to 1836. He worked out a new theory of evolution by natural selection which aroused a great deal of controversy, as did his theory that humans were descended from an ape-like ancestor.

1862 England cricket team visit Australia
First Roman Catholic monastery in England since the Reformation founded in Suffolk
John Speke becomes the first European to enter Uganda

1863 Football Association founded
Work begins on London Underground Railway (world's first)
James Clerk Maxwell suggests existence of electromagnetic waves
Broadmoor opened for criminally insane prisoners

1864 Britain cedes Ionian Isles to Greece
Octavia Hill begins reform of tenement buildings in London
Metropolitan Railway, London, opens
Sir Samuel White Baker discovers Lake Albert
Metric system approved in Britain, but only for scientific work
Chimney Sweeps Act forbids use of children
Clifton Suspension Bridge, Bristol, is opened

1865 William Booth founds Christian Mission
Lewis Carroll publishes *Alice's Adventures in Wonderland*

1866 First successful transatlantic cable
Elizabeth Garrett Anderson opens dispensary for women
Dr T.J. Barnardo opens home for waifs
Marquess of Queensberry's boxing rules adopted

1867 Canada becomes the first Dominion
Parliamentary Reform Act gives more people the vote

Dr David Livingstone arrives at Lake Ngami in southern Africa in 1849. Africa was the last great continent to be explored by Europeans, who were put off exploration of the interior by the climate, the dangers of disease and the difficulties of travel inland. In 1788 the Association for Promoting the Discovery of the Interior Parts of Africa was set up in London which began to send expeditions to explore the continent. Livingstone, who went to Africa as a missionary, travelled far into unknown parts of the continent, exploring the Zambezi and Congo rivers and discovering the Victoria Falls and Lake Nyasa. He died in 1873. Europeans decided to set up colonies in Africa and at one time war between them was only narrowly averted. The Africans could do little to stop this. Britain acquired much of southern and eastern Africa.

Transportation

The punishment of transportation, which ended in 1868, began in the reign of Elizabeth I. It was an extension of the older punishment of banishment or exile. The British established penal settlements, to which convicts could be sent, in North America. After the American War of Independence this area was closed to such use, so Australia was opened up as a new place for penal colonies. More than 174,000 convicts were sent there, for varying periods from a few years to life. Many settled there after their release.

The Growth of Unions

The first trade unions came into existence early in the 1700s. They ran into trouble in 1799 when they were banned because they might be a revolutionary danger – at a time when the excesses of the French Revolution were on people's minds.

This ban was lifted in 1824, and after that unions grew apace, as did strikes against poor wages and bad conditions.

Some were ruthless in their methods: Sheffield cutlery workers were known to drop a keg of gunpowder down the chimney of a fellow-worker who did not follow the line. But most were prudent and responsible, and the Trade Union Act of 1871, making the unions officially and finally legal, also gave them certain rights and protection for their funds. The law was the result of pressure from the newly formed Trades Union Congress.

Victorian Literature
The literature of the late Hanoverian period was Romantic, as exemplified in the novels of Sir Walter Scott and the poems of William Wordsworth. Victorian novelists, poets and other writers reflected much more the social changes and problems of the day. The abject life of the poor was drawn with brutal skill by Charles Dickens in books such as *Oliver Twist*. William Thackeray wrote satires on the life of high society, and Mrs Gaskell depicted life in the new manufacturing cities of the north.

The strong and sometimes austere religious faith of the time was mirrored by many lesser writers, especially those aiming at young readers. A typical such author was A.L.O.E. (A Lady of England, the pen-name of Charlotte Maria Tucker). Her highly moral tales were often given as Sunday School prizes. The stories of Charlotte M. Yonge, in contrast, conveyed High Church teachings. Anna Sewell's one book, *Black Beauty* did much to awaken people to the cruel treatment often meted out to horses.

1868 Transportation to Australia ends
Benjamin Disraeli (Tory) becomes PM for the first time
Britain annexes Basutoland
Third Maori War in New Zealand
General Election: William Gladstone (Liberal) becomes PM
Trades Union Congress formed
Whitaker's Almanack first issued
Semaphore traffic signals installed near Westminster Abbey
No under-8s allowed to work on farms
1869 Irish Church disestablished
Debtors' prisons abolished
Slum clearance begins
Clipper *Cutty Sark* launched
1870 Married Women's Property Act gives women greater control of their own property
Education Act sets up school boards
1871 Local Government Boards set up in England
Trades unions formally legalized
Army reorganized: purchase of commissions abolished
Kimberley diamond field annexed
H.M. Stanley meets David Livingstone at Ujiji, Lake Tanganyika
Bank holidays introduced in England and Wales
FA Cup competition established
Oceanic: first large luxury liner
1872 Secret ballot for elections introduced by the Ballot Act
HMS *Challenger* begins mapping the ocean bed (to 1876)
First international football match, England v Scotland
1873 Supreme Court and Court of Appeal established
Anglo-Ashanti War
W.C. Wingfield invents game of *Spharistiké* (now lawn tennis

Via Kew to the Far East

A royal gift was indirectly responsible for a major industry in Malaysia, Indonesia and other Far Eastern countries. In 1759 Princess Augusta, mother of George III, set aside part of the gardens of Kew Palace for plant experiments. It is now the Royal Botanic Gardens, Kew, world famous as a centre of botanical studies.

The demand for rubber grew rapidly in the 19th century, but the only source of supplies was South America. The British government decided to cultivate rubber in its newly acquired lands in the Far East. Rubber seeds were collected in Brazil and shipped to Kew Gardens, where they were raised. In 1877 2000 young plants were shipped to Ceylon (Sri Lanka) in special containers, and from there distributed to other countries. Today Malaysia and Indonesia between them produce 90 per cent of the world's supply of natural rubber.

The Suez Canal

When France and the Turkish rulers of Egypt undertook the construction of the Suez Canal in 1859 – it opened ten years later – British traders welcomed it, but the British government opposed it as a threat to communications with India.

Sixteen years later the spendthrift khedive (viceroy) of Egypt was short of money, and offered his shares in the Suez Canal Company to Britain. The Prime Minister, Benjamin Disraeli, was more farseeing than his predecessors or than the Foreign Office and the foreign secretary, Lord Derby, who poohpoohed the idea. Disraeli overruled

The two outstanding political leaders of the 1870s and 1880s were William Ewart Gladstone (1809-98; above) and Benjamin Disraeli (1804-81; opposite). Gladstone was a sound financier and an earnest philanthropist. Leader of the Liberal Party from 1867, he was Prime Minister 1868-74, 1880-85, in 1886, and 1892-94. Disraeli was of Jewish descent; he was Conservative Prime Minister in 1868 and from 1874 to 1880. He introduced a number of reforms and had an active foreign policy; on his own responsibility he bought the khedive of Egypt's interest in the Suez Canal for Britain, and had Queen Victoria assume the title Empress of India. He was a most witty and attractive man, and was adept in dealing with Queen Victoria who personally much preferred him to Gladstone.

Derby, and promptly bought the shares for £4,080,000. He borrowed the money from the international bankers Rothschilds until Parliament could vote the necessary funds.

Wars in Africa

Britain was involved in two wars in southern Africa in three years.

The Zulu War began when a large Zulu army under King Cetewayo threatened the Transvaal. The Boers of the Transvaal sought British protection. The local commander sent a force into Zululand, only to have it cut up by the Zulus. Reinforcements from Britain had to be brought in to subdue the Zulus.

The First Boer War broke out when the Boers of the Transvaal tried to recover their independence, which they had given up when they sought aid against the Zulus. After they defeated the British at Majuba Hill the independence of the Transvaal was again recognized, though the British kept control of its external relations.

1874 Conservatives win election: first clear majority since 1841
Britain annexes Fiji
1875 Public Health Act: rules for sanitation for all house-owners
Britain buys shares in Suez Canal
Plimsoll Line introduced to stop overloading of ships
Artisans' Dwellings Act: local councils empowered to clear slums
Food and Drugs Act controls substances added to food
Matthew Webb: first man to swim the English Channel
First Gilbert and Sullivan opera: *Trial by Jury*
1876 Disraeli becomes Earl of Beaconsfield
Grey squirrel introduced from US
1877 Queen Victoria is proclaimed Empress of India
Britain annexes Walvis Bay and the Transvaal
First Wimbledon championships
1878 Irish National Land League formed
Electric street lighting in London
First British telephone company
William Booth names his mission the Salvation Army
Red Flag Act: Steam road vehicles limited to 4 mph (6.4 kph), and to be preceded by a man with a red flag
1879 Zulu War
Afghans murder British legation: Britain invades Afghanistan
Worst crop failure of the century
London's first telephone exchange
First railway dining-car in Britain
Tay Bridge collapses in gale
William Crookes develops the cathode ray tube

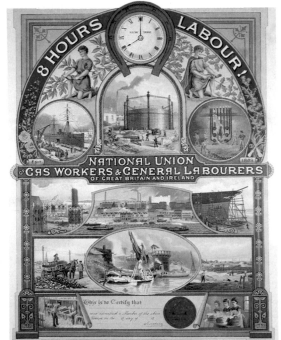

The 19th century saw the growth of the trades union movement in Britain. In 1834 the 'Tolpuddle Martyrs', six agricultural workers, were sentenced to seven years' transportation for swearing an illegal oath; they had sworn an initiation oath when forming a branch of a union. They became symbols of the demand for freedom to form associations; and there were many protests against their sentence, such as the procession shown above. After this time initiation oaths were dropped, and permanent organizations of workers increased steadily.

Left: The banner of the National Union of Gas Workers and General Labourers, one of the mass workers' organizations founded in the 1880s.

The Bradlaugh Case

In English Law, an oath is an appeal to God to witness the truth of a statement. To help people whose religion is against oaths, the Law allows affirmation – a solemn declaration of truth. But when the freethinker Charles Bradlaugh was elected a Member of Parliament it was found that the rules of the House of Commons did not allow affirmation, and he was excluded.

Bradlaugh offered to take the oath – and was again excluded on the grounds that as he was a freethinker the oath would not be binding. His constituents re-elected him three times, and each time he was ejected from the House, on one occasion by ten policemen. Finally in 1886 Mr Speaker Peel ruled that he could take the oath. As an MP, Bradlaugh persuaded the Commons to change the rules to allow affirmation.

The First Boycott

When crop failures in 1879 threatened a new Irish famine, the Irish Land League was formed to fight for tenants' rights. The next year the land agent for the Earl of Erne's estates in County Mayo refused a call by the League to cut rents, and instead proceeded to evict a number of tenants. The League organized a conspiracy to 'send him to Coventry'; nobody spoke to him, and shops refused to serve him. He had to call in volunteers from Ulster, guarded by troops, to bring in the harvest. He soon went back to England. His name was Charles Cunningham Boycott, and the verb 'to boycott' has since passed into common use.

1880 Flogging abolished in navy
Relief of Distress Act for Ireland
Employers' Liability Act
Education up to age 12 compulsory
Parcel post introduced in England
Transvaal declares independence
1881 Transvaal Boers defeat the British, who recognize their independence
Land Act attempts to give fairer deal to Irish tenants. Charles Stewart Parnell, MP, and others jailed for opposing the Act
Flogging abolished in the army
Postal orders first issued
1882 Phoenix Park murders: Fenians kill Lord Frederick Cavendish, chief secretary for Ireland, and Thomas Burke, permanent under-secretary
British troops crush revolt in Egypt against Ottoman khedive
Preliminary work on Channel Tunnel
1883 Irish terrorists try to blow up *The Times* office in London
Boys' Brigade founded
Royal College of Music established
Royal Red Cross Order founded
1884 Third Reform Bill: electorate increased to 5,000,000
Fabian Society founded
Work starts on *New English Dictionary* (to 1928; now Oxford E.D.)
Charles Parsons makes first practical steam turbine generator
1885 The Mahdi revolts in Sudan: British governor General Charles Gordon slain
First Secretary of State for Scotland appointed
Francis Galton proves individuality of fingerprints

Scramble for Africa

The interior of Africa was largely unexplored by Europeans until the 19th century. Then it was opened up by a series of British, French and German explorers. Among them were the Scottish missionary David Livingstone, Henry Morton Stanley, who went to look for Livingstone when he was feared lost, Samuel White Baker, Dixon Denham, and the brothers John and Richard Lander.

Britain and France were the first in the field in what became a race to grab colonies. Other colonial powers included Italy, Germany, Spain, Belgium, and Portugal. By 1902, there were only two independent countries left, Ethiopia and Liberia. The Union of South Africa was then part of the British Empire. The European powers even held a conference in Berlin in 1884-85 to divide Africa between them.

Ruined by Divorce

For 13 years the Irish Home Rule movement was led by Charles Stewart Parnell, a Member of Parliament regarded as the 'uncrowned king' of Ireland. He was, unexpectedly, a landlord, Anglo-Irish and a Protestant. But his deep love of Ireland, matched by an equally strong loathing for Britain, won him the support of all Irish Catholics. William Gladstone, the Liberal statesman, relied on him for support in his campaign to get Home Rule through the House of Commons.

At the height of his power and influence, Parnell was cited in a divorce action brought by Captain W.H. O'Shea against his wife, Katherine. At first Parnell's Party supported him, but when Gladstone opposed him on moral grounds they turned against him, and his political career came to a sudden end.

The Widow of Windsor

After the death of Prince Albert, Queen Victoria went into deep and apparently permanent mourning. Though she dealt with Ministers and State papers as assiduously as before, she made few public appearances, refusing even to open Parliament each year. She was irreverently dubbed 'the Widow of Windsor'. Her Golden Jubilee, however, brought her out of her seclusion, and she was seen in public more after that time.

In the late 19th century a second Industrial Revolution took place. Coal and iron were still important but were overtaken by steel, electricity, oil and chemicals. Many of the chemicals were produced from the by-products of coal, including explosives, fertilizers, dyes and later drugs and fibres. Electricity provided a new source of light, heat and power, and was used to drive machinery and to provide lighting for streets, factories and homes. It brought power into the home for small appliances. Left: A South Wales coalfield; below: London's first Deptford power station.

1886 British annex Upper Burma
Irish Home Rule Bill defeated
Liberals split: some form Liberal Unionist Party
Severn Tunnel opened
Tilbury Docks, Essex, opened

1887 Queen Victoria's Golden Jubilee
Britain annexes Zululand
Bloody Sunday: Trafalgar Square protest over jailing of Irish nationalist William O'Brien
Sir Thomas More, John Fisher, and other English martyrs canonized
Coal Mines Act: no boys under 13 allowed to work underground

1888 County councils established
John Boyd Dunlop re-invents the pneumatic tyre
The Financial Times first issued
Football League is founded
Jack the Ripper murders prostitutes in Whitechapel, London
Miners' Federation founded

1889 Major London dock strike
London County Council set up
Secondary Education for Wales established

1890 Parnell sued for divorce: Liberal Party disowns him
Elementary education is made free
First London Tube Railway opened
Forth Bridge (rail) opened

1891 Liberals adopt programme dedicated to Home Rule
Leeds has Britain's first electric tramcar system

1892 Dam across river Vyrnwy, North Wales, to supply water to Liverpool
C.F. Cross develops viscose rayon
William Gladstone (Liberal) forms his last government at 80

Father of the Labour Party

Keir Hardie, more than anyone else, helped in the formation of the Labour Party and its early growth. Hardie had an arduous upbringing. He never went to school, but from the age of 10 worked in the Lanarkshire mines. He educated himself at night school.

Hardie learned public speaking on temperance platforms, and became an active trade unionist and a journalist. In 1888 he founded the Scottish Parliamentary Labour Party. In 1892 he was elected Independent Socialist MP for West Ham, and a year later started the Independent Labour Party (ILP). A few years later he was the prime mover in founding the Labour Representation Committee, which evolved into the modern Labour Party.

'The Chief'

Modern popular journalism was founded by Alfred Harmsworth (1865-1922), who became Lord Northcliffe in 1905. Sensing that with free education there was a growing public for newspapers, he launched the *Daily Mail*, described as 'a penny newspaper for one half-penny'.

Though the *Daily Mail's* early issues, with advertisements on the front page and small, staid headlines, would look 'heavy' by today's standards, the news was clearly displayed and tightly edited. In three years it had double the circulation of any other paper. 'The Chief', as Northcliffe was known to his staff, kept a close eye on everything. At his insistence, the *Daily Mail* backed motoring, aviation and polar exploration.

The Empire Builder

One of the most influential men in the history of southern Africa was Cecil Rhodes. A parson's son, he went to Natal from England at the age of 17 because his health was poor. He made a fortune in the Kimberley diamond mines, while paying frequent visits to Oxford to study for a degree. When gold was discovered in the Transvaal, Rhodes made another fortune. He went into politics, and by 1890 was premier of Cape Colony. He acquired the rights

to develop Matabeleland and Mashonaland and formed them into the colony of Rhodesia (now Zimbabwe).

Rhodes was brought down by his friend, Dr Leander Starr Jameson. Jameson led an armed raid into the Transvaal to try to overthrow the Boer government, which was denying voting and other rights to the *Uitlanders,* or foreign workers, in the goldfields. Jameson's raid failed. Rhodes was blamed for the raid, and had to resign as premier. Ironically Jameson, after serving a jail sentence in Britain for his act of aggression, returned to Cape Colony and became its premier.

Rhodes, who died in 1902 aged 49, left his fortune to create the Rhodes Scholarships to Oxford University, open to Commonwealth, German and US students.

Below: In 1897 Queen Victoria celebrated her Diamond Jubilee – 60 years on the throne, which had seen Britain developing into the leading industrial and colonial nation. The Queen had brought the country great stability, and while she had learnt not to take part in Party politics, her experience and advice were greatly valued by her ministers.

1893	Keir Hardie forms Independent Labour Party
	Uganda becomes a British protectorate
	Lords reject second Home Rule Bill
	University of Wales formed
	Manchester Ship Canal completed
	Liverpool overhead railway built
1894	Death Duties introduced
	Parish councils established
	James Dewar liquifies oxygen
	Blackpool Tower opened
1895	Togoland annexed by Britain
	Cecil Rhodes creates Rhodesia
	London School of Economics founded
	National Trust established
	Westminster cathedral begun
	First Promenade Concert season
	First London motor-car exhibition
	Jameson Raid
1896	Fourth Ashanti War
	Matabeles rebel in Rhodesia
	Guglielmo Marconi patents wireless in England
	Alfred Harmsworth (later Lord Northcliffe) starts the *Daily Mail*
	Red Flag Act repealed: speed limit raised to 14 mph (23 kph)
1897	Victoria's Diamond Jubilee
	Britain occupies Benin in protest at human sacrifices
	Royal Automobile Club founded
	Joseph Chamberlain's suggestion of Anglo-German alliance is poorly received
	Battle of Omdurman gives Anglo-Egyptian control of Sudan
	Sale of Church livings ends
	Waterloo-City Railway electrified
	W. Ramsay and M.W. Travers discover neon, krypton and xenon gases

The Second Boer War

The Second Boer War followed from the Jameson Raid of 1895, and had much the same cause. Britain supported the political rights of the *Uitlanders* (foreign workers) which the Boer rulers of the Transvaal refused. Thousands of the Uitlanders were British, and they sent a petition to Queen Victoria asking for help. Prolonged talks broke down, and the Boers declared war. They were supported by the Orange Free State, also Boer-governed.

The Boers, who greatly outnumbered the British, invaded Cape Colony and laid siege to Kimberley, Ladysmith and Mafeking. Mafeking was defended by Col. Robert Baden-Powell, later renowned as the founder of the Boy Scout movement. When it was relieved rejoicing in London was so extreme that a new verb, *to maffick*, or rejoice riotously, was coined.

Reinforcements were sent from England, and gradually the British conquered the country, though the Boers carried on a guerrilla campaign for 18 months. Boer farms were burned and women and children were concentrated in internment camps known as *concentration camps* – the first use of the term.

The peace treaty ending the war annexed Transvaal and Orange Free State, but promised them self-government, which they were given in 1907.

The Boxers

European traders became increasingly active in China at the end of the 19th century and many Chinese feared that they threatened the country's independence. A secret society called 'The Society of Harmonious Fists' (popularly called Boxers by the Europeans) was formed to fight this supposed threat. In 1900 the Boxers and other societies rose against the foreigners, killing 231 civilians and many Chinese Christians. An international force restored order, and China agreed to pay compensation.

The Prince of Wales boards a motor car for the first time in July 1900. He was a genial man who loved racing, shooting and the theatre; he was immensely popular with his people, and perhaps surprisingly conscientious in undertaking his public duties. His mother had allowed him to play little real part in affairs of state; when he came to the throne as Edward VII, he was particularly careful to see that his heir, the future George V, should be fully aware of what was going on.

The 'Entente Cordiale'

Several years of disputes between Britain and France over overseas territories – which at one stage almost led to war – were ended by the signing of an *entente* (understanding), which became popularly known as the *Entente cordiale*. The French, who had been most hostile, were won over by the charm of Edward VII during a State visit to Paris in 1903.

The Australian Commonwealth

The success of the first independent Dominion – Canada – paved the way for the creation of a second. The six Australian states were separate colonies, but their leaders came to realize that some form of union was needed. None of the colonies was willing to give up its independence, so in the end a federal form of government was agreed on.

The Commonwealth of Australia came into being on the first day of 1901. It was the last major event in the long reign of Queen Victoria, which came to an end 21 days later.

The Wireless

Radio communication, on which scientists from many countries had been working for years, was finally achieved by an Italian, Guglielmo Marconi. Receiving little encouragement in Italy, Marconi went to England, where he found all the help he needed. He patented his invention in Britain, and set up a company to exploit it. It was from Britain – Poldhu in Cornwall – that he sent the first transatlantic message by 'wireless telegraphy', the Morse letter S, picked up in Newfoundland.

1899 Second Boer War begins (to 1902)
London borough councils established
First motor-buses in London
First radio transmission from England to France
1900 Labour Representation Committee: to work for Labour group in Parliament
British relieve sieges of Ladysmith and Mafeking
Britain annexes Tonga, Orange Free State and Transvaal
Boxer Rising against foreigners in China: Britain helps suppress it
Quaker George Cadbury founds Bourneville Village Trust
Arthur Evans begins excavations in Crete
Daily Express founded
New university: Birmingham
1901 Queen Victoria dies; succeeded by son, Edward VII (to 1910)
Australia becomes a Dominion
First petrol-driven motor-cycle
First British submarine launched
Marconi sends radio signal from Cornwall to Newfoundland (letter S)
1902 Order of Merit established
Oliver Heaviside discovers ionosphere
1903 Britain conquers northern Nigeria
Beginning of *Entente Cordiale*
Car speed limit set at 20 mph (32 kph)
Emmeline Pankhurst starts suffragettes
Letchworth Garden City established
First motor-taxis in London
Liverpool cathedral begun
Daily Mirror founded
Universities of Liverpool and Manchester established

New Zealand

The third of the great Dominions, which were in time to transform the British Empire into the British Commonwealth of Nations, was New Zealand. The country had its own government from 1852, and Britain transferred more and more power to it over the years.

Finally in 1907 New Zealand was proclaimed as a Dominion, with full internal self-government. Britain retained control over defence and external affairs. But in practice, though it relied on Britain for defence, New Zealand was free to conduct its own external

Right: In 1909, when the House of Lords tried to block Lloyd George's tax reforms, he threatened to have enough Liberal peers created to defeat the Conservative majority. After two general elections the Parliament Act of 1911 limited the power of the Lords to stop them blocking such legislation.

affairs, a position regularized by the Statute of Westminster in 1931.

Much of New Zealand's progress to independence was the work of Richard Seddon, its prime minister from 1893 to his death in 1906. Seddon introduced votes for women in 1893, 25 years before Britain.

UNDER WHICH FLAG?

THE PEOPLE'S BUDGET

THE POOR BUT PITY HONEST DUKES

Which is your side in the great fight—

PEERS OR PEOPLE?

Opposite: Suffragettes in 1908 celebrating the release of two of their members from Holloway prison. These militant campaigners for votes for women tried to draw attention to their cause by interrupting political meetings, chaining themselves to railings, breaking windows, and later even by arson, slashing pictures and throwing bombs. When imprisoned, many went on hunger strike. Their violence turned people against them and more valuable work was done by the National Union of Women's Suffrage Societies, who kept within the law. The First World War proved the essential part women could play outside the home, and in 1918 women over 30 who were householders or wives of householders were given the vote.

1904 Workers' Educational Association begins
Frederick Kipping discovers silicones
J.A. Fleming invents thermionic valve
London Symphony Orchestra founded
Leeds University founded

1905 Automobile Association established
First public cinema shows in London
Sheffield University founded

1906 Liberals win landslide election. 29 Labour MPs elected: Labour Representation Committee changes its name to the Labour Party
Bakerloo and Piccadilly tubes open in London
China and Britain agree to reduce opium production
F.G. Hopkins discovers vitamins

1907 New Zealand becomes a Dominion
Motor-racing starts at Brooklands
Northern tube line opened

1908 H.H. Asquith becomes Liberal PM
Anglo-German tension grows
Port of London Authority set up
Phosphorus matches banned
Robert Baden-Powell founds the Boy Scout movement
Old Age Pensions for over 70s
New universities: Belfast and University of Ulster

1909 House of Lords reject Chancellor of the Exchequer David Lloyd George's budget proposals, precipitating constitutional crisis
Girl Guides established in Britain
Selfridge's store opens
A.V. Roe begins building aeroplanes in Britain
New university: Bristol

The Edwardian Age

On the surface, the Edwardian Era, under a genial and pleasure-loving king, was a much brighter and more glamorous time than the closing years of Victoria's reign. But underneath the apparent calm and settled order of things, there was growing unrest. Political strife was bitter, the Labour movement was growing in strength, women were battling for emancipation and over Europe the clouds of war were gathering fast.

The 'Titanic' Disaster

When she set out from Britain on her maiden voyage in 1912 the liner *Titanic* was the biggest ship in the world. She was described as 'unsinkable' because she had a double-bottomed hull with 16 watertight compartments and could still float with any four flooded.

Ascot races, 1910 followed soon after the death of Edward VII: ladies were dressed in mourning shades of black, white or purple. The death of the King heralded the end of the secure, untroubled world of British Society.

On her way to New York the liner hit an iceberg, which ripped open five of the watertight compartments. She sank 2½ hours later, with the loss of 1513 lives. The other 711 people on board were picked up by the liner *Carpathia*, which arrived on the scene 20 minutes later.

As a result of the disaster safety rules were tightened up: every ship must now carry enough lifeboats for everyone on board, whereas the *Titanic* had spaces for only half; and ships must maintain a 24-hour radio watch. Another ship nearer than the *Carpathia* had had no radio operator on duty to hear the *Titanic*'s SOS call for help.

Scott of the Antarctic

The British expedition of Robert Falcon Scott to the South Pole ended in tragedy. On his way to Antarctica Scott heard that a Norwegian expedition led by Roald Amundsen, believed to be to the Arctic, was also heading for the South Pole.

Amundsen used Husky dogs to draw his sledges. Scott unwisely used ponies, which were not suited to the severe conditions. Eventually Scott and four companions reached the Pole, pulling their own sledges, to find that Amundsen had got there 34 days earlier. On their way back Scott's party ran into unexpected blizzards, and died of cold and hunger only 18 kilometres from ample stores.

The Crippen Case

The trial of Dr Harvey Hawley Crippen for the murder of his wife in 1910 gained unusual publicity because of the manner of his arrest. When police inquiries became too close Crippen fled to Canada by ship, taking with him his girl-friend, Ethel Le Neve, disguised as a boy.

Aboard the ship the captain realized Le Neve was a girl, guessed who the couple were and radioed London. A Scotland Yard detective crossed the Atlantic in a faster ship, and Crippen was arrested before his ship reached Canada. This was the first time radio had been used to help catch a criminal. Crippen was brought back to England, tried and hanged for murder, but Le Neve was acquitted of a charge of helping him.

1910 Union of South Africa a dominion
Two General Elections over Budget: Liberal majority cut
Parliament Bill to curb powers of Lords: Conservative peers resist it
Edward VII dies; succeeded by son, George V (to 1936)
First Labour Exchanges opened
Halley's Comet observed
Louis Paulhan wins prize for London to Manchester powered flight
George V gives secret pledge to create enough Liberal peers to force the Parliament Bill through

1911 Ramsay MacDonald becomes leader of the Labour Party
Parliament Bill passed; Lords give way
South Wales miners end 10-month strike
Railwaymen strike
Shops Act: employees to have half a day off every week in addition to Sunday
First Official Secrets Act
William Morris (later Lord Nuffield) makes first Morris car
August 9: 100°F in London
First women members of the Royal College of Surgeons

1912 Miners and London dockers strike
Commons reject votes for women; protests increase
National Health Insurance introduced
R.F. Scott dies reaching South Pole

1913 Lords reject Home Rule and Welsh Church disestablishment Bills
Emily Dawson: first woman magistrate
Arms to Ireland are banned
New Statesman magazine founded

189

The Modern World

To those who lived through it, the First World War – the Great War, as it was known – hung like a curtain between the settled world of Victoria and Edward VII and the uncertain future. Yet those uncertainties were all present before the War. Labour was becoming steadily better organized, and strikes were frequent. Unemployment meant that more than 400,000 people a year were emigrating in search of work. Suffragettes demonstrated constantly in their demand for women's rights, many of them enduring prison, hunger strikes and force feeding.

The rapid growth in technology begun before the War accelerated after it. New machines radically altered not only the techniques of industrial production, but also life in the home. More astonishing still was the increasing speed of communications, until people and goods could cross the world in a matter of hours and pictures and speech could be almost instantaneously transmitted.

After the Second World War Britain's Empire disappeared; the countries belonging to it were almost all independent by 1970. They remained linked in the Commonwealth of Nations. Britain became a member of other groupings too – the United Nations, the North Atlantic Treaty Organization, the European Economic Community. In the modern world, it has become apparent, a small country can no longer stand alone.

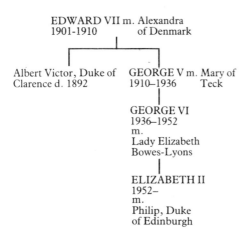

EDWARD VII m. Alexandra
1901-1910   of Denmark

Albert Victor, Duke of   GEORGE V m. Mary of
Clarence d. 1892   1910–1936   Teck

GEORGE VI
1936–1952
m.
Lady Elizabeth
Bowes-Lyons

ELIZABETH II
1952–
m.
Philip, Duke
of Edinburgh

The Growth of Aviation

Aviation has been one of the greatest forces for change in the modern world. Only a dozen years after the Wright Brothers made their pioneering flight aircraft were being used in warfare, although control of the air was not a deciding factor in the First World War as it was in the Second World War and subsequent wars.

In peacetime, aviation has done a great deal to shrink the world, and in particular to make Britain less insular. Every year millions of people fly abroad on holiday or business, and as a result people today have much more knowledge of other lands and peoples than did earlier generations.

Opposite: A 'dogfight' between fighter aircraft during the Second World War, when the Royal Air Force won the Battle of Britain for air supremacy and prevented a German invasion of England.

ELSEWHERE IN THE WORLD

1914 World War I begins (to 1918)
     Panama Canal opened
1915 Albert Einstein: *General Theory of Relativity*
1917 Russian Revolutions: Bolsheviks (Communists) seize power
1919 League of Nations formed
1920 Palestine set up as Jewish state
     Prohibition in US (to 1933)
1922 Fascists take power in Italy
1923 Turkey becomes a republic under Mustafa Kemal (Ataturk)
1926 First demonstration of television
1927 First solo transatlantic flight
1931 Sino-Japanese War (to 1945)
1933 Nazis take power in Germany
1936 Spanish Civil War (to 1939)
1939 World War II begins (to 1945)
1945 United Nations formed
     First atomic bomb set off
1948 State of Israel established
1949 Apartheid in South Africa
1950 Korean War (to 1953)
1953 Egypt becomes a republic
1956 Suez Canal is blocked
1957 *Sputnik 1*, first space satellite
     Vietnam War begins (to 1975)
1960 Seventeen colonies in Africa become independent
1961 Yuri Gagarin, first man in space
1963 US President John F. Kennedy is assassinated
1967 Six-Day War: Israel v Arabs
1969 First men reach the Moon
1973 October War: Israel v Arabs: as a result, Arabs restrict oil, starting world economic crisis
1978 John Paul II, first non-Italian Pope since 1522
     Smallpox is eradicated
1979 Russians invade Afghanistan
1980 Iran-Iraq War begins
1983 US Marines invade Grenada to drive out Communists

The Start of the First World War

For some years the rivalry between European powers over trade, colonies and military power had been growing, and they had grouped in defensive alliances. The First World War was triggered off by the assassination of the Archduke Franz Ferdinand, heir to the Austro-Hungarian throne, by a Serbian student. Austria-Hungary demanded an explanation, and then declared war on Serbia, though with little intention of fighting. Russia, Serbia's ally, immediately mobilized its army, also with no intention of fighting. At this point the game of bluff went wrong. Germany, Austria's ally, demanded that Russia should stop mobilization, and almost at once declared war. For good measure the Germans also declared war on France, Russia's ally.

The Germans believed that attack was the best form of defence. Dreading a war on two fronts, they decided to knock out France first, and launched an attack. It was based on a plan drawn up by a former Chief of Staff, General von Schlieffen. It involved bypassing the French frontier defences by going through Belgium. This move drew in Britain, which had guaranteed Belgium's safety. From Austria-Hungary's declaration of war to Britain's involvement took just ten days.

Britain was the only country without a huge reserve of trained men. The British Expeditionary Force contained less than 100,000 men.

The Schlieffen Plan called for a swift advance. But movement was on foot or with horse-transport, and was slow.

Opposite: The first aircraft used in war were used for observation and reconnaissance work; before long, guns were mounted on them.

The French rail network allowed defensive positions to be reinforced more quickly. Within three months a line of trenches ran from the border of neutral Switzerland to the sea. The war had reached deadlock, and in the next four years the western front did not move more than 32 kilometres. In a series of major battles hundreds of thousands of lives were lost for the gain of at most a few kilometres.

An attempt in 1915 to capture the Dardanelles Straits from Turkey, which had entered the war on Germany's side, was carried out half-heartedly and not surprisingly failed.

Britain's Empire came to its aid during the First World War; here Indian troops ride through a French village.

The Easter Rising

After years of wrangling, an Act giving Home Rule to Ireland was finally passed at the beginning of the war. It was immediately suspended until after the war, which few people then expected would last long. This Act gave Home Rule to the whole island, ignoring the wish of the Protestant North to stay part of the United Kingdom.

A group of extremists in Ireland, dismayed at the delay, decided to start a rebellion with German aid. Sir Roger Casement, a former British consul, was landed from a German submarine on Good Friday, 1916, to warn that no help was forthcoming. Despite efforts to stop the rebellion, about a thousand men seized the General Post Office and other buildings in Dublin and proclaimed the Irish Republic. The rebellion was crushed after four days of fighting. Fifteen of the leaders were shot under martial law: only Éamon de Valera was spared, because he was nominally a US citizen. Casement was executed for treason.

1914 Lords reject votes for women
Commons pass Irish Home Rule Bill
Irish rebel in Dublin
Britain declares war on Germany; British troops land in France
Britain declares war on Austria-Hungary
Battle of Namur and Mons
Retreat from Mons
First battle of the Marne
Battle of the Aisne
Irish Home Rule suspended
Boers rebel
First battle of Ypres
Britain declares war on Turkey
British protectorate in Egypt
First Treasury notes: £1 and 10s

1915 HMS *Formidable* sunk
German airship bombs Britain
German blockade of Britain
Battle of Neuve Chapelle
Second battle of Ypres: Germans use gas for the first time
Allied troops land at Gallipoli
British liner *Lusitania* is sunk; 124 Americans drowned
Asquith forms coalition
Zeppelin airships raid London
British take Mesopotamia
Boers surrender in South Africa
Allies withdraw from Gallipoli

1916 Conscription comes into force
Clydeside munition workers strike
Easter rebellion in Dublin
Battle of Jutland
HMS *Hampshire* sunk: British War Minister Lord Kitchener dies
National Savings begin
Daylight Saving (summer time) begins
Battle of the Somme: first tanks used
Germans shell English coast
Lloyd George becomes PM

The War in the Trenches

Generals on both sides on the Western Front (in France and Belgium) believed in frontal attacks. The result was a series of huge battles in which heavy casualties were sustained to no real purpose. One of the worst was the Third Battle of Ypres, also called Passchendaele. It was fought in torrential rain, and the troops had to wade through mud up to their waists. In 102 days the British advanced about 8 kilometres at a cost of 400,000 lives. They captured the site of Passchendaele, a village which was completely destroyed in the fighting.

The War at Sea

There were only two major sea battles in the old style in the First World War. In 1914 a German fleet was destroyed

This painting by C.R.W. Nevinson, entitled 'The Harvest of Battle', shows wounded soldiers struggling across a landscape of complete devastation.

off the Falkland Islands; two years later the main German fleet engaged a British fleet off Jutland. The British lost more ships, but the German fleet never left harbour again.

Instead, the Germans concentrated on a relatively new weapon: the submarine. The German U-boats attacked all shipping, even that of neutral countries, bound for Britain and France. This brought the US into the war with its vast resources of arms and men. But losses of shipping were so high that disaster loomed until Lloyd George, overruling the admirals, insisted that ships sailed in convoys, which were easier to protect.

The Home Front

The war began with a Liberal government in power – the last to hold office. It was headed by H.H. Asquith, a quiet and scholarly statesman. His conduct of the war drew criticism, largely that it was not dynamic enough. In 1915 a chronic shortage of shells prompted Asquith to create a Ministry of Munitions under David Lloyd George, hitherto Chancellor of the Exchequer. Lloyd George solved the shell shortage, and, with the aid of Conservative leaders in what had now become a coalition, ousted Asquith as Prime Minister in 1916.

The professional army was lost in the costly battles of 1914. Volunteers flocked to join up, urged on by silly girls who offered white feathers to anyone of military age not seen in uniform. Eventually, to see fair play, conscription was introduced.

The war brought many quiet revolutions. With so many men in the forces, women had to take over their jobs, gaining at a stroke a big step towards the equality many of them sought. Food was rationed, largely to prevent hoarding. National Savings were introduced to help finance the war.

The End of the War

The British campaign in the Near East against Turkey helped to end the war by defeating Turkey, and another of Germany's allies, Bulgaria. With an attack in the rear pending the German army commanders realized they could no longer win the war, and urged their government to ask for an armistice.

1917 British capture Baghdad
Imperial War Cabinet formed
US declares war on Germany
Battle of Arras: Canadians capture Vimy Ridge
Sinn Fein riots in Dublin
Irish rebels of 1916 get amnesty
Royal Family adopt name of Windsor, drop German names and titles
Third battle of Ypres
Balfour Declaration: Britain promises Palestine home for Jews
British take Gaza and Jaffa
Battle of Cambrai
British capture Jerusalem
Order of the British Empire and Companions of Honour founded

1918 Second battle of the Somme
Royal Air Force formed, replacing Royal Flying Corps of the army
Major German offensive
Home Rule for Ireland abandoned
Food rationing begins (ends 1919)
British land at Vladivostok to fight the Bolsheviks
British occupy Damascus
Influenza epidemic rages
Armistice with Austria-Hungary
Armistice with Germany (Nov. 11)
Labour Party quits coalition
'Khaki' Election: Liberal-Conservative coalition majority 262
Women over 30 get the vote

1919 War with Afghanistan
German East Africa mandated to Britain: renamed Tanganyika
German fleet scuttled at Scapa Flow
Lady Astor becomes first woman MP to take her seat
First Atlantic aeroplane crossing by J.W. Alcock and A.W. Brown
First flight to Australia (Ross Smith), in 135 hours

Turmoil in Ireland

In the general election of 1918 the *Sinn Féin* (Ourselves Alone) party won 73 seats, and promptly formed themselves into a separate parliament in Dublin. Although Home Rule was already law, only waiting to go into effect, the British government decided to bow to the wishes of the Protestant North and split off six counties of Ulster with a parliament of their own, the northern and southern Irish to combine in a Council of Ireland.

Meanwhile an old secret society, the Irish Republican Brotherhood, reconstituted itself as the Irish Republican Army (IRA). Without authority from Sinn Féin the IRA began a guerrilla war against the British, financed by American Irish. The British sent over auxiliary forces to combat the IRA, the Black and Tans (called so from the colour of their uniforms), who became noted for brutality.

A treaty signed at the end of 1921 confirmed the partition, with the 26 southern counties forming a new Dominion, the Irish Free State. Civil war then broke out in the Free State between those members of Sinn Féin who supported the new Dominion and those who wanted a republic.

Workers at Crewe demonstrate during the General Strike of 1926; it began with the coal-mining industry and spread rapidly to other workers. The government was able to defeat it with the help of volunteers who kept essential services running.

The General Strike

The General Strike of 1926 lasted nine days. It was called in support of the miners, who were fighting threatened wage cuts. It failed because the government was able to organize volunteers to run essential services, and could use the radio to keep people informed. The miners' strike went on for another six months, and also ended in failure.

Barricades in the streets of Dublin in January 1921, when IRA guerrillas were fighting the British to achieve complete Irish independence.

1920   Former East African Protectorate becomes Kenya colony
Riots in Belfast against Irish independence
Irish Republican Army (IRA) begins guerrilla war
Government of Ireland Act: North and South each to have a parliament, with a joint council
Church of Wales disestablished
Women awarded Oxford degrees
Unknown Soldier buried in Westminster Abbey

1921   Unemployment payments increased – nearly one milllion jobless
Elections in Ireland: North accepts new government; Sinn Féin wins in South and refuses
George V opens Ulster Parliament and appeals for reconciliation; truce in guerrilla war
British Legion of ex-servicemen founded
Irish Free State set up

1922   Guerrillas attack new Irish rulers
Lloyd George coalition falls: Bonar Law (Con.) is PM
British Broadcasting Company is founded

1923   Stanley Baldwin becomes PM (Con.)

1924   First Labour Government: Ramsay MacDonald PM; General Election after only 8 months returns Conservatives
British Empire Exhibition

1925   Cyprus becomes a Crown colony
Unemployment Insurance Act passed

1926   Éamon de Valera founds Fianna Fáil (Soldiers of Destiny) party
General Strike in Britain (9 days)
Reading University founded
J.L. Baird invents television

The Great Depression

The world economic crisis known as the Great Depression started in the US in 1929. Factories had been producing more goods than people could afford; they had to work part time and the reduced wages meant people could afford still less. Speculators had been buying shares and forcing their price up. Suddenly investors realized that although stock prices were rising, production was falling. In a panic, they began to sell their shares. Prices of shares plummeted, and thousands of people were ruined.

The US, and countries relying on it, stopped buying goods. British exporters saw their markets disappear. Unemployment rose sharply, reaching almost 3,000,000 by 1931. A run on the pound sterling was precipitated by the collapse of an Austrian bank, which led to the freezing of British assets overseas. The economy recovered only slowly through the 1930s.

The Statute of Westminster

Imperial Conferences, forerunners of today's Commonwealth Conferences, were held in 1926 and 1930. As a result of their deliberations the British Parliament passed in 1931 the Statute of Westminster, which defined more clearly than earlier laws the independent nature of the Dominions. The Dominions then were Canada, Australia, New Zealand, South Africa, the Irish Free State, and Newfoundland. The Crown was, as now, the unifying factor. The statute also laid down that changes to

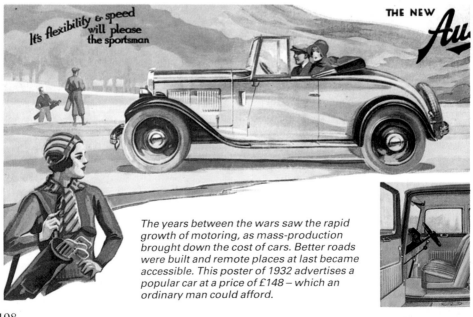

It's flexibility & speed will please the sportsman

THE NEW *Au*

The years between the wars saw the rapid growth of motoring, as mass-production brought down the cost of cars. Better roads were built and remote places at last became accessible. This poster of 1932 advertises a popular car at a price of £148 – which an ordinary man could afford.

This poster was designed to advertise the Conservative Party. It was altered to popularize the National Government, formed in 1931 under the Labour Prime Minister Ramsay MacDonald to try to combat the grave financial difficulties which overtook Britain and the other industrial countries in the 1930s. Unemployment was widespread, and in 1936 a report found that half the nation was ill-fed, the worst areas being parts of Scotland, the north of England and south Wales.

the royal titles and the succession to the throne had to be decided by the parliaments of all Dominions as well as that of the United Kingdom.

1927 IRA kill Kevin O'Higgins, Irish Minister of Justice
Trades Disputes Act: certain strikes and lockouts declared illegal; political levy to be 'contracted in'
British Broadcasting Corporation takes over from B.B. Company
Coypu introduced from Argentina

1928 Women get the vote at 21
Alexander Fleming discovers penicillin mould in his laboratory
J.L.Baird demonstrates colour TV

1929 General Election: Labour wins, Ramsay MacDonald PM
Wall Street Crash starts the Great Depression (to 1940s)
Margaret Bondfield, first woman Privy Councillor
First crease-resistant cotton fibre made by Tootal's of St Helen's

1930 Youth Hostels Association founded
Acrylic plastic invented
Amy Johnson flies solo from London to Australia
Airship R101 crashes: end of airship building in Britain
Daily Worker (now Morning Star) first issued

1931 National Coalition formed under MacDonald
Britain abandons gold standard
Whipsnade Zoo opened
First London trolley bus
Statute of Westminster

1932 Éamon de Valera elected President of Ireland
Former Labour MP Oswald Mosley starts British Union of Fascists
James Chadwick discovers neutrons
Jobless organize hunger marches
Unemployment reaches 3,000,000

INSTRUMENT OF ABDICATION

I, Edward the Eighth, of Great Britain, Ireland, and the British Dominions beyond the Seas, King, Emperor of India, do hereby declare My irrevocable determination to renounce the Throne for Myself and for My descendants, and My desire that effect should be given to this Instrument of Abdication immediately.

In token whereof I have hereunto set My hand this tenth day of December, nineteen hundred and thirty six, in the presence of the witnesses whose signatures are subscribed.

SIGNED AT
FORT BELVEDERE
IN THE PRESENCE
OF

Edward VIII reigned for only a few months; in December 1936 he abdicated in order to marry a twice-divorced American, Mrs Wallis Simpson. He was made Duke of Windsor and retired to live abroad.

Ireland Severs Links

The links between the Irish Free State and the United Kingdom were gradually broken during the 1930s. In 1932 the government of Éamon de Valera ousted the governor-general, the King's representative, and abolished appeals to the Privy Council; following the Abdication Ireland removed mention of the Crown from its constitution, and in 1937 Ireland ended the Free State and proclaimed itself the independent republic of Ireland, or Eire. The British handed over three Irish ports which it held under the 1921 treaty.

The Abdication

When George V died in 1936 he left the monarchy strong in the affections of the people. His eldest son, who inherited the Crown as Edward VIII, was 41 and unmarried. As Prince of Wales he had acquired great personal popularity, both at home and in the Empire.

Though Edward was well aware of the social problems of the time – he had made trenchant remarks about both slums and unemployment – he spent much of his time in a rather shallow social life. The closest of his friends was Mrs Wallis Simpson, an American with one divorced husband still living, and another whom she hoped to divorce.

Edward's infatuation for Mrs Simpson was the talk of the world's Press, but by a voluntary agreement the British newspapers avoided all mention of it. The Prime Minister, Stanley Baldwin, tackled the King about Mrs Simpson. Edward declared that he wanted to marry her, and proposed a *morganatic* marriage, in which Mrs Simpson would be his wife but not queen. Baldwin, mindful of the 1931 Statute of Westminster, consulted the Dominions. They were against the idea, and so were most people in Britain. They wanted a monarchy they could respect, with higher-than-average standards of behaviour. Faced with the choice of his throne or 'the woman I love', Edward chose to abdicate.

His successor was his brother Albert, Duke of York, who took the title of George VI. The new king was a quiet, shy man with a speech impediment who had seen service at the battle of Jutland. But he had the great advantage of a beautiful and popular wife, Elizabeth (later the Queen Mother), and together they gained the respect and affection of the people.

Neville Chamberlain, British Prime Minister, leaves to meet German leader Hitler in September 1938. Hitler was granted substantial concessions but ignored the terms of this Munich agreement.

1933	Fianna Fáil gains majority of 1 in Irish elections
	British disarmament plan fails
	Oxford Union votes 'not to fight for King and Country'
	ICI invents Polythene
1934	Driving tests introduced
	Liner *Queen Mary* launched with aid from government to help unemployment
	First Mersey Tunnel opened
1935	Anti-Catholic riots in Belfast
	Green Belt around London established
	Robert Watson-Watt builds first practicable radar
	Paperback revolution: Allen Lane founds Penguin Books
	30 mph (48 kph) speed limit and crossing beacons introduced
	Ramsay MacDonald retires: Stanley Baldwin (Cons) heads coalition
	General Election: sweeping Conservative majority
1936	George V dies: succeeded by son, Edward VIII
	BBC starts regular TV service
	Edward VIII abdicates: succeeded by brother, George VI (to 1952)
1937	Air Raid precautions planned
	Irish Free State becomes Eire
	Frank Whittle: first jet engine
	Baldwin retires: Neville Chamberlain becomes PM
1938	National register for war service
	Women's Voluntary Service founded
	Queen Elizabeth (largest-ever liner) is launched
	Sulphanilamide drugs developed
	Munich Crisis: Chamberlain meets Hitler and with policy of appeasement claims to achieve 'peace for our time'

A painting showing the destruction of a German U-boat. Supplies from abroad were brought to Britain by convoys of ships, many of which were destroyed by these German submarines.

The Phoney War

War between Britain and Germany became inevitable when it was obvious that the Nazi government of Germany, led by the megalomaniac Jew-hater Adolf Hitler, was set on a course of conquest and of exterminating the Jews. The Nazi assault on Poland, a country which Britain had pledged to help, provided the final spark.

In fact Britain could do nothing to help Poland. For the first seven months there was a 'Phoney War', in which little happened that affected Britain directly, except that a black-out was in force against possible air-raids, and food rationing was introduced.

His Finest Hour

The sudden unleashing of Hitler's war machine on Denmark and Norway led to a crisis of confidence in the government of Neville Chamberlain. An all-Party coalition was called for, and Labour refused to serve under Chamberlain. By general consent the choice fell on Winston Churchill.

Churchill had been in the political wilderness from 1929 to 1939, and had a reputation, largely unjustified, for irresponsibility. But throughout the 1930s he had been a lone voice warning of the perils ahead. He had boundless energy and a fertile mind.

This, to use a phrase from one of Churchill's later speeches, was his finest hour. A born orator, he provided as he put it the roar for the British lion, which heartened the people in the days of disaster ahead. He took the title

Minister of Defence as well as Prime Minister, and so acquired almost dictatorial powers, which he used to hack through red tape and incompetence.

The War in the Air

Having overrun the Netherlands, Belgium and France, Hitler planned to invade Britain. He began with a series of daylight air-raids to cripple the island's defences. In the Battle of Britain the German raids were fought off by the pilots of RAF Fighter Command. Foiled, Hitler cancelled his invasion plans.

The Germans then switched to a series of night bombing raids, first on London and then on other industrial centres. This became known as the 'Blitz' – short for *Blitzkrieg* (lightning war). It went on sporadically until May 1941, when the Nazi bombers were switched to attack Russia.

Once again, women workers played a vital part in war work. Here they assemble a barrage balloon – a defence against attack from the air.

1939	Morden-Finchley tube railway constructed (27 km)
	Britain and France promise to support Poland, Greece, Romania
	Conscription introduced for men
	George VI visits Canada and US
	John Cobb sets land speed record of 594 kph
	Russo-German pact
	First British transatlantic airmail service begins
	Blackout introduced
	Germans invade Poland
	Britain and France declare war
	Leaflet raids on Germany: the 'Phoney War' period
	Battle of the River Plate
1940	Food rationing starts
	Women get old age pension at 60
	Germans invade Norway and Denmark
	Chamberlain resigns: Winston Churchill forms coalition
	Germans invade Netherlands, Belgium and France
	The Home Guard formed
	Fire-watching compulsory
	British forces evacuated from Dunkirk
	Penicillin developed as antibiotic
	French surrender
	Battle of Britain
	The Blitz: London the main target
	George Cross instituted
1941	Double Summer Time introduced
	House of Commons destroyed
	Lend-Lease: US aid for Britain
	Churchill and US President Roosevelt sign Atlantic Charter
	Clothes rationing begins (to 1949)
	Conscription for women
	Japanese attack Pearl Harbor: US brought into the war
	British Eighth Army advances and retreats in Egypt and Libya

British troops land on a Normandy beach on D-Day – June 6th 1944 – at the start of the liberation of France. Stormy weather and unexpectedly strong resistance in places pinned the invading forces down for some weeks before they could advance eastwards to Germany.

The War in the East

War broke out in eastern Asia in the last weeks of 1941 when without warning the Japanese attacked American and British territories. This brought the US into the war against Germany, which was Japan's ally.

By May 1942 the Japanese had overrun the British territories of Hong Kong, Burma, Malaya, Singapore, Borneo, most of New Guinea and many smaller islands, and were menacing Australia. They also controlled the Philippines, the Dutch East Indies (now Indonesia) and French Indo-China. Two major British battleships, *Prince of Wales* and *Repulse*, were sunk.

A great deal of the Allied counter-attack in the Far East was carried out by American and Australian forces. The British 14th Army fought its way back through Burma, aided by a commando force, the *Chindits*, commanded by Brigadier Orde Wingate.

The Battle of the Atlantic

The battle which nearly brought Britain to its knees was the Battle of the Atlantic, which raged from 1941 through the war. German U-boats sank hundreds of ships bringing supplies. Convoys, and help from America even before it entered the war, gradually brought the losses down and the rate of U-boat sinkings up.

The War in Africa

Italy, which joined the war in 1940, tried to capture Egypt and the Suez Canal from its colony in Libya. The fighting raged to and fro in the Western Desert, until by July 1942 a combined

Italian and German force had advanced to within 100 kilometres of Alexandria.

Three months later the British and Commonwealth armies, under new commanders (Generals Alexander and Montgomery), broke the German/ Italian forces in the battle of El Alamein, and then rolled steadily westwards. Meanwhile an Allied force had landed in French North Africa. By May 1943 North Africa was clear of the enemy, and two months later the Allies landed in Sicily. By October Italy had surrendered and changed sides.

D-Day
The invasion of Europe took 18 months to prepare, from the time the US entered the war. D-Day, the first assault, came on June 6th, 1944, when an Allied force stormed ashore on the Normandy coast. A force of 3,000,000 men assembled in Britain; and 11,000 aircraft and 9000 ships and landing craft took them across the Channel.

Planning For Peace
Even when the war was at its height the government found time to begin planning for peace. In 1942 the economist Sir William Beveridge brought out a government report on *Social Insurance and Allied Services*, which laid the foundations for today's Welfare State. Two years later the Minister of Education, R.A. Butler, sponsored an Act (the 'Butler Act') providing for three stages of education – primary, secondary and further – and for the school-leaving age to be gradually raised from 14 to 16.

1942 Term 'United Nations' first used
Japanese take Malaya, Singapore and Burma
'Baedeker raids': Germans bomb Bath and other cultural centres
British invade Madagascar
Malta resists continual attack: island awarded the George Cross
Oxfam founded
British retreat to El Alamein
Commando raid on Dieppe
Battle of El Alamein: Allies begin final advance across Libya
Allies land in western North Africa
Economist Sir William Beveridge produces plan for social security

1943 Winston Churchill and US President Roosevelt meet at Casablanca
North Africa cleared of Germans and Italians
Allies land in Sicily
Allies invade mainland Italy
Italy surrenders, joins the Allies
Churchill, Roosevelt and Joseph Stalin of Russia meet at Teheran

1944 Pay-As-You-Earn tax scheme introduced
New air-raids on London
National Health Service proposed
D-Day: Allied armies invade Normandy
Flying-bomb (V1) raids on London begin
Education Act plans to raise school-leaving age
Blackout restrictions lifted
Antwerp and Brussels liberated
British land on French Riviera
Battle of the Bulge (last major German offensive)
First V2 rocket bombs launched
British paratroop attack on Arnhem (Netherlands) fails

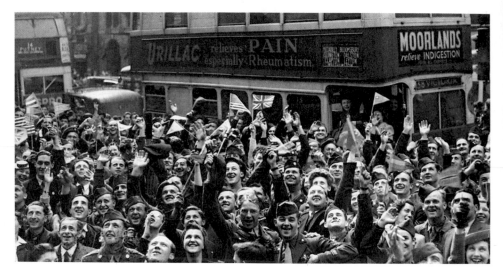

Cheering crowds in Piccadilly Circus greet the news of the German surrender on May 7th 1945.

The End of the War

The war in Europe dragged on until the beginning of May, 1945. Then, with his armies everywhere retreating, and constant bombing knocking out his oil supplies and industries, the Nazi dictator Adolf Hitler committed suicide, and the Germans surrendered. Britain celebrated May 8th as VE-day (Victory in Europe).

The war with Japan threatened to be a much longer affair. But in August the Allies launched a new and terrifying weapon. They dropped two atomic bombs on Japan, and within days the Japanese surrendered. British and American scientists had been working on the bomb for several years, in the greatest secrecy. September 2nd was celebrated as VJ-day.

Labour Sweeps to Power

The coalition government which had fought the war did not long survive the end of fighting in Europe. There had been no election for nearly 10 years, twice the normal time allowed. The rank and file of the Labour Party demanded a vote. So Churchill resigned, and an election was held.

The result was a sweeping victory for Labour, which was returned with a majority of 146. Its leader, Clement Attlee, who had been deputy to Churchill, became Prime Minister. Labour won with a policy of social and economic reconstruction, while the Conservatives bore the blame for much that had gone wrong in the 1930s.

Labour's plans for the future were greatly hampered by the financial burden left by the war. Britain's exports had dropped sharply, while it had had to borrow hugely to pay for supplies. It had also had to sell off a quarter of its overseas investments, thereby losing the income from them, and other 'invisible' earnings such as profit from tourism had stopped. Worse still, the Lend-Lease scheme by which the US provided goods on a more or less free-gift basis abruptly ended. A huge loan from the Americans went only part way towards bridging the financial gap. For a time, the ordinary citizen had to face greater austerities than in the war.

Despite this Labour managed to carry through part of its programme, in particular nationalization of the mines, civil aviation, road transport and the Bank of England.

Lord Louis Mountbatten, Viceroy of India, puts forward the plan to partition the subcontinent into Hindu India and Muslim Pakistan on granting it independence. Behind him sits his adviser Lord Ismay; on the left of the picture is the Hindu leader Mr Nehru, on the right Mr Jinnah, President of the All-India Muslim League. Independence and partition saw appalling bloodshed and refugee problems as people living in the state of the other religion tried to make their way to the state of their own religion.

1945 British 14th Army opens offensive in Burma
Churchill, Roosevelt and Stalin confer at Yalta, Crimea
Last of 1050 V2s falls on London
Germans surrender (May 7)
Coalition breaks up: Churchill forms Conservative caretaker government
General Election: Labour landslide (Labour 393, Conservatives 213, Liberals 12, others 22): Clement Attlee PM
Atomic bombs dropped on Hiroshima and Nagasaki, Japan
Japan surrenders: World War II ends
Lend-lease ends: financial crisis
United Nations inaugurated
US lends Britain $3.75 billion
Family allowances begin

1946 Trade Disputes Act (1927) repealed
Bank of England nationalized
New Towns Act passed
Civil Aviation nationalized
BBC resumes TV (suspended since 1939), with 12,000 viewers
Bread rationed (world shortage)
BBC Third Programme begins (forerunner of Radio 3)
Arts Council set up
National Health Act passed

1947 Coal Mines nationalized
Fuel crisis: shortage of coal
Road transport nationalized
India partitioned to form independent India and Pakistan
First atomic pile installed at Harwell
John Cobb sets new land speed record: 634.38 kph
Princess Elizabeth marries Philip, Duke of Edinburgh
School-leaving age raised to 15

Change of Government

After five difficult years the Labour Party went into the general election of 1950 considerably divided, and its overall majority was cut to only five. It struggled on for 20 months, then went to the country with a manifesto which made little mention of further nationalization, once the main plank of the Labour platform. The Conservatives were returned with a majority of 16. Winston Churchill, now 76, became Prime Minister again.

Hardly had the dust of the election settled than George VI, who had survived an operation for lung cancer, died suddenly in his sleep. He was succeeded by his 25-year-old daughter Elizabeth II, who had been training for the monarchy since childhood.

The Empire Crumbles

With the 'Old Dominions' the transfer of power from Britain to its former colonies had been a slow and peaceful affair. After the Second World War a wave of nationalism, accompanied by a growing belief among the British that having an empire was morally unjustified and uneconomic, meant that a slow transfer was no longer possible.

The Indian Empire was the first to go; it was split into two countries (India and Pakistan) along religious and racial lines. This was accompanied by mass emigration and hideous massacres.

Burma and Ceylon (now Sri Lanka) both became independent in 1948. Burma opted to leave the Commonwealth, as did Eire, which declared itself an independent republic.

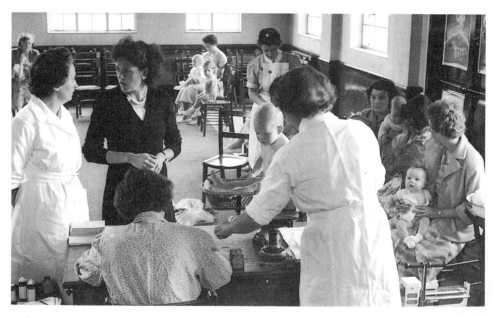

Change and Reform

The Labour Government introduced many changes and reforms in its first term of office. Two were of constitutional importance.

The first reduced the power of the House of Lords to delay Bills which the Commons had passed. In 1911 this power was set at two years; the new Act reduced it to one. Labour feared, with some reason, the enormous built-in Conservative majority in the Upper House. The second reform swept away 12 university seats in the Commons, and the right of businessmen to have a vote for their business premises as well as at home. Thenceforth one person, one vote was the rule.

Other changes included the foundation of the National Health Service, foreshadowed in the wartime Beveridge Report; the nationalization of railways, power and gas; and the abolition of corporal punishment. The iron and steel industry was also nationalized, but as this measure did not take effect until after the Conservatives had been returned to power, the Tories reversed it.

The wartime controls slowly disappeared. Labour abolished clothes rationing and eased food rationing; their successors ended the necessity for citizens to have identity cards.

The early post-war years saw the setting up of the Welfare State, through which the government hoped that the state would care for its citizens 'from the cradle to the grave' through a system of health care, unemployment and sickness benefits, and pensions. Here children are brought to a National Health Service infant welfare clinic in 1951.

1948 Railways, power, gas nationalized
British mandate in Palestine ends
Act declares that Commonwealth citizens are automatically British
Bread rationing ends
Corporal punishment abolished
National Health Service begins
Antibiotics aureomycin and chloromyatin are prepared
Olympic Games held in London
Nottingham University founded

1949 Clothes rationing ends
Republic of Ireland proclaimed
Britain reaffirms position of Northern Ireland in the UK
Power of Lords is reduced

1950 Scottish Nationalists take Stone of Scone from Westminster (found 1952)
General Election: Labour majority cut to five
National Service extended to two years (from 18 months)

1951 Festival of Britain
Charges for teeth and spectacles introduced: Labour split
Comet, first jet airliner, developed
General Election: Conservatives win majority of 16: Churchill PM
Steel nationalization comes into force and is at once halted

1952 George VI dies; succeeded by daughter, Elizabeth II
Identity cards abolished: numbers remain on NH medical cards
Britain makes its first atom bomb
Oil dispute with Iran
Mau Mau disturbances in Kenya
Last London tram runs

1953 Disastrous floods on east coast
Myxomatosis reduces rabbit numbers
Commonwealth team climbs Everest
Road transport denationalized

Life Peerages

Reform of the House of Lords had been a talking point for many years. It was criticized because all its members, apart from the bishops and the Law Lords, inherited their titles and the right to sit in the Upper House. These hereditary peers were largely Conservative. The numbers of peers were growing, since new peerages were being created faster than old ones were dying out; and fewer than half a dozen peeresses in their own right were entitled to sit in the Lords. The Conservatives introduced the concept of life peerages for people other than bishops and judges, and extended them to women as well as men.

The coronation of Queen Elizabeth in 1953 seemed to herald a new era of British prestige and prosperity. It was a scene of glorious pageantry, attended by armed forces from all over Britain's empire – soon to become its Commonwealth – and rulers of many countries.

Nuclear Protest

Britain's testing of nuclear weapons aroused much fear and opposition. From 1956, protesters marched each Easter from the atomic research station at Aldermaston to Trafalgar Square to urge that tests be stopped. Two years later the Campaign for Nuclear Disarmament was founded; it sought to stop Britain having nuclear weapons.

The Suez Crisis

After the Second World War Britain retained a garrison in Egypt to guard the Suez Canal, which was a vital link between Britain and the Far East. Egypt's new ruler, Colonel Nasser, demanded that the British withdraw, and in June 1956 the last troops left the Canal Zone. Meanwhile Nasser was trying to obtain a loan, jointly from the World Bank, the US and Britain, to finance the Aswan High Dam across the Nile.

Anti-British radio attacks from Egypt, plus a doubt of the country's ability to repay the loans, led to the withdrawal of all offers of help. At this Nasser nationalized the Canal.

The newly formed state of Israel, always at loggerheads with its Arab neighbours, proposed a plan whereby Israel would attack Egypt, giving Britain and France, the chief shareholders in the Suez Canal, an excuse to intervene and restore order. This plan was welcomed by the Prime Minister, Anthony Eden, who had succeeded Churchill in 1955.

Eden had been, for two spells, a brilliant and skilful foreign secretary. In this instance his skill deserted him, possibly because he was a sick man. Israel attacked: Britain and France demanded a withdrawal of troops on both sides, with an Anglo-French garrison for the Canal. Egypt refused, and Anglo-French troops went in. Pressure from the United Nations, led by the US, forced an immediate withdrawal. A few months later, his health worse, Eden resigned.

1954 Tenants gain security of tenure
Hull University founded
'Flying Bedstead' – first vertical take-off aircraft – developed
Roger Bannister runs mile in under 4 minutes (3 min 59.4 sec)
Food rationing ends

1955 Churchill retires: Anthony Eden succeeds as PM
General Election: Conservatives increase majority to 67
Ruth Ellis is last woman executed for murder
Attlee retires as Labour leader: succeeded by Hugh Gaitskell
Exeter University founded
Duke of Edinburgh's Award Scheme starts
ITV and VHF broadcasts begin

1956 Premium bonds introduced
First Aldermaston march
Suez Canal crisis: Anglo-French intervention fails to stop its nationalization

1957 Eden ill, retires: succeeded by Harold Macmillan as PM
International Geophysical Year
Jodrell Bank radio telescope tracks *Sputnik 1* (first satellite)
Leicester University founded

1958 Life peerages introduced
Race riots in London and Nottingham
Charles created Prince of Wales
Last débutantes presented at Court
Fishing dispute with Iceland
British party under Vivian Fuchs makes first transantarctic crossing

1959 Christopher Cockerell invents the Hovercraft
First part of M1 motorway opened
General Election: Conservatives increase majority to 100

The Reluctant Viscount

A further reform of the House of Lords resulted from a campaign by Anthony Wedgwood Benn. Political power had come to rest more and more with the Commons, and certain offices, including prime minister, are now regarded as unavailable to peers. Benn succeeded to the title of Viscount Stansgate on the death of his father, thus ending his career in the Commons. He fought to stay in the Lower House, but came up against the rule that peers are not eligible for election as Members of Parliament (along with lunatics, judges, most clergymen, bankrupts, and holders of certain offices).

The Peerage Act of 1963 allowed all peers to disclaim their titles when they inherit them (though their heirs can inherit if they want). It also allowed any existing peers to disclaim within a year of the Act becoming law. A number did, among them Lord Stansgate, the Earl of Home, who was chosen to be Prime Minister and Lord Hailsham, a candidate for the premiership. Home and Hailsham later returned to the Lords – as life peers.

The University Boom

In an increasingly complex world the need for more people with higher education became steadily greater; so in the 1950s and 1960s successive governments embarked on a programme of university expansion. Existing universities were given government aid to erect

The 1960s saw a number of British colonies achieve independence. Here the Tanganyikan leader Julius Nyerere is carried shoulder-high from Government House after the announcement of Tanganyikan independence in April 1961.

new buildings, take on more staff and absorb more students.

In addition 19 new universities received their charters in the 1960s. Some were completely new creations. Others were colleges of advanced technology which received university status.

A more daring innovation was the Open University, started to provide degrees for mature students by a mixture of correspondence courses, radio and television programmes, and a limited number of tutorials. It was the idea of Michael Young, founder of the Consumers' Association and its magazine *Which?*, and was enthusiastically taken up by the Labour Prime Minister Harold Wilson and his Minister of Education, Jennie Lee. In its first ten years the OU produced 45,000 graduates, average age 38.

Independence in Africa

The winding up of the British Empire continued apace during the 1960s and 1970s. By 1968 all but one of Britain's African colonies had achieved independence. The exception was Rhodesia, formerly Southern Rhodesia, where the white minority held power and was reluctant to give it up.

Britain insisted that the black people should have a greater say before Rhodesia could be independent. Negotiations broke down, and on November 11th, 1965, Rhodesia's premier Ian Smith declared independence. Britain ruled the declaration illegal, and organized an economic blockade of Rhodesia. Britain was supported by the United Nations.

1960 Pacemaker for hearts developed
      Cyprus, Nigeria independent
1961 Volcanic eruption on island of Tristan da Cunha: population evacuated to Britain
      Farthings cease to be legal tender
      Francis Crick and James Watson solve the structure of DNA
      South Africa leaves Commonwealth
      New universities: Essex and Sussex
      Sierra Leone, Tanganyika independent
1962 New Coventry cathedral opened
      Thalidomide tragedy: babies born with deformities
      Independent: Jamaica, Trinidad and Tobago, Uganda
      New Act controls immigration from West Indies and Pakistan
      New university: Keele
1963 Common Market rejects Britain
      'Beeching Report' begins rail closures
      Beatles pop group win international fame
      Peerage Act gives peers right to disclaim on inheritance
      Independent: Kenya, Malaysia, Zanzibar
      Macmillan retires: succeeded as PM by Sir Alec Douglas-Home
      New universities: Newcastle, York
1964 Malawi and Zambia independent
      New universities: East Anglia, Kent, Lancaster, Strathclyde, Warwick
      General Election: Labour victory; Harold Wilson becomes PM
1965 New university: Ulster
      Oil, gas found in North Sea
      Greater London created
      White Rhodesians declare UDI

Capital Punishment

The death penalty, the most extreme that can be exacted by society against a criminal, had been in steady decline since the 18th century. In the early 1700s several hundred crimes could be punished by hanging, including many forms of theft. By 1861, thanks to the campaigning of reformers, the list had been reduced to four: murder, high treason, piracy and the destruction of such military establishments as arsenals and dockyards.

A long campaign by abolitionists raged through the 1950s and 1960s. It was reinforced by serious doubts of the guilt of at least one man executed for murder. The last executions took place in 1964, after which all people sentenced to hang were reprieved. In 1969 a free vote of Members of Parliament finally abolished the death penalty, though there have been several attempts to bring it back for the more barbarous crimes.

Race Relations

Until the late 1950s Britain was an almost exclusively white community. Then a flood of immigrants from the West Indies, India and Pakistan came in to supply much-wanted labour, of which there was a shortage. Their presence in large numbers soon brought racial tensions which the country had

In 1965 Sir Winston Churchill, a controversial politician for many years but undoubtedly a great war leader, died. He was given the rare honour of a state funeral in St Paul's cathedral; here his coffin is drawn through the city.

not previously known; by 1970 their numbers had risen to more than one million.

To protect these people against discrimination, of which there was all too much evidence, Parliament passed Acts to inflict penalties on people found showing open discrimination, and set up a Race Relations Board to hear complaints and act on them.

At the same time, 'Women's Liberation' movements pointed out that women, too, were the victims of discrimination in terms of pay and job opportunities, and various Acts were passed to try to right this injustice.

Northern Ireland

Discrimination was also at the root of the troubles in Northern Ireland which broke out in 1969. The partition of Ireland, which split off the six Protestant and Loyalist counties from the rest of the predominantly Catholic south, left a large number of Catholics north of the border. This Catholic minority found itself discriminated against in terms of housing, job opportunities and influence in local affairs, and began a Civil Rights movement to press for better conditions.

Civil Rights demonstrations were met by counter-demonstrations from the Protestants, who feared any movement which might bring them into association with the Republic of Ireland rather than with Great Britain. Demonstrations quickly turned into mob violence, with deaths and destruction of property on a scale so serious that troops were sent in to try to keep order.

1966 Barbados, Botswana, Guyana and Lesotho gain independence
Aberfan disaster: landslip kills 116 children, 28 adults
New universities: Aston, Bath, Bradford, Brunel, City, Heriot-Watt, Loughborough, Stirling, Surrey
First Ombudsman appointed
Severn and Tay road bridges open

1967 Pirate radios outlawed: BBC launch Radio 1 as 'pop' station
Breath tests introduced
Homosexuality between consenting adults no longer offence
Liner *Queen Elizabeth 2* launched
Economic blockade of Rhodesia
Gibraltar votes to stay British
Francis Chichester sails around the world and is knighted
Steel industry renationalized
£ devalued by 14.3 per cent
New universities: Dundee, Salford

1968 Mauritius, Swaziland independent
Welsh nationalists set bombs
Martin Ryle discovers pulsars
Race Relations Act passed
Student riots in London
Two-tier postal system introduced

1969 Voting age reduced from 21 to 18
School leaving age up to 16
Rhodesia declares itself a republic
Concorde makes its first flight
Robin Knox-Johnston sails round world in first non-stop solo voyage
Wally Herbert leads first trans-arctic expedition
Riots and terrorism in Northern Ireland: troops sent to keep peace
Capital punishment abolished

British soldiers in Northern Ireland embarked on the thankless task of peacekeeping between the Roman Catholics and Protestants in 1970. Here a lorry burns as British troops move in during riots in Belfast's Falls Road area.

The Common Market

The main achievement of Edward Heath's administration was Britain's entry into the European Economic Community (EEC), usually called the Common Market. Britain stood aloof when the EEC was formed in 1957, and had been rebuffed when it tried to join in the 1960s.

The timing of Britain's entry was not ideal, and seemed to involve heavy payments for little benefit. Harold Wil-son, when Labour returned to power, negotiated revised terms, then invited the public to vote on membership in Britain's first referendum. The vote was a clear-cut 'yes' for staying in the EEC.

Terrorism in Ireland

The tensions between Protestants and Catholics were seized upon by the Irish Republican Army, a militant group with support in Ireland and the United States, dedicated to the reunification of Ireland by any means. The IRA and a splinter group, the Provisional IRA, launched a campaign of terrorism, with frequent bombings and murders, which continued well into the 1990s. Their actions hardened the attitudes of

Ulster's Protestants and Protestant extremists retaliated by killing Catholics.

Election Fortunes

Economics and labour relations dominated the General Elections of the 1970s. The first, in 1970, was confidently expected by everyone to return Labour to power. But in a shock result the Conservatives, under their new leader Edward Heath, won a majority of 31. Britain's heavy international debt was one cause of the defeat.

The miners triggered off the next election. Offered 16 per cent against their claim for a pay rise up to 40 per cent, they threatened to strike. Heath called an election, to get the country's backing for his tough line on wages. The result was a 'hung' Parliament, neither of the two big parties having a majority. Labour took office under Harold Wilson, who after nine months called a second election which gave him a majority of three.

Babies in the News

Three births made news in Britain in the late '70s and early '80s.

The first was Louise Brown, born on July 25th, 1978. She was the world's first test-tube baby.

The second birth was a new heir to the throne: Prince William, born to the Prince and Princess of Wales on June 21st, 1982.

The third birth was that of Britain's first surviving sextuplets, born on November 18th, 1983 to Janet and Graham Walton of Wallasey, in Merseyside.

1970 Equal Pay for men and women decreed by law
General Election: Conservatives win majority of 31: Edward Heath becomes PM

1971 Open University starts teaching
Decimal currency introduced
Trade union reform introduced

1972 'Bloody Sunday': 13 killed in Londonderry riots
N Ireland comes under direct rule from Whitehall
Uganda Asians expelled, flee to UK
Industrial Relations Court set up
'Bloody Friday' in Belfast: bombs kill 11, wound 120

1973 Britain joins Common Market
IRA car bomb in London kills 1, injures 216, damages Old Bailey
Counties abolished in N Ireland
Power cuts lead to 3-day week
Bahamas gain independence
N Irish vote to stay in UK

1974 Miners vote to strike: Heath calls General Election, and loses. Harold Wilson heads minority Labour government
Miners get 35 per cent pay rise
English and Welsh counties reorganized
Second General Election: Labour majority 3

1975 Scottish counties abolished
'Cod War' with Iceland (to 1976)
Britain's first referendum: 60 per cent vote to stay in EEC

1976 Wilson retires: James Callaghan becomes PM
Betty Williams and Mairead Corrigan form Ulster peace movement (Nobel peace prize, 1977)
Worst drought for 200 years

1977 Labour and Liberals form pact

1978 First test-tube baby born

1981 saw the marriage of Prince Charles to the Lady Diana Spencer who became much loved by the British people. In 1982 their son Prince William was born. The young prince is seen here with his parents during their tour of Australia and New Zealand.

The Social Democrats

A new political party, the Social Democratic Party (SDP) was formed in 1981 by four former senior Labour Ministers: Roy Jenkins, William Rodgers, David Owen and Shirley Williams. The 'Gang of Four', as they were called, had become disenchanted with the Leftward drift of the Labour Party, and its antagonism to the Common Market. Other Labour rebels, one Conservative, and some by-election victories swelled

the number of SDP Members of Parliament to 27, but most of them lost their seats in the General Election of 1983, which returned Margaret Thatcher's government to power with a landslide majority of 144.

For all elections the SDP formed an alliance with the Liberal Party, so that only one candidate from the Alliance would fight any seat, and each party would help the other.

Papal Visits

Pope John Paul II made religious history with visits to Ireland and the United Kingdom. In the predominantly Catholic Ireland he received, as expected, a rapturous welcome: 2,800,000 people (out of a population of

3,300,000) attended the religious ceremonies he held.

In Protestant Britain the Pope's reception was less overwhelming, but more significant. He took part with Robert Runcie, the Archbishop of Canterbury, in an ecumenical service in Canterbury cathedral, marking a healing of the rift opened by Henry VIII.

The Falklands War
Argentina had claimed the Falkland Islands – ruled by Britain since 1833 – for many years, but its sudden invasion of the islands took the world by surprise. Lord Carrington, the Foreign Secretary, and two of his Ministers resigned, feeling that they had seriously misjudged the situation.

Theirs was not the only misjudgment: Argentina's rulers did not expect the swift retaliation. With a speed which astonished everyone, Britain sent a task force on its way within three days of the invasion, and in a determined and bloody series of battles recaptured the Falklands 73 days after the invasion. The resolute stand of Margaret Thatcher's government brought it, and her, increased popularity and respect.

The war also caused some rethinking of Britain's defence strategy, since several of the warships sent to the Falklands had been on the brink of being scrapped or sold.

At the end of the war, the problem of the Falkland Islands remained unsolved. Britain refused to negotiate on the sovereignty question, insisting that the islanders' wish to remain British be respected.

1979 'Winter of discontent': massive series of strikes
Welsh referendum rejects devolution plans; Scots accept by too small a margin
Callaghan loses vote of confidence
General Election: Conservatives win overall majority of 43. Margaret Thatcher, first woman PM
IRA bomb kills Earl Mountbatten
Pope John Paul II visits Ireland
Jack Lynch resigns as Irish PM: succeeded by Charles Haughey
1980 Steel workers strike for 14 weeks
Commandos storm Iranian Embassy to free 19 hostages held there by terrorists
Rhodesia becomes officially independent as Zimbabwe
Callaghan succeeded by Michael Foot as Labour leader
Jobless top 2,000,000
1981 Labour rebels form SDP
Ten IRA hunger strikers die
Unemployment tops 2,500,000
Irish General Election: Garret Fitzgerald is new Taoiseach (PM)
1982 Irish coalition falls: Haughey is again PM
Argentina seizes Falkland Islands: recaptured in 10 weeks
The Pope visits Britain
Unemployment tops 3,000,000
Irish General Election: Garret Fitzgerald again PM
1983 General Election: Conservatives have majority of 144
Michael Foot succeeded by Neil Kinnock as Labour leader
IRA car bomb outside Harrods, London kills 6, injures 90
1984 IRA bomb at Brighton's Grand Hotel, aimed at Conservative leaders, kills 6, injures 31

At last, the Chunnel

After more than a century of indecision, Britain and France agreed in 1986 to bore the Channel Tunnel. By 1992 the boring of the running and service tunnels was complete.

But geological and financial difficulties led the programme to fall behind schedule, and the planned opening date of July 1993 had to be put back into 1994. Arguments over the route of the new high-speed rail link between Folkestone and London caused more problems.

Storms and Heat

The Great Hurricane of October 16, 1987, was the country's worst storm for 250 years. It swept across southern England from Cornwall to East Anglia, killing 18 people, leaving a £300 million trail of damage and uprooting about 9 million trees.

In 1989 Britain had its warmest year since records began in 1659. Severe droughts followed, especially in the south east and East Anglia. They continued into 1990 and 1991, but eased slightly when the summer of 1992 proved to be wet.

Severe storms in 1990 and 1991 led to further damage, though not on the same scale as that of 1987.

Margaret Thatcher Goes

The Conservative Prime Minister, Mrs Margaret Thatcher, had two triumphs in the late 1980s. In June 1987 she won a third term in power, and on May 3, 1988 she celebrated ten continuous years as premier.

But a succession of Cabinet disagreements led to resignations by senior ministers. In 1986 Michael Heseltine (Defence) and Leon Brittan (Trade and Industry) quit. In a Cabinet reshuffle in 1989 Mrs Thatcher replaced Sir Geoffrey Howe as Foreign Secretary by John Major, provoking a row. A few months later the Chancellor of the Exchequer, Nigel Lawson, resigned. He was succeeded by Major.

In October 1990 Major and the Prime Minister decided to join the European Exchange Rate Mechanism, tying the pound to other European currencies. A few days later Howe resigned, and attacked the Government's policies.

Heseltine then challenged Mrs Thatcher for election as Conservative party leader. Voting was not decisive, but Mrs Thatcher felt obliged to resign. Major was chosen as leader and became Prime Minister.

Economic Gloom

By the time John Major went to No 10 Downing Street Britain was sinking into recession, which was a world-wide problem. The official end of the Cold War and the collapse of the Soviet Union did not lift the economic gloom.

Major won a general election in the spring of 1992, but with a greatly reduced majority. He and his Chancellor, Norman Lamont, staked their reputations on staying within the Exchange Rate Mechanism, but were forced to leave it in September 1992 when the value of the pound nose-dived.

By this time businesses were failing at an ever increasing rate, thousands of people were falling behind with their mortgage repayments and losing their homes, and unemployment soared.

Author Denounced
British author Salman Rushdie's book *The Satanic Verses* was described as blasphemous by Muslims in 1989. Iran's leader, Ayatollah Khomeini, pronounced sentence of death on him, and Rushdie had to go into hiding.

Years of Disasters
The late 1980s and early 1990s were years of disasters in transport and sport. In 1987 the car ferry *Herald of Free Enterprise* left Zeebrugge with its bow door open. Water poured in and the ferry capsized, killing 193 people. A fire at King's Cross Underground station killed 30 people.

In 1988 a triple rail crash at Clapham Junction, south London, killed 36 people. Ten days later a terrorist bomb blew up an American jumbo jet which crashed on the little Scottish town of Lockerbie, killing 270 people. In January 1989 an engine fire in an airliner flying from London to Belfast led to a crash in which 46 people died.

Sport was marred by a fire at Bradford City football stadium, which led to the deaths of 55 fans in 1985; by the deaths of 38 people in Brussels following fights between supporters of Liverpool and Juventus (Italy) a fortnight later; and by overcrowding and panic at Hillsborough Stadium Sheffield, in which 94 fans were crushed to death.

1985 Bradford soccer ground blaze kills more than 50 fans; Liverpool fans riot in Belgium, 38 people die
Anglo-Irish agreement signed
1986 Michael Heseltine and Leon Brittan resign from Cabinet
1987 Ferry *Herald of Free Enterprise* capsizes at Zeebrugge; nearly 200 people die
Conservatives win third term
Worst storm for 250 years kills 18 people, fells 9 million trees
1988 Fire ravages North Sea oil rig Piper Alpha; 166 crew men die
Sabotaged airliner crashes on Lockerbie, 270 people die
1989 Britain's warmest year since 1659
1990 A violent storm lashes southern Britain, killing 46 people
Margaret Thatcher fails to win clear vote to remain Tory leader; John Major succeeds her as prime minister
1991 Gulf War: British forces help to restore Kuwaiti independence
Recession bites; jobless rise to more than 2 million; 48,000 businesses collapse
1992 Conservatives win fourth term with greatly reduced majority
Neil Kinnock resigns as Labour leader; succeeded by John Smith
Recession continues; jobless near 3 million and more businesses collapse
1993 The Queen celebrates 40 years since her coronation
Nigel Short beaten by Gary Kasparov in World Chess Championship held in London
Britain ratifies Maastricht Treaty and becomes member of European Union

Reference Section

SOME BRITISH ARTISTS

Bacon, Francis (1910–1992), Dublin-born of English parents, became a leading 20th century artist. Many of his portraits distort the human figure; he said he believed in portraying feeling rather than just illustrating an object.

Blake, William (1757–1827), was a painter, engraver, poet and mystic. He produced books of his own poems in which he engraved text and illustrations together, the first being *Songs of Innocence*. Blake was a religious man. He did not paint from nature but his work was inspired by visions.

Bonington, Richard Parkes (1801–1828), was born near Nottingham but from the age of 15 lived the rest of his short life in France. He is noted for his richly-coloured landscapes.

Burne-Jones, Sir Edward (1833–1898), produced detailed pictures of medieval and mythological subjects, such as the Arthurian legends. He conjured up a dream-like, unreal world.

Constable, John (1776–1837), the foremost English landscape painter of his time, specialized in Suffolk scenes. He painted natural subjects in a realistic way. His work reflects his interest in the effects of light and shadow on nature and, in this way, he foreshadowed the Impressionists. His most famous paintings are *The Hay Wain* and *Salisbury Cathedral*.

Cotman, John Sell (1782–1842), a water-colour landscape artist, was born in Norwich and was a leading member of a group known as the Norwich School. Many of his best paintings are of Norfolk scenes.

Fuseli, Henry (1741–1825), was a Swiss painter who settled permanently in London and became Keeper of the Royal Academy. Many of his paintings are Romantic but grotesque.

This picture of Weymouth Bay was painted in 1816 by John Constable, when he was on his honeymoon.

Gainsborough, Thomas (1727–1788), a Suffolk landscape artist, became a fashionable London painter of elegant portraits. Among his best-known pictures are *The Blue Boy*; *Mrs Siddons*; and *Queen Charlotte*.

Hockney, David (1937–   ), was born in Bradford. His paintings are bold and unconventional. He uses acrylic paint to achieve flat areas of colour in works such as *A Bigger Splash*. He has designed film and theatre sets.

Hogarth, William (1699–1764), was born and worked in London. There he gained inspiration for his satirical paintings, which usually point to a moral. They include the series *The Rake's Progress*; *The Election*; *Marriage à la Mode*.

Holbein, Hans (1497–1543), was a German artist who settled in England in 1532 and became a court painter to Henry VIII. Portraits include those of Henry, Thomas Cromwell, Anne of Cleves, Jane Seymour and Catherine Howard.

Kneller, Sir Godfrey (1646–1723), was born in Germany but became a portrait artist in England, and court painter to Charles II. His studio produced slick, fashionable portraits.

Knight, Dame Laura (1877–1970), a Derbyshire-born artist, is known for her paintings of the circus, Russian ballet, and gypsies. In 1936 she became the first woman Royal Academician for more than a century.

Landseer, Sir Edwin (1802–1873), London-born, painted many Scottish scenes. He is famous for his animal studies, and the sculptures of the lions in Trafalgar Square at the foot of Nelson's Column.

Lawrence, Sir Thomas (1769–1830), born in Bristol, became the most successful portrait painter of his day, and was court artist to George III.

Lowry, Laurence Stephen (1887–1976), was Manchester born and painted the stark landscapes of the industrial north of England. His figures are tall and thin.

Millais, Sir John Everett (1829–1896), was a popular Victorian artist, many of whose pictures have an almost photographic quality.

Morland, George (1763–1804), was born in London, but became known for his scenes of rustic village life.

Munnings, Sir Alfred (1878–1959), was born in Mendham, Suffolk. He vigorously opposed modern abstract art, and himself specialized in pictures of horses and racecourse scenes.

Nicholson, Ben (1894–1982), was a leading English abstract painter. He maintained that abstract art brought art into everyday life.

Piper, John (1903–   ), was at first an abstract painter, then became a representational artist. He served as a war artist during World War II. He also designed theatre sets and stained glass windows.

Raeburn, Sir Henry (1756–1823), was the leading portrait painter of his birthplace, Edinburgh. He was appointed George IV's Limner (painter), for Scotland in 1823.

Reynolds, Sir Joshua (1723–1792), was the first President of the Royal Academy, and the most important English portrait painter of the 18th century. He did much to raise the status of artists in Britain.

Rossetti, Dante Gabriel (1828–1882), London-born of Italian descent, was one of the founders of the Pre-Raphaelite Brotherhood. His paintings are full of rich colours and romantic imagery. He was also a poet.

Sutherland, Graham (1903–1980), was a leading English landscape and portrait painter. Not all his portraits found favour; that of Sir Winston Churchill was destroyed by the Churchill family.

Turner, Joseph Mallord William (1775–1851), anticipated the French Impressionists in his atmospheric pictures, mostly water-colours. His work reveals the drama and power of nature. He is noted for his sunsets and storms.

BRITISH RULERS

Rulers of England (to 1603)
Saxons
Egbert	827–839
Aethelwulf	839–858
Aethelbald	858–860
Aethelbert	860–865
Aethelred I	865–871
Alfred the Great	871–899
Edward the Elder	899–924
Aethelstan	924–939
Edmund	939–946
Edred	946–955
Edwy	955–959
Edgar	959–975
Edward the Martyr	975–978
Aethelred II the Unready	978–1016
Edmund Ironside	1016

Danes
Cnut	1016–1035
Harold I Harefoot	1035–1040
Harthacnut	1040–1042

Saxons
Edward the Confessor	1042–1066
Harold II	1066

House of Normandy
William the Conqueror	1066–1087
William II	1087–1100
Henry I	1100–1135
Stephen	1135–1154

House of Plantagenet
Henry II	1154–1189
Richard I	1189–1199
John	1199–1216
Henry III	1216–1272
Edward I	1272–1307
Edward II	1307–1327
Edward III	1327–1377
Richard III	1377–1399

House of Lancaster
Henry IV	1399–1413
Henry V	1413–1422
Henry VI	1422–1461

House of York
Edward IV	1461–1483
Edward V	1483
Richard III	1483–1485

House of Tudor
Henry VII	1485–1509
Henry VIII	1509–1547
Edward VI	1547–1553
Mary I	1553–1558
Elizabeth I	1558–1603

Rulers of Scotland (to 1603)
Malcolm II	1005–1034
Duncan I	1034–1040
Macbeth	1040–1057
Malcolm III Canmore	1058–1093
Donald Bane	1093–1094
Duncan II	1094
Donald Bane (restored)	1094–1097
Edgar	1097–1107
Alexander I	1107–1124
David I	1124–1153
Malcolm IV	1153–1165
William the Lion	1165–1214
Alexander II	1214–1249
Alexander III	1249–1286
Margaret of Norway	1286–1290
Interregnum	1290–1292
John Balliol	1292–1296
Interregnum	1296–1306
Robert I (Bruce)	1306–1329
David II	1329–1371

House of Stewart
Robert II	1371–1390
Robert III	1390–1406
James I	1406–1437
James II	1437–1460
James III	1460–1488
James IV	1488–1513
James V	1513 -1542
Mary	1542–1567
James VI	1567–1625

Became James I of England in 1603.

Rulers of Britain
House of Stuart
James I	1603–1625
Charles I	1625–1649
Commonwealth	1649–1660

House of Stuart (restored)
Charles II	1660–1685
James II	1685–1688
William III jointly	1689–1702
Mary II	1689–1694
Anne	1702–1714

House of Hanover
George I	1714–1727
George II	1727–1760
George III	1760–1820
George IV	1820–1830
William IV	1830–1837
Victoria	1837–1901

House of Saxe-Coburg
Edward VII	1901–1910

House of Windsor
George V	1910–1936
Edward VIII	1936
George VI	1936–1952
Elizabeth II	1952–

BRITISH PRIME MINISTERS

W = Whig, T = Tory, Cln = Coalition, P = Peelite, L = Liberal,
C = Conservative, L = Labour

Sir Robert Walpole (W)	1721–42
Earl of Wilmington (W)	1742–43
Henry Pelham (W)	1743–54
Duke of Newcastle (W)	1754–56
Duke of Devonshire (W)	1756–57
Duke of Newcastle (W)	1757–62
Earl of Bute (T)	1762–63
George Grenville (W)	1763–65
Marquess of Rockingham (W)	1765–66
Earl of Chatham (W)	1766–67
Duke of Grafton (W)	1767–70
Lord North (T)	1770–82
Marquess of Rockingham (W)	1782
Earl of Shelburne (W)	1782–83
Duke of Portland (Cln)	1783
William Pitt (T)	1783–1801
Henry Addington (T)	1801–04
William Pitt (T)	1804–1806
Lord Grenville (W)	1806–07
Duke of Portland (T)	1807–09
Spencer Perceval (T)	1808–12
Earl of Liverpool (T)	1812–27
George Canning (T)	1827
Viscount Goderich (T)	1827–28
Duke of Wellington (T)	1828–30
Earl Grey (W)	1830–34
Viscount Melbourne (W)	1834
Sir Robert Peel (T)	1834–35
Viscount Melbourne (W)	1835–41
Sir Robert Peel (T)	1841–46
Lord John Russell (W)	1846–52
Earl of Derby (T)	1852
Earl of Aberdeen (P)	1852–55
Viscount Palmerston (L)	1855–58
Earl of Derby (C)	1858–59
Viscount Palmerston (L)	1859–65

Earl Russell (L)	1865–66
Earl of Derby (C)	1866–68
Benjamin Disraeli (C)	1868
William Gladstone (L)	1868–74
Benjamin Disraeli (C)	1874–80
William Gladstone (L)	1880–85
Marquess of Salisbury	1885–86
William Gladstone (L)	1886
Marquess of Salisbury (C)	1886–92
William Gladstone (L)	1892–94
Earl of Rosebery (L)	1894–95
Marques of Salisbury (C)	1895–1902
Arthur Ballfour (C)	1902–05
Sir Henry Campbell-Bannerman (L)	1905–08
Herbert Asquith (L)	1908–15
Herbert Asquith (Cln)	1915–16
David Lloyd-George (Cln)	1916–22
Andrew Bonar Law (C)	1922–23
Stanley Baldwin (C)	1923–24
James Ramsay MacDonald (Lab)	1924
Stanley Baldwin (C)	1924–29
James Ramsay MacDonald (Lab)	1929–31
James Ramsay MacDonald (Cln)	1931–35
Stanley Baldwin (Cln)	1935–37
Neville Chamberlain (Cln)	1937–40
Winston Churchill (Cln)	1940–45
Winston Churchill (C)	1945
Clement Attlee (Lab)	1945–51
Sir Winston Churchill (C)	1951–55
Sir Anthony Eden (C)	1955–57
Harold Macmillan (C)	1957–63
Sir Alec Douglas-Home (C)	1963–64
Harold Wilson (Lab)	1964–70
Edward Heath (C)	1970–74
Harold Wilson (Lab)	1974–76
James Callaghan (Lab)	1976–79
Margaret Thatcher (C)	1979–90
John Major (C)	1990–

THE COMMONWEALTH OF NATIONS

Commonwealth Independence date		Country	Independence date	Country	Independence date
		Jamaica	1962	St Vincent	1979
Antigua & Barbuda	1981	Kenya	1963	Seychelles	1976
Australia	1901	Kiribati	1979	Sierra Leone	1961
Bahamas	1973	Lesotho	1966	Singapore	1965
Bangladesh: (from Pakistan)	1971	Malawi	1964	Solomon Islands	1978
Barbados	1966	Malaysia	1957	Sri Lanka	1948
Belize	1981	Maldives	1982	Swaziland	1968
Botswana	1966	Malta	1964	Tanzania	1961
Brunei	1984	Mauritius	1968	Tonga	1970
Canada	1931	Namibia	1990	Trinidad & Tobago	1962
Cyprus	1960	Nauru	1968	Tuvalu	1978
Dominica	1978	New Zealand	1907	Uganda	1962
Fiji	1970	Nigeria	1960	United Kingdom	—
Gambia	1965	Pakistan	1947	Vanuatu	1980
Ghana	1957	Papua New Guinea	1975	Western Samoa	1962
Grendada	1974	St Christopher & Nevis	1983	Zambia	1964
Guyana	1966	St Lucia	1979	Zimbabwe	1980
India	1947				

Index

N

Nagasaki 207
Namur, battle of 193
Nanking, Treaty of 166
Nantes, Edict of 95, 115
Napoleon I, emperor of France 135, 152, 155, 156, 159
Naseby, battle of 123
Nasser, Colonel 211
National Government 199, *199*
National Health Act 207
National Health Insurance 189
National Health Service 205, *208*, 209
Nationalization 207, 208, 209, 211
National Portrait Gallery 171
National Service 209
National Trust 183
National Union of Gas Workers and General Labourers *178*
National Union of Women's Suffragette Societies *186*
Natural selection *173*
Navy 141, 143, 150, 152, 153
Nazis 191, 202
Nehru, Jawaharlal *207*
Nelson, Horatio 152, 153, 155, *155*
Nennius *20*, 25
Netherlands *see also* Dutch Republic 95, 115, 127, 131, 135, 137, 149, 152, 153, 203
Neutrons 199
Neuve Chapelle, battle of 193
Neville's Cross, battle of 71
Nevison, C. R. W. *194*
New Brunswick 172
Newbury, battle of 123
Newcastle University 213
Newcastle-upon-Tyne 33, 57
Newfoundland 111
New Lanark Mills *148*
New Model Army 122, 125
New Orleans, battle of 156, 159
News of the World 165
Newspapers 133, 149, 151, 153, 157, 159, 165, 169, 182
New Statesman 189
Newton, Isaac *128*
New Towns Act 207
New York 128, 149
New Zealand 145, 165, 169, 171, 175, 186, 187
Niall of the Nine Hostages 17
Nicaea, Council of 17
Nigeria 185, 213
Nightingale, Florence 169, *172*
Nile, battle of the 152, 153
Nonconformists 127, 131
Nore mutiny, 152, 153
Norfolk, dukes of 76, 109
Normandy 19, 28, 30, 33, 35, 37, 39, 41, 43, 44, 52, 55, 83, 89, *204*, 205
Normandy landing *204*, 205
Normans 30-46, 48, 49, 63
North, Lord 147
North African campaign 205
Northampton 59
Northampton, battle of 89
Northcliffe, Lord *see* Harmsworth, Alfred
Northern Ireland 196, 197, 209, 215, *216*, 217

Northmen *see* Vikings
North Pole 163
North Sea oil 213
Northumberland 43, *45*, 49, 51, 59, 97, 101
Northumberland, Duke of *106*, 107, 109
Northumberland, Earl of *see* Percy, Henry
Northumbria, Kingdom of 21, 23, *23*, 25, 27, 33
North Wales 48, 49, 56, 80
North-West Passage 112
Norway 29, 30, 33, 35, 37, 61, 65, 163, 202, 203
Norwich 40
Norwich cathedral 35
Nottingham University 209
Nova Scotia 172
Novel 141, *157*, *169*, 175
Nuclear Disarmament, Campaign for 210
Nuffield, Lord *see* Morris, William
Nuffield Foundation 205
Nuremberg, Peace of 95
Nursing *169*, *172*
Nyerere, Julius *212*

O

Oaks horse race 149
Oates, Titus 129
Oblivion, Act of 117
O'Brien, Smith 167
O'Brien, William 181
Observer, The 153
Oceanic (liner) 175
O'Connell, Daniel 167
O'Connor, Aedh 63
O'Connor, Rory 49
O'Connor, Turloch 49
O'Donnell, Hugh 113
Odo of Bayeux *30*, 35
Offa of Mercia *24*, 25
Offa's Dyke *24*, 25
Official Secrets Act 189
Oglethorpe, James 139
O'Higgins, Kevin 199
Oil 191, 209, 213
Olaf of Norway 29
Old Age Pensions 187, 203
Oldcastle, John 83
Old Pretender *see* James Edward
Old Sarum 160
Olympic Games 11, 209
Ombudsman 215
Omdurman, battle of 183
Omnibus 161
O'Neill, Hugh 113
O'Neill, Shane 107, 109
Ontario 172
Open University 213, 217
Opium 166, 187
Opium War 164, 165
Orange Free State 184, 185
Order of Merit 185
Order of the British Empire 195
Order of the Garter 71
Ordnance Survey 153
Oriana, The Triumphs of 112
Orinoco river 113
Orkney *10*, 91
Orléans 79, 82, 84, 85

Ormonde, Duke of 137
O'Shea, W. H. 180
Oswald of Northumbria 23
Otterburn 77
Ottoman Empire 162, 179
Oudenarde, battle of 133
Oughtred, William 121
Owain Glyndwr 80, *80*, 81
Owain Gwynedd 48, 49
Owen, David 218
Owen, Robert *148*
Oxfam 205
Oxford, Earl of 76, 77
Oxford, Provisions of 60, 61
Oxford English Dictionary 179
Oxford University 49, 61, *68*, 105, 197
Oxygen 135, 149, 183

P

Pacific Ocean 95
Paine, Thomas 153
Pakistan 11, 207, *207*, 208
Palestine *42*, 52, 53, 170, 191, 195, 209
Pankhurst, Emmeline 185
Paper tax 147, 149
Parcel post 179
Paris 85, 15
Paris, Matthew *55*, *57*, *58*, *61*
Paris, Peace of 145
Paris, Treaty of 157
Parker, Hyde 152
Parkes, Alexander 169
Parliament 46, *46*, 59, 60, *113*, 121, 122, *122*, 124
Parliament Act 187, *187*, 189
Parliamentarians 122, *124*
Parliamentary reform 160
Parnell, Charles Stewart 179, 180, 181
Parr, Catherine 104
Parsons, Charles 179
Parsons, Robert 111
Pasteur, Louis 172
Paston family 83
Patay, battle of 85
Paulhan, Louis 189
Paviland Man *13*
Paxton, Joseph *168*
Pay-As-You-Earn 205
Pearl Harbor 203
Peasants' Revolt 47, 74, 75, *75*
Pedro the Cruel, of Portugal 74, 75
Peel, Robert 159, 167
Peerage 43, 210, 212, 213
Pembroke, Richard, Earl of (Strongbow) 48, 49
Penal settlement *150*, 151, 174
Penda of Mercia 23
Pendulum 139
Penicillin 199, 203
Peninsular War 135, 155, 156, *158*
Penn, William 129
Pennsylvania 129
Penny post 129, 165
Pensions 187, 203
Penzance 113
People's Charter 164, 165
Pepys, Samuel 127
Perceval, Spencer 157
Percy, Henry 77, 81, 97
Percy family 81
Perkins, William H. 171
Perrers, Alice 75

ACKNOWLEDGEMENTS

Cover: top left COI, centre Tate Gallery, right Michael Holford, bottom left British Museum, centre Michael Holford, right Picturepoint; half title: By Gracious Permission of Her Majesty The Queen; title: top National Army Museum, centre By Gracious Permission of Her Majesty The Queen, bottom National Portrait Gallery, right Camera Press; contents: far left Keystone, centre left Fotomas, centre right Mansell Collection, far right Hulton Picture Library; page 10 left Aerofilms, right Photo Library International; 11 top National Museum of Wales, centre British Museum; 12 British Tourist Authority; 13 centre Peter Clayton, bottom Scottish Tourist Board; 14 British Tourist Authority; 15 Picturepoint; 17 Peter Clayton; 18 bottom left Cooper Bridgeman, right British Museum; 19 Trinity College Library, Dublin; 20 Fotomas; 22 top British Museum, bottom Cooper Bridgeman; 24 Janet & Colin Bord; 26 Michael Holford; 27 Ashmolean Museum; 28 British Museum; 30 Mansell; 32 Aerofilms; 35 Bodleian Library; 36 Edwin Smith; 38 top Corpus Christi College, Oxford, bottom British Museum; 39, 40, 42 British Museum; 44 Janet & Colin Bord; 45 National Galleries Scotland; 46 By Gracious Permission of Her Majesty The Queen; 48 Mansell; 49 Picturepoint; 52, 53, 54, 55, British Museum; 56 Derek Widdicombe; 57 top Mansell; bottom British Museum; 58 British Museum; 60 Hulton Picture Library; 61 Mansell; 62 top British Tourist Authority, bottom By Gracious Permission of Her Majesty The Queen; 64 Janet & Colin Bord; 65 Sir David Ogilvy; 66 British Museum; 67 Dr Duncan Thomson, 68 top British Museum, bottom Mervyn Blatch; 71 Bodleian Library; 72 British Tourist Authority; 73 National Portrait Gallery; 74 British Tourist Authority; 75 Mary Evans Picture Library; 76 Fotomas; 77 Fotomas; 80 Archives Nationales, Paris; 81 National Galleries of Scotland/Tom Scott; 83 Michael Holford; 84 Hulton Picture Library; 85 British Museum; 86 Bodleian Library; 88 Edwin Smith; 90 British Museum; 92 Fotomas; 93, 94 British Museum; 96 Mansell; 97 British Museum; 98 National Portrait Gallery; 99 Public Records Office; 100 top Tony Morrison, bottom J. Allan Cash; 102, 103 National Portrait Gallery; 104 National Maritime Museum; 106, 107 National Portrait Gallery; 108 Mansell; 109 British Museum; 110 National Maritime Museum; 113 Fotomas; 114 By Permission of the Earl of Rosebery; 116 top Mansell; bottom Fotomas; 118 By Gracious Permission of Her Majesty The Queen; 120 top Fotomas, bottom Hulton Picture Library; 123 Fotomas; 124 top Mansell, bottom Public Record Office; 126 top National Portrait Gallery; 128 top Hulton Picture Library, bottom Fotomas; 130 By Gracious Permission of Her Majesty The Queen; 131 Peter Clayton; 132 By Gracious Permission of Her Majesty The Queen; 133 Hulton Picture Library; 134 National Army Museum; 136 top Fotomas, bottom Hulton Picture Library; 137 Hulton Picture Library; 138 Holkham Estate Office; 139 Fotomas; 140 Hulton Picture Library; 141 National Portrait Gallery; 142 National Army Museum; 143 India Office Library; 144 National Maritime Museum; 145 National Portrait Gallery; 146 Michael Holford; 148 top Ironbridge Museum, bottom Mansell; 150 Axel Poignant; 151, 152 Hulton Picture Library; 154 Cooper Bridgeman; 155 National Portrait Gallery; 156 Mansell; 157 top National Portrait Gallery, bottom Hulton Picture Library; 158 Mansell; 159 National Portrait Gallery; 160 Science Museum; 162 Camera Press; 163 Fotomas; 164 By Gracious Permission of Her Majesty The Queen; 165 Science Museum; 166 National Army Museum; 167 Hulton Picture Library; 168 Mansell; 169 Hulton Picture Library; 170, 172 Mansell; 173, 174, 176, 177 Hulton Picture Library; 178 top Fotomas; 180 Mary Evans Picture Library; 181, 184 Mansell; 186 Mary Evans Picture Library; 187 Fotomas; 188 Mansell; 190 Imperial War Museum; 192 India Office Library; 193 Imperial War Museum; 194 Imperial War Museum; 196, 197 Hulton Picture Library; 198 National Motor Museum; 199 Conservative Central Office; 200, 201 Hulton Picture Library; 202 National Maritime Museum; 203 Imperial War Museum; 204 John Topham; 206, 207 Keystone; 208 Henry Grant; 210 COI; 212 Keystone; 214 Camera Press; 216 Keystone; 218 Camera Press; 222 National Gallery; 225 Ronald Sheridan.
Picture Research: Penny J. Warn